WE THE STATES

☆　　☆　　☆　　☆　　☆　　☆

WE THE STATES

An Anthology of Historic Documents
and Commentaries thereon, *Expounding
the State and Federal Relationship*

☆　　☆　　☆　　☆　　☆　　☆　　☆

Published by the
VIRGINIA COMMISSION ON
CONSTITUTIONAL GOVERNMENT

THE WILLIAM BYRD PRESS, INC.
RICHMOND, VIRGINIA

MEMBERS OF THE COMMISSION

DAVID J. MAYS, *Chairman*

JAMES JACKSON KILPATRICK, *Vice Chairman*

☆ ☆ ☆ ☆ ☆ ☆ ☆ ☆ ☆ ☆ ☆ ☆ ☆

PREFACE

T HE SEVERAL separate publications here bound together were distributed seriatim by the Virginia Commission on Constitutional Government between 1959 and 1963. The Commission itself was created by act of the Virginia General Assembly in 1958; it is made up of four members of the House of Delegates, three members of the State Senate, and eight members named by the Governor from the State at large. Its functions are to work through the processes of public education for a restoration of a balanced and responsible federalism in the United States.

The Virginia Declaration of Rights, with which this book begins, was the work of George Mason (1725-1792), one of the most interesting figures in that company of great men remembered as the "founding fathers." He was planter, statesman, thinker, pamphleteer, a critic of ideas. The "fundamental principles" he set forth in the Declaration of Rights found their way into the Constitution of Virginia, and into the Bill of Rights of the Constitution of the United States.

An excerpt from Thomas Jefferson's autobiography begins on page 5; here Jefferson described the day-by-day events that led to adoption of the Declaration of Independence in 1776. The version of the Declaration found on page 9 shows Jefferson's original draft with the deletions and insertions made by the Continental Congress. On page 17 appears Jefferson's famed letter of 1826 to Roger C. Weightman—the last Jefferson letter extant—in which the aging Virginian looked back upon his Declaration from the vantage point of 50 years.

The Articles of Confederation follow. Historian Allan Nevins has remarked of this forgotten compact that its provisions "should not be regarded with contempt: They served as a steppingstone to a new order." The careful reader of the Articles will find a dozen phrases later embodied in the Constitution of 1788.

We have retained in this volume the original Foreword prepared by Mr. Denys P. Myers to the Commission's definitive edition of the Constitution of the United States. A new section has been added to cover ratification by the States in 1964 of the 24th Amendment to the Constitution, prohibiting the imposition of a poll tax as a prerequisite to voting.

The Bill of Rights became operative, as a part of our supreme law, in September of 1789. Less than a decade passed before the First Amendment, forbidding the Congress to make any law abridging freedom of speech, was gravely violated by enactment of the sedition laws. These unconscionable statutes were denounced by Kentucky and Virginia in the famed Resolutions of 1798; and these resolutions in turn were followed by the Report of James Madison to the Virginia General Assembly of 1799. In this great political treatise, Madison defended the principles enunciated in the Virginia Resolution of the preceding year. The text here presented is taken directly from the Archives of the Commonwealth of Virginia.

The Commission is indebted to Dr. Noble C. Cunningham, of the University of Richmond, for selecting the group of Jefferson's letters that appear on pages 225-281. His introduction to these letters also has been retained in this collection.

The Jefferson letters are here followed by John C. Calhoun's "Fort Hill Address," in which Calhoun established what he termed the great and leading principle, "that the General Government emanated from the people of the several States, forming distinct political communities, and acting in their separate and sovereign capacity, and not from all of the people forming one aggregate political community." The South Carolinian brought to the philosophy of American government one of the great intellects of our history; he may be read with much profit today.

Coming to more contemporary affairs, we have here included the text of a statement delivered before a subcommittee of the Senate Judiciary Committee by the Commission's chairman, Mr. David J. Mays. The statement examines one of the grave constitutional questions involved in the Supreme Court's decision in the School Segregation Cases: In terms of a State's power to operate racially separate public schools, what was the intention of those who framed and ratified the Fourteenth Amendment? A more extended essay on the same theme, prepared by the Commission's staff, follows upon Mr. Mays' statement.

This volume concludes by providing the full text of the widely acclaimed Report adopted by the Conference of Chief Justices at Pasadena in August of 1958. It was through this Report that the State Chief Justices, by overwhelming vote, urged upon the Supreme Court of the United States a renewed dedication to the wisdom of judicial restraint.

In offering this anthology to students, teachers, and friends of the Constitution, the Virginia Commission on Constitutional Government ventures a prayer that responsible ways and means will be found for adapting the "fundamental principles" of our past to the social and political problems that lie ahead. These principles were sound when our Republic was created, for they were based upon eternal truths of man's behavior—and the state's behavior also. However greatly our society has changed, the principles endure.

The Commission's grateful appreciation is expressed to Miss May Gee, for labors beyond the call of duty as the Commission's secretary, and to Mr. Willis Shell of William Byrd Press, whose good taste and ingenuity as designer and typographer made the book possible.

JAMES J. KILPATRICK, *Chairman*
COMMITTEE ON PUBLICATIONS

TABLE OF CONTENTS

The Articles of Amendment:

INTRODUCTION

N MONDAY, August 6, South Carolina's John Rutledge submitted to the Philadelphia convention of 1787 the first full draft of a tentative Constitution. His "Committee of Detail" had been hard at work, during a three-day recess, trying to knit together a hundred different provisions for fashioning a new government for the United States of America.

History does not record that anyone paid much attention to the Committee's draft of a preamble. It read:

We the people of the States of New Hampshire, Massachusetts, Rhode-Island and Providence Plantations, Connecticut, New-York, New-Jersey, Pennsylvania, Delaware, Maryland, Virginia, North-Carolina, South-Carolina, and Georgia, do ordain, declare, and establish the following Constitution for the Government of Ourselves and Our Posterity.

On the following day, as Madison's Notes of the Convention of 1787 disclose, the preamble was approved in that form "nem. con." Not until Thursday, August 30, when the weary delegates worked their way to the very end of the tentative document, did a disturbing uncertainty creep into the debate: How many States were likely to ratify any Constitution at all? This was a *Union* being formed—a voluntary union of separate, sovereign States. Maryland's Daniel Carroll thought that the ratification of all thirteen States should be required. Roger Sherman of Connecticut was willing to settle for ten. James Wilson of Pennsylvania pointed out that the Constitution would be binding only upon the States that agreed to it; he thought eight ratifications would be sufficient to start a new Union. James Madison proposed that the operative clause be based upon the ratifications of seven States entitled collectively to 33 members of the House. In the end, the convention compromised upon the ratifications of nine States as a sufficient number to establish the Constitution among themselves. The following week, debate moved on to other issues.

But as one reads over the notes of these historic conversations, one senses that some intensely practical questions of political tactics were beginning to assume larger proportions. By the first of September, the convention plainly was drawing to a close. There seemed no hope whatever that Rhode Island would ratify. North Carolina was most uncertain. Virginia's George Mason had just remarked "that he would sooner chop off his right hand than put it to the Constitution as it now stands." The vote in New York predictably would be close.

With all these considerations in mind, it becomes easier to grasp the prudent deletions recommended on September 12, when the Committee on Style and Arrangements, headed by Connecticut's conciliatory Samuel Johnson, brought in a new and substantially final draft of a Constitution. This time the preamble read:

We, the people of the United States, in order to form a more perfect union, to establish justice, insure domestic tranquility, provide for the common defence, promote the general welfare, and secure the blessings of liberty to ourselves and our posterity, do ordain and establish this Constitution for the United States of America.

The diplomatic change, from "we, the people of [certain named] States," to "we, the people of the United States," aroused no recorded debate in the Philadelphia convention. As the context of their daily discussion makes clear, the delegates were perfectly well aware that the Constitution would have to be voted up or down by the States, acting individually; there was no thought of any "nationwide" referendum among the people as a whole. But the change did not escape the angry eye of Patrick Henry. The following June, in Virginia's great Convention of 1788, he seized upon the revised preamble as evidence that the Philadelphia delegates had sought to fashion a consolidated government.

"I have the highest veneration for those gentlemen," he cried, "but, sir, give me leave to demand, what right had they to say *We, the People?* My political curiosity, exclusive of my anxious solicitude for the public welfare, leads me to ask, who authorized them to speak the language of, *We the People*, instead of *We the States?* States are the characteristics and the soul of a confederation. If the States be not the agents of this compact, it must be one great consolidated national government, of the people of all the States."

One by one, proponents of the Constitution arose to assure the suspicious Henry that no such thing as a consolidated national government was being proposed. Edmund Pendleton, one of the Constitution's strongest advocates, agreed with Henry that a consolidated government, annihilating the States, necessarily would "terminate in despotism." Colonel Henry Lee said that "we the people" obviously meant, "we the people on whom the Constitution would operate"—that is, the people within each separate State. "It is not binding on the people until it becomes their act." Madison gave positive assurances: The people who were mentioned in the preamble were "not the people as composing one great body," but rather "the people composing thirteen sovereignties."

The question thus raised by Patrick Henry, and thus answered by the foremost spokesmen for the Constitution, provides a useful title and a pervading theme for the anthology of documents, statements, and essays here compiled. The principal concern of the Virginia Commission on Constitutional Government, a century and three-quarters later, is to raise again some of those warnings against centralism voiced by Henry and Mason, and to urge a renaissance of those sound principles of federation advanced by Madison, Pendleton, Franklin, Hamilton, Jay and others.

We speak here for the States, *qua* States, and for the people who are by constitutional definition citizens of each of them. Our dedication is to the structure of constitutional union erected by the ratifying States of 1788, and to the beautiful plan of checks and balances by which this house of our fathers was designed. We take the view that neither the Reconstruction amendments, nor any other amendments, have altered the statement of historic truth approved by the United States Senate in 1837:

In the adoption of the Federal Constitution, the States acted severally as free, independent and sovereign States. Each for itself, by its own voluntary assent, entered the Union with a view to its increased security against all dangers, domestic as well as foreign, and the more perfect and secure enjoyment of its natural political and social advantages.

In delegating a portion of their powers to be exercised by the Federal government, the States retained, individually and respectively, the exclusive and sole right over their own domestic institutions and police, and are alone responsible for them.

Today it is apparent to even the most casual eye that the house of our fathers has fallen into decay. The great beams that gave it strength—the separation of powers within the central government, the division of responsibility between the States and the Federal authority—now tend to crumble under subtle and insidious attack. The men who framed our Constitution built tight doors against the despotism they knew so well; now the doors hang awry, and a cold wind of judicial construction sweeps along the corridors. The States themselves, falling into impotence, often seem helpless to halt the destruction. And too many Americans, afflicted with the ills of an affluent society, are indifferent to the fundamental principles by which the greatness of the American Republic was achieved.

II

In the fifteenth article of Virginia's Declaration of Rights, George Mason in 1776 laid down a maxim for the sound guidance of our own generation: "Be it declared," he said, "that no free government, or the blessings of Liberty, can be preserved to any People but by a firm adherence to Justice, Moderation, Temperance, Frugality, and Virtue, and by frequent Recurrence to fundamental Principles."

We often tend to imagine, today, that our fundamental principles are to be dated from the Declaration of Independence or from the Constitution of 1787. Yet, clearly, Mason in 1776 was urging a recurrence to fundamental principles much older than this. What was he talking about? What did he ask the people to recur to?

Mason's fundamental principles, we submit, were grounded in the rights of man and the duties of government. Man was free; government's first duty was to keep that freedom inviolate. There was never much more than this. Man had rights; government had a duty to secure those rights. These were the fundamental principles, the alpha and the omega of the American Republic.

"All men are by nature equally free and independent," said Mason, "and have certain inherent rights, of which, when they enter a State of Society, they cannot, by any Compact, deprive or divest their posterity."

What were these inherent rights? They were in essence as Jefferson was to proclaim them in the Declaration of July 4: "Namely, the enjoyment of life and liberty, with the means of acquiring and possessing property, and pursuing and obtaining happiness and safety."

Consider, if you will, Mason's clear and simple definition. He did not hesitate to define the inherent rights of man, in part, in terms of "the means of possessing *property*." In our own day, "property" has become a dirty word; it was not so in Mason's time. Property rights meant something then; they do not seem to mean as much now.

What were some of Mason's other "fundamental principles" to which he urged man's frequent recurrence?

"That all power is vested in, and consequently derived

from, the People; that magistrates are their trustees and servants, and should at all times be amenable to them. . . . That government is, or ought to be, instituted for the common benefit, protection, and security of the people, nation, or community. . . . That the legislative and executive powers of the State ought always to be separate and distinct from the judiciary. . . . That the people ought never to be taxed or deprived of their property [again that word!] for public uses without their consent. . . ."

There were other fundamental principles important to Mason—trial by jury, freedom of the press, freedom of religion—but the first principles he set forth went to the liberty of man and to the nature of the state. These were the essential relationships he asked us to reflect upon; we cannot do better than to act upon his sage advice today.

Once the thoughtful citizen clarifies this relationship in his own mind—once he grasps the fundamental flow of power in its sure and proper channels—contemporary questions of political conflict lose some of their obscurity. In our Republic, political power springs from the people in their States—or as Madison said, from the people in their separate sovereignties—and out of the reservoirs of the States, some of this power flows on to the Federal sea. But the source is always in the people themselves; and it is a part of the beauty of the Constitution, when it is taken with the first ten amendments and treated as a whole, that it begins with the people—"We the People"—and it ends with the people, in that familiar reservation of power "to the States respectively, or to the people."

"All authority belongs to the people," said Jefferson, but he knew this principle would be forgotten. "The spirit of our times may alter," he wrote in his *Notes on Virginia*; and then he corrected "*may* alter" to read "will alter." The spirit of our times will alter: "Our rulers will become corrupt, our people careless. They will be forgotten and their rights disregarded. They will forget themselves, but in the sole faculty of making money, and will never think of uniting to effect a due respect for their rights."

Contemporary examples of the truth of Jefferson's prophecy may be found at every hand. Yet the people have become careless not only of abstract principle but also of the political machinery by which our rights and powers are distributed. "The capital and leading object of the Constitution," said Jefferson, "was to leave with the States all authorities which respected their own citizens only, and to transfer to the United States those which respected citizens of foreign or other States: To make us several as to ourselves, but one as to all others."

It was this aspect of the Constitution that most captivated Tocqueville. He thought the Constitution of 1787 "the most perfect Federal constitution that ever existed," the work of a small convention that contained "the finest minds and the noblest characters that had ever appeared in the new world." No aspect of their genius seemed to him more appealing than the plan by which "each colony became an independent republic, assumed an absolute sovereignty," and then took its place as one of the United States that form "not only a Republic, but a confederation." When Tocqueville wrote, in the 1830's, he gazed with admiration on what he termed "the 24 small sovereign nations, whose agglomeration constitutes the body of the Union." And he added: "The great political principles which now govern American society undoubtedly took their origin and their growth in the State. We must know the State, then, in order to gain a clue to the rest." To

Tocqueville, the sovereignty of the Union was "an abstract being," but the sovereignty of the States was "perceptible by the senses, easily understood, and constantly active."

Yet this perceptive French critic, though some of his prophecies have proved as wrong as some of Madison's and Hamilton's, shrewdly foresaw the dangers to the federal plan he praised so warmly. The most fatal defect he saw in the Constitution at the time was "the relative weakness of the government of the Union." He was certain this defect would be corrected in time, but then a greater danger would arise: "I cannot conceive," he wrote, "that a nation can live and prosper without a powerful centralization of government. But I am of the opinion that centralized administration is fit only to enervate the nations in which it exists, by incessantly diminishing their local spirit." The trouble, he added, is that when the social power is centralized in legislative hands, it often forgets "the maxims of wisdom and foresight in the consciousness of its strength. Hence arises its danger. *Its vigor, and not its impotence, will probably be the cause of its ultimate destruction.*"

One hundred and thirty-five years after Tocqueville wrote, the acuity of his insight commands our admiration. It is indeed the vigor of our central government, and not its impotence, that steadily threatens to destroy the American confederation. We are encountering, in our own own time, the very persuasive arguments Tocqueville anticipated: It would be said, he predicted, that the central government in Washington could manage local affairs much more efficiently and more uniformly, than local governments could manage them on their own. But he added reflectively: "It profits me but little, after all, that a vigilant authority always protects the tranquillity of my pleasures and constantly averts all dangers from my path, without my care or concern, if this same authority is the absolute master of my liberty and my life, and if it so monopolizes movement and life that when it languishes everything languishes around it; that when it sleeps, everything must sleep, and that when it dies the state itself must perish."

III

It is important, in this discussion, to ask ourselves the key question of why? Why did the people, as the source of all political power, devise the finely balanced mechanism of the Constitution of 1787? The abstractions of sovereignty and the legalities of ratification to one side, *why* the States? The most cursory reading of the Constitution will disclose the vital role assigned them. Under the compact, they were to have equal representation in the Senate; their electors were to choose a President—or if that failed, the States themselves, voting as equals, were to choose a President; the final power of constitutional amendment was to rest in the States as States, and not in a mere majority of the States but in not fewer than three-fourths of them; and finally, in that ringing amendment insisted upon by New Hampshire and New York as firmly as by Virginia and North Carolina, the States wanted it known that all powers not delegated to the central government by the Constitution, nor prohibited by the Constitution to the States, were reserved to the States *respectively*, or to the people.

The architecture of the Constitution is familiar to us all. The question that occupies our reflection is *why* the structure was designed this way. Two reasons suggest themselves, one negative, the other affirmative, and these are as applicable to our Union today as they were at the time of its formation. First, the founding fathers feared the excessive centralization of power; second, they wanted to secure the advantages of political experiment that arise from a diversified control of political authority.

Both doctrines are old; they were part of the fundamental principles Mason and Jefferson and Patrick Henry had in mind. Aristotle warned of the dangers that arise when a government of laws is corrupted by a government of men. In his *Politics*, Aristotle praises the rule of the law and says this: "Therefore, he who bids the law rule may be deemed to bid God and Reason alone rule, but he who bids man rule adds an element of the beast; for desire is a wild beast, and passion perverts the minds of rulers, even when they are the best of men. The law is reason unaffected by desire."

Two thousand years later, in the Virginia Convention of 1788, the same abiding truths were to be eloquently expressed. One of the most interesting men in that constellation of greatness was a rough countryman, William Grayson. On June 21, he arose to respond to the pleas of Madison, Marshall, Edmund Randolph, and others that greater trust and confidence should be reposed in the men —and especially the judges—who would occupy high office under the new Constitution.

"Mr. Chairman," said Grayson, "it seems to have been a rule with the gentlemen on the other side, to argue from the excellency of human nature, in order to induce us to grant away the rights and liberties of our country. I have no doubt the same arguments were used in a variety of occasions. I suppose, Sir, that same argument was used when Cromwell was invested with power. The same argument was used to gain our assent to the stamp act. I have no doubt it has been invariably the argument in all countries, when the concession of power has been in agitation. But power ought to have such checks and limitations as to prevent bad men from abusing it. It ought to be granted on a supposition that men will be bad; for it may be eventually so."

This same theme was sounded relentlessly by Patrick Henry: "I may be thought suspicious," he cried, "when I say our privileges and rights are in danger. But, Sir, suspicion is a virtue, as long as its object is the preservation of the public good, and as long as it stays within proper bounds.... Guard with jealous attention the public liberty! Suspect every one who approaches that jewel!" Henry was not persuaded that "we need not fear, because those in power, being our representatives, will not abuse the powers we put in their hands."

"I am not well versed in history," he said at another point, "but I will submit to your recollection, whether liberty has been destroyed most often by the licentiousness of the people, or by the tyranny of rulers? I imagine, Sir, you will find the balance on the side of tyranny."

George Mason was still another who sounded this alarm repeatedly in the Virginia Convention: "It is ascertained by history," he said, "that there never was a government over a very extensive country without destroying the liberties of the people; history also . . . shows us that monarchy may suit a large territory, and despotic governments ever so extensive a country; but that popular governments can only exist in small territories. Is there a single example, on the face of the earth, to support a contrary opinion? Where is there one exception to this general rule? Was there ever an instance of a general national government extending over so extensive a country, abounding in such a variety of climates, where the people retained their liberty?"

So, too, with Jefferson. In a letter sent from Paris to Madison the December preceding the Virginia convention in June, he discussed at length the features he did not like in the proposed Constitution. There was no bill of rights; there was no positive provision for rotation of the presidential office; there was no clause expressly reserving to the States the powers not delegated to the central government. Jefferson was suspicious that too much authority would be concentrated in Federal hands. "I own I am not a friend to a very energetic government," he said, "It is always oppressive."

How were the oppressions of centralized authority to be avoided? Jefferson provided a thundering answer in his famed Kentucky Resolution: "In questions of power, let no more be heard of confidence in man, but bind him down from mischief by the chains of the Constitution!"

The chains rust. The prudent warnings of these great men go unheeded now. They looked upon government with a suspicious, jealous eye. "Too much suspicion may be corrected," said Henry. "If you give too little power today, you may give more tomorrow. But the reverse of the proposition will not hold. If you give too much power today, you cannot retake it tomorrow; for tomorrow will never come for *that* purpose." In our own time, a trustful and gullible people daily yield more of their liberties and responsibilities to the state, until government, like the Minotaur, feeds upon the very body of our freedoms.

What were the links the founding fathers forged—or thought they forged—that were to bind down our magistrates? The powers delegated to the Congress were accompanied at every hand by powers specifically withheld. The executive was set in check against the legislature, with a power in two-thirds of the legislature to override the executive. The President's power to negotiate treaties was to be checked by the Senate's right of advice and consent. Against both of these branches of government, the judiciary was to provide still a third check and balance, but the jurisdiction of the Supreme Court was to be made subject, in certain particulars, to the powers of the Congress. And standing watchfully over the whole apparatus were to be the States themselves, holding the power of amendment, and ready (as they thought) to reassume their powers and withdraw from the Union if the peoples' liberties should appear in danger. "Our peculiar security," said Jefferson in 1803, "is in possession of a *written* Constitution." Then he added a fateful warning: "Let us not make it a blank paper by construction."

So much, then, for the first, negative, reason that explains the "why" of the States: The structure of the American Union was intended to prevent the accretion of excessive political power in the hands of the central government. With sound reason, our fathers feared such power. It was not that they loved order less, but they loved freedom more.

IV

There is a second, affirmative, reason for the reservation of undelegated powers to the States. Jefferson once summed it up in a blunt declaration that, *"Our country is too large to have all its affairs directed by a single government."*

The country was too large then; it is much larger now.

The strength of our Federal super-structure lies in the fact that it rests upon fifty pillars, not upon one. Former Justice Burton remarked in a famous opinion that "the differing needs and customs of the respective States and even of the respective communities within each State emphasize the principle that familiarity with, and complete understanding of, local characteristics, customs and standards are foundation stones of successful self-government. . . . No national government, however benevolent, that governs over 130 million people in 48 States can be as closely in touch with those who are governed as can the local authorities in the several States and their subdivisions."

Many writers have referred to the States as "fifty separate laboratories for experimenting in self-government." The metaphor is apt. Political wisdom is not concentrated in Congressional retorts alone. It exists also in State capitals from coast to coast, and in the offices of State agencies. Here ideas may be tested individually: Georgia and Kentucky may experiment with an extension of the franchise to 18-year-olds; Nevada may experiment with gambling laws that seem unwise to other States; legislation dealing with highway safety, medical care, the regulation of labor, civil rights, air and stream pollution—in all these fields, the States, familiar with the needs and desires of their own people, may experiment with varying remedies. Some experiments will fail. Of course they will fail. Who should imagine otherwise? But if an experiment does fail, the consequences may be confined; and if an experiment succeeds, the good may be emulated.

This is one of the great "whys" of the States: Diversity in political solution, experimentation, refinement, innovation, the testing of governmental process on the hard anvil of trial and error. And to the extent the States are deprived of their powers in this regard, or discouraged in the use of their powers, the vitality of the Union as a whole inevitably must decline. More than this, the freedom of the people, and their responsibility for their own destinies, surely must be diminished. Uniformity is a benevolent god; smiling gently, he snuffs out the human spirit.

But it is often objected, by the advocates of a greater centralism, that "the States have failed to meet the needs of the people." And if the States continue to fail to meet the needs of the people, it is said, the people must turn to Washington. This is a specious line of reasoning. The power to act embraces the power not to act; the power "to provide for a need" includes the power to conclude that a need does not exist. If a town or county or State refuses to build a certain school house, after public hearing and debate by the processes of representative government, is it to be said that the town or county or State has "refused to meet a need," and therefore, the correcting hand of Washington must be summoned? This is nonsense. When the desires of articulate pressure groups become confused with the genuine needs of a prudent and thrifty people, the very essence of self-government is corrupted. We of Virginia have in the Congress 12 able men. What do they know of the local needs of Arizona or of Indiana? By what arrogance may they assume a wisdom superior to that of a State legislature in acting upon State needs? No. Organized blocs turn to Washington primarily for this reason: Because that is where the money is; and second, because the Congress is an easy mark. City Councils and State legislatures, close to their people, sensitive to reality, know when to resist. But the Congress is conscious of Aristotle's maxim that a proposal "which is common to the greatest number has the least care bestowed upon it." Accountability is spread thin on Capitol Hill.

Within the realm of their domestic concerns, the States have a right to be wrong—wrong, that is, in the view of other States and other peoples. This is not to say that the States have a right to be unconstitutional; they have a right to be "wrong," and it is a travesty upon the political and judicial process that an action thought wrong or unwise is held to be, *for that reason,* unconstitutional. Courts ought never to concern themselves with the wisdom of the lawmaker, but solely with his power to enact. "State constitutions and State laws," said Holmes, "may regulate life in many ways which we might think injudicious, or if you like, tyrannical." This is the States' prerogative, and judges have no authority to substitute their own policies out of some personal convictions of social or economic propriety. The States have an unquestioned right, Holmes said again, to engage in experiments that "may seem futile or even noxious to me and to those whose judgment I most respect." Nothing in the Constitution requires Virginia to accept the social experiments that delight the California eye. Arizona is not bound in her domestic policies by visiting experts from the East. Indiana has the power to bring to the local problems of Indiana the political wisdom of Indiana. Among many friends of individual liberty, the rent control that lingers in New York is seen as a violation of every great principle of property right and personal freedom. But this is New York's business, not ours; and we of Virginia sometimes wish that New York would take the same tolerant view of matters that are our business and none of New York's.

V

Now, if these ancient principles of government are sound (as we believe they are); and if they have been eroded by the avidity of our magistrates and the apathy of our people (as we believe they have); and if a responsibility exists to attack this erosion, what do we do about it?

We of this Commission have no warrant to serve as some platform committee for a Conservative party, assigned to set forth a complete statement of political objectives. We do suggest a few areas by way of example.

First, we would urge that everything possible be done, at whatever sacrifice, to stop the Federal juggernaut in its tracks. Let us press for a moratorium on new programs of Federal grants in aid, and insist that existing programs be held at present levels until a judicious and responsible rollback can be attempted.

We would propose further, that a plan be devised for gradual reduction, over a period of several years, of certain Federal programs that have distorted our structure in the past few decades. These cannot be abandoned summarily, and it is the worst sort of naivete to cherish some illusion that they can. States and localities have been nursing on the Federal breast too long; the weaning process takes time.

But suppose it were said, for instance, that Federal grants for urban renewal—a program of the most doubtful constitutionality—would be steadily reduced in the future; suppose it were said that Federal shares of aid to various welfare recipients steadily would be decreased, that grants for local sewerage would decline, that schools would be expected to pay more of the cost for "free" hot lunches.

Obviously, a terrible cry would go up from the State and local officials charged with raising money and administering the many plans now subject to Federal aid. But their anguish might be quieted—and this is a necessary corollary to the whole proposal—if simultaneously tax sources now preempted or dominated by the central government also were relinquished to the States. Mr. Eisenhower once urged precisely this approach: He was agreeable to seeing the Federal tax on telephones repealed, so that the States could reenact it, if they chose, without additional burden to telephone subscribers. Nothing came of his plan, and Mr. Eisenhower did not push it. But the approach was essentially sound.

Other objectives present themselves for candid review: Existing tax policies make the formation of capital exceedingly difficult, and capital supports the entire economic structure. Those who would recur to fundamental principles should take the lead in seeking a continuing program of tax reduction and reform—a program that would leave to the people more of their earnings, make available to the private economy new reservoirs of capital, and in the end augment the revenues of government itself.

On another front, a determined effort should be made to get the government out of some of its business-type enterprises. Again, the divestiture of billions of dollars in property, involving the entrenched jobs of thousands of persons, cannot be accomplished in a twinkling. But in our despair at solving the problem as a whole, we ought not to abandon attempts to solve bits of it piecemeal. It is the very vastness of the Federal machine that overwhelms and defeats so many efforts to bring government under better control: Why save a million dollars, it is wearily asked, when a billion is being wasted away somewhere else? The answer is of course to resist the outpouring of non-essential billions, but to realize that a flooded river is not brought back in its channels by dropping a single great boulder in its path. A levee is built one bag at a time. An orderly disposition of Federal surplus property, and a planned suspension of various Federal enterprises, provide reasonable goals for reasonable men to aim at.

Many other specific objectives could be enumerated. Senator Tower has suggested, for example, in his excellent covenant of conservative pledges, a renewed effort to obtain enactment of Representative Howard Smith's "anti-pre-emption" resolution. This resolution passed in the House by a large vote in 1960 and narrowly failed in the Senate. Several amendments to the Constitution merit affirmative support: The old Mundt-Coudert plan, for instance, by which presidential electors would be chosen by congressional districts within each State, instead of by States at large, has much to commend it. Sound principles of federalism support a revision of Article V by which the States themselves, without the intercession of the Congress, could submit proposed amendments to the Constitution directly to their sister States, which amendments would become part of the Constitution on approval of three-fourths of the States. A renewed dedication to old ideals would embrace a program of greater freedom for the farmer, greater freedom for the railways, greater freedom for the businessman, greater security for a worker's right to work—and yet make it quite clear that we propose a return of neither dust bowls nor robber barons.

Finally, it may be suggested that no positions that might be taken at the national level will amount to much unless simultaneously, in every State, a truly determined and active effort is made to promote constructive programs within our own bailiwick. The Governor of New York said in 1962:

"We stand upon the threshold of a new test of leadership at the State level. For so great and urgent are the demands of national defense and foreign policy upon all resources of the national government that now, as never in our history, are State governments challenged to face and meet the pressing domestic concerns of our society. We stand, in short, at an historic point in the long evolution of our federal idea. It summons us to remember and to apply a basic truth of American political history—the truth that our States are designed to be our great centers for political experiment. The time is upon us to assert again the older and more vital tradition, to call upon our States to be active where they have been passive, progressive where they have been timid, creative where they have been merely cautious. In a word, it is time for the States to lead."

Virginia subscribes wholeheartedly to this view. If we will work in our States for genuinely constructive programs; if we will look forward to the 21st Century as often as we look back to the 18th, we may again see the great beacon light of constitutional government shining through the clouds that now obscure it. The eternal truths that govern man's best and happiest relationship with the state are not dead. They are sleeping, and need only to be awakened and applied to the political problems of our own day and time.

—J. J. K.

Richmond,
June, 1964

WE THE STATES

THE VIRGINIA
DECLARATION OF RIGHTS

THE VIRGINIA
DECLARATION of RIGHTS

Drawn originally by GEORGE MASON and then adopted unanimously by the *Convention of Delegates* at the *Capitol* in *Williamsburg* on June 12, 1776.

I.

THAT all Men are by Nature equally free and independent, and have certain inherent Rights, of which, when they enter into a State of Society, they cannot, by any Compact, deprive or divest their Posterity; namely, the Enjoyment of Life and Liberty, with the Means of acquiring and possessing Property, and pursuing and obtaining Happiness and Safety.

II.

That all Power is vested in, and consequently derived from, the People; that Magistrates are their Trustees and Servants, and at all Times amenable to them.

III.

That Government is, or ought to be, instituted for the common Benefit, Protection, and Security, of the People, Nation, or Community; of all the various Modes and Forms of Government that is best, which is capable of producing the greatest Degree of Happiness and Safety, and is most effectually secured against the Danger of Mal-administration; and that, whenever any Government shall be found inadequate or contrary to these Purposes, a Majority of the Community hath an indubitable, unalienable, and indefeasible Right, to reform, alter, or abolish it, in such Manner as shall be judged most conducive to the public Weal.

IV.

That no Man, or Set of Men, are entitled to exclusive or separate Emoluments or Privileges from the Community, but in Consideration of public Services; which, not being descendible, neither ought the Offices of Magistrate, Legislator, or Judge, to be hereditary.

V.

That the legislative and executive Powers of the State should be separate and distinct from the Judicative; and, that the Members of the two first may be restrained from Oppression, by feeling and participating the Burthens of the People, they should, at fixed Periods, be reduced to a private Station, return into that Body from which they were originally taken, and the Vacancies be supplied by frequent, certain, and regular Elections, in which all, or any Part of the former Members, to be again eligible, or ineligible, as the Laws shall direct.

VI.

That Elections of Members to serve as Representatives of the People, in Assembly, ought to be free; and that all Men, having sufficient Evidence of permanent common Interest with, and Attachment to, the Community, have the Right of Suffrage, and cannot be taxed or deprived of their Property for public Uses without their own Consent or that of their Representatives so elected, nor bound by any Law to which they have not, in like Manner, assented, for the public Good.

VII.

That all Power of suspending Laws, or the Execution of Laws, by any Authority without Consent of the Representatives of the People, is injurious to their Rights, and ought not to be exercised.

VIII.

That in all capital or criminal Prosecutions a Man hath a Right to demand the Cause and Nature of his Accusation, to be confronted with the Accusers and Witnesses, to call for Evidence in his Favour, and to a speedy Trial by an impartial Jury of his Vicinage, without whose unanimous Consent he cannot be found guilty, nor can he be compelled to give Evidence against himself; that no Man be deprived of his Liberty except by the Law of the Land, or the Judgment of his Peers.

IX.

That excessive Bail ought not to be required, nor excessive Fines imposed; nor cruel and unusual Punishments inflicted.

X.

That general Warrants, whereby any Officer or Messenger may be commanded to search suspected Places without Evidence of a Fact committed, or to seize any Person or Persons not named, or whose Offence is not particularly described and supported by Evidence, are grievous and oppressive, and ought not to be granted.

XI.

That in Controversies respecting Property, and in Suits between Man and Man, the ancient Trial by Jury is preferable to any other, and ought to be held sacred.

XII.

That the Freedom of the Press is one of the greatest Bulwarks of Liberty, and can never be restrained but by despotic Governments.

XIII.

That a well regulated Militia, composed of the Body of the People, trained to Arms, is the proper, natural, and safe Defense of a free State; that standing Armies, in Time of Peace, should be avoided, as dangerous to Liberty; and that, in all Cases, the Military should be under strict Subordination to, and governed by, the civil Power.

XIV.

That the People have a Right to uniform Government; and therefore, that no Government separate from, or independent of, the Government of *Virginia*, ought to be erected or established within the Limits thereof.

XV.

That no free Government, or the Blessings of Liberty, can be preserved to any People but by a firm Adherence to Justice, Moderation, Temperance, Frugality, and Virtue, and by frequent Recurrence to fundamental Principles.

XVI.

That Religion, or the Duty which we owe to our Creator, and the Manner of discharging it, can be directed only by Reason and Conviction, not by Force or Violence; and therefore, all Men are equally entitled to the free exercise of Religion, according to the Dictates of Conscience; and that it is the mutual Duty of all to practise Christian Forbearance, Love, and Charity towards each other.

☆ ☆ ☆ ☆ ☆ ☆ ☆ ☆ ☆ ☆ ☆ ☆ ☆

THE DECLARATION OF INDEPENDENCE

An Excerpt from the AUTOBIOGRAPHY of Thomas Jefferson

ON the 15th of May, 1776, the convention of Virginia instructed their delegates in Congress, to propose to that body to declare the colonies independent of Great Britain, and appointed a committee to prepare a declaration of rights and plan of government.

In Congress, Friday, June 7, 1776. The delegates from Virginia moved, in obedience to instructions from their constituents, that the Congress should declare that these United colonies are, and of right ought to be, free and independent states, that they are absolved from all allegiance to the British crown, and that all political connection between them and the state of Great Britain is, and ought to be, totally dissolved; that measures should be immediately taken for procuring the assistance of foreign powers, and a Confederation be formed to bind the colonies more closely together.

The House being obliged to attend at that time to some other business, the proposition was referred to the next day, when the members were ordered to attend punctually at ten o'clock.

Saturday, June 8. They proceeded to take it into consideration, and referred it to a committee of the whole, into which they immediately resolved themselves, and passed that day and Monday, the 10th, in debating on the subject. . . .

It appearing in the course of these debates, that the colonies of New York, New Jersey, Pennsylvania, Delaware, Maryland, and South Carolina were not yet matured for falling from the parent stem, but that they were fast advancing to that state, it was thought most prudent to wait a while for them, and to postpone the final decision to July 1st; but, that this might occasion as little delay as possible, a committee was appointed to prepare a Declaration of Independence. The Committee were John Adams, Dr. Franklin, Roger Sherman, Robert R. Livingston, and myself. Committees were also appointed, at the same time, to prepare a plan of confederation for the colonies, and to state the terms proper to be proposed for foreign alliance.

The committee for drawing the Declaration of Independence, desired me to do it. It was accordingly done, and being approved by them, I reported it to the House on Friday, the 28th of June, when it was read, and ordered to lie on the table. On Monday, the 1st of July, the House resolved itself into a committee of the whole, and resumed the consideration of the original motion made by the delegates of Virginia, which, being again debated through the day, was carried in the affirmative by the votes of New Hampshire, Connecticut, Massachusetts, Rhode Island, New Jersey, Maryland, Virginia, North Carolina and Georgia. South Carolina and Pennsylvania voted against it. Delaware had but two members present, and they were divided. The delegates from New York declared they were for it themselves, and were assured their constituents were for it; but that their instructions having been drawn near a twelvemonth before, when reconciliation was still the general object, they were enjoined by them to do nothing which should impede that object. They, therefore, thought themselves not justifiable in voting on either side, and asked leave to withdraw from the question; which was given them.

The committee rose and reported their resolution to the House. Mr. Edward Rutledge, of South Carolina, then requested the determination might be put off to the next day, as he believed his colleagues, though they disapproved of the resolution, would then join in it for the sake of unanimity. The ultimate question, whether the House would agree to the resolution of the committee, was accordingly postponed to the next day, when it was again moved, and South Carolina concurred in voting for it. In the meantime, a third member had come post from the Delaware counties, and turned the vote of that colony in favor of the resolution. Members of a different sentiment attending that morning from Pennsylvania also, her vote was changed, so that the whole twelve colonies who were authorized to vote at all, gave their voices for it; and, within a few days, the convention of New York approved of it, and thus supplied the void occasioned by the withdrawing of her delegates from the vote.

Congress proceeded the same day to consider the Declaration of Independence, which had been reported and lain on the table the Friday preceding, and on Monday referred to a committee of the whole. The pusillanimous idea that we had friends in England worth keeping terms with, still haunted the minds of many. For this reason, those passages which conveyed censures on the people of England were struck out, lest they should give them offence. The clause too, reprobating the enslaving the inhabitants of Africa, was struck out in compliasance to South Carolina and Georgia, who had never attempted to restrain the importation of slaves, and who, on the contrary, still wished to continue it. Our northern brethren also, I believe, felt a little tender under those censures; for though their people had very few slaves themselves, yet they had been pretty considerable carriers of them to others. The debates, having taken up the greater parts of the 2d, 3d, and 4th days of July, were, on the evening of the last, closed; the

Declaration was reported by the committee, agreed to by the House, and signed by every member present, except Mr. Dickinson. As the sentiments of men are known not only by what they receive, but what they reject also, I will state the form of the Declaration as originally reported. The parts struck out by Congress shall be distinguished by a black line drawn under them;* and those inserted by them shall be placed in the margin, or in a concurrent column.

• • •

* The text of the Declaration of Independence that follows is taken, as to capitalization and punctuation, from the broadside that was printed on the night of July 4, 1776. The portions of Jefferson's draft that were deleted by the Congress are bracketed in struck type; the passages added by the Congress are shown in italics. This was the official text of the Declaration. A copy of the broadside itself was wafered into the manuscript minutes of the Continental Congress by Charles Thomson, the secretary. In August of 1776, an engrossed copy, differing slightly from the official text, was made for signing. This second version is the one most often seen.

☆ ☆ ☆ ☆ ☆ ☆ ☆ ☆ ☆ ☆ ☆ ☆ ☆

In CONGRESS, July 4, 1776.

A DECLARATION

By the REPRESENTATIVES of the UNITED STATES OF AMERICA, In GENERAL CONGRESS assembled.

WHEN in the Course of human Events, it becomes necessary for one People to dissolve the Political Bands which have connected them with another, and to assume among the Powers of the Earth, the separate and equal Station to which the Laws of Nature and of Nature's God entitle them, a decent Respect to the Opinions of Mankind requires that they should declare the causes which impel them to the Separation.

WE hold these Truths to be self-evident, that all Men are created equal, that they are endowed by their Creator with [inherent and] *certain* unalienable Rights, that among these are Life, Liberty, and the Pursuit of Happiness—That to secure these Rights, Governments are instituted among Men, deriving their just Powers from the Consent of the Governed, that whenever any Form of Government becomes destructive of these Ends, it is the Right of the People to alter or to abolish it, and to institute new Government, laying its Foundation on such Principles, and organizing its Powers in such Form, as to them shall seem most likely to effect their Safety and Happiness. Prudence, indeed, will dictate that Government long established should not be changed for light and transient Causes; and accordingly all Experience hath shewn, that Mankind are more disposed to suffer, while Evils are sufferable, than to right themselves by abolishing the Forms to which they are accustomed. But when a long Train of Abuses and Usurpations ~~[begun at a distinguished period and]~~, pursuing invariably the same Object, evinces a Design to reduce them under absolute Despotism, it is their Right, it is their Duty, to throw off such Government, and to provide new Guards for their future Security. Such has been the patient Sufferance of these Colonies; and such is now the Necessity which constrains them to ~~[expunge]~~ *alter* their former Systems of Government. The History of the present King of Great-Britain is a History of ~~[unremitting]~~ *repeated* Injuries and Usurpations, ~~[among which appears no solitary fact to contradict the uniform tenor of the rest, but all have]~~ *all having* in direct Object the Establishment of an absolute Tyranny over these States. To prove this, let Facts be submitted to a candid World ~~[for the truth of which we pledge a faith yet unsullied by falsehood]~~.

HE has refused his Assent to Laws, the most wholesome and necessary for the public Good.

HE has forbidden his Governors to pass Laws of immediate and pressing Importance, unless suspended in their Operation till his Assent should be obtained; and when so suspended, he has utterly neglected to attend to them.

HE has refused to pass other Laws for the Accommodation of large Districts of People, unless those People would relinquish the Right of Representation in the Legislature, a Right inestimable to them, and formidable to Tyrants only.

HE has called together Legislative Bodies at Places unusual, uncomfortable, and distant from the Depository of their public Records, for the sole Purpose of fatiguing them into Compliance with his Measures.

HE has dissolved Representative Houses repeatedly ~~[and continually]~~, for opposing with manly Firmness his Invasions on the Rights of the People.

12

HE has refused for a long Time, after such Dissolutions, to cause others to be elected; whereby the Legislative Powers, incapable of Annihilation, have returned to the People at large for their exercise; the State remaining in the mean time exposed to all the Dangers of Invasion from without, and Convulsions within.

HE has endeavoured to prevent the Population of these States; for that Purpose obstructing the Laws for Naturalization of Foreigners; refusing to pass others to encourage their Migrations hither, and raising the Conditions of new Appropriations of Lands.

HE has [suffered] *obstructed* the Administration of Justice [totally to cease in some of these States], *by* refusing his Assent to Laws for establishing Judiciary Powers.

HE has made [our] Judges dependent on his Will alone, for the Tenure of their Offices, and the Amount and Payment of their Salaries.

HE has erected a Multitude of new Offices [by a self-assumed power], and sent hither Swarms of Officers to harrass our People; and eat out their Substance.

HE has kept among us, in Times of Peace, Standing Armies [and ships of war], without the consent of our Legislatures.

HE has affected to render the Military independent of and superior to the Civil Power.

HE has combined with others to subject us to a Jurisdiction foreign to our Constitution, and unacknowledged by our Laws; giving his Assent to their Acts of pretended Legislation:

FOR quartering large Bodies of Armed Troops among us:

FOR protecting them, by a mock Trial, from Punishment for any Murders which they should commit on the Inhabitants of these States:

FOR cutting off our Trade with all Parts of the World:

FOR imposing Taxes on us without our Consent:

FOR depriving us, *in many Cases,* of the Benefits of Trial by Jury:

FOR transporting us beyond Seas to be tried for pretended offences:

FOR abolishing the free System of English Laws in a neighbouring Province, establishing therein an arbitrary Government, and enlarging its Boundaries, so as to render it at once an Example and fit Instrument for introducing the same absolute Rule into these [States] *Colonies*:

FOR taking away our Charters, abolishing our most valuable Laws, and altering fundamentally the Forms of our Governments:

FOR suspending our own Legislatures, and declaring themselves invested with Power to legislate for us in all Cases whatsoever.

HE has abdicated Government here, [withdrawing his governors, and declaring us out of his allegiance and protection] *by declaring us out of his Protection and waging War against us.*

HE has plundered our Seas, ravaged our Coasts, burnt our Towns, and destroyed the Lives of our People.

HE is, at this Time, transporting large Armies of foreign Mercenaries to compleat the Works of Death, Desolation and Tyranny, already begun with circumstances of Cruelty and Perfidy, scarcely paralled in the most barbarous Ages, and totally unworthy the Head of a civilized Nation.

HE has constrained our fellow Citizens taken Captive on the high Seas to bear Arms against their Country, to become the Executioners of their Friends and Brethren, or to fall themselves by their Hands.

HE has *excited domestic Insurrections amongst us, and has*

14

endeavoured to bring on the Inhabitants of our Frontiers, the merciless Indian Savages, whose known Rule of Warfare, is an undistinguished Destruction of all Ages, Sexes and Conditions ~~[of existence]~~.

~~[He has incited treasonable insurrections of our fellow-citizens, with the allurements of forfeiture and confiscation of our property.~~

~~He has waged cruel war against human nature itself, violating its most sacred rights of life and liberty in the persons of a distant people who never offended him, captivating and carrying them into slavery in another hemisphere, or to incur miserable death in their transportation thither. This piratical warfare, the opprobrium of INFIDEL powers, is the warfare of the CHRISTIAN King of Great-Britain. Determined to keep open a market where MEN should be bought and sold, he has prostituted his negative for suppressing every legislative attempt to prohibit or to restrain this execrable commerce. And that this assemblage of horrors might want no fact of distinguished die, he is now exciting those very people to rise in arms among us, and to purchase that liberty of which he has deprived them, by murdering the people on whom he also obtruded them: thus paying off former crimes committed against the LIBERTIES of one people with crimes which he urges them to commit against the LIVES of another.]~~

IN every stage of these Oppressions we have Petitioned for redress in the most humble Terms: Our repeated Petitions have been answered only by repeated Injury. A Prince, whose Character is thus marked by every act which may define a Tyrant, is unfit to be the Ruler of a *free* People ~~[who mean to be free. Future ages will scarcely believe that the hardiness of one man adventured, within the short compass of twelve years only, to lay a foundation so broad and so undisguised for tyranny over a people fostered and fixed in principles of freedom.]~~

15

Nᴏʀ have we been wanting in Attentions to our British Brethren. We have warned them from Time to Time of Attempts by their Legislature to extend ~~[a]~~ *an unwarrantable* jurisdiction over ~~[these our States]~~ *us*. We have reminded them of the Circumstances of our Emigration and Settlement here ~~[, no one of which could warrant so strange a pretension: that these were effected at the expense of our own blood and treasure, unassisted by the wealth or the strength of Great-Britain: that in constituting indeed our several forms of government, we had adopted one common king, thereby laying a foundation for perpetual league and amity with them: but that submission to their parliament was no part of our Constitution, nor ever in idea, if history may be credited: and,]~~. We *have* appealed to their native Justice and Magnanimity ~~[as well as to]~~ *and we have conjured them by* the Ties of our common Kindred to disavow these Usurpations, which, ~~[were likely to]~~ *would inevitably* interrupt our Connections and Correspondence. They too have been deaf to the Voice of Justice and of Consanguinity ~~[, and when occasions have been given them, by the regular course of their laws, of removing from their councils the disturbers of our harmony, they have, by their free election, reestablished them in power. At this very time too, they are permitting their chief magistrate to send over not only soldiers of our common blood, but Scotch and foreign mercenaries to invade and destroy us. These facts have given the last stab to agonizing affection and manly spirit bids us to renounce forever these unfeeling brethren. We must endeavor to forget our former love for them, and hold them as we hold the rest of mankind, enemies in war, in peace friends. We might have been a free and a great people together; but a communication of grandeur and of freedom, it seems, is below their dignity. Be it so, since they will have it. The road to happiness and to glory is open to]~~

us too. ~~We will tread it apart from them, and~~]. We must, therefore, acquiesce in the Necessity, which denounces our [~~eternal~~ Separation, *and hold them, as we hold the rest of Mankind, Enemies in War, in Peace, Friends.*

We therefore the Representatives of the UNITED STATES OF AMERICA in GENERAL CONGRESS, Assembled, *appealing to the Supreme Judge of the World for the Rectitude of our Intentions*, do, in the Name, and by the Authority of the good People of these [~~States reject and renounce all allegiance and subjection to the kings of Great-Britain and all others who may hereafter claim by, through, or under them; we utterly dissolve all political connection which may heretofore have subsisted between us and the people or parliament of Great-Britain: and finally we do assert and declare these Colonies to be free and independent States,~~] *Colonies, solemnly Publish and Declare, That these United Colonies are, and of Right ought to be,* FREE AND INDEPENDENT STATES; *that they are absolved from all Allegiance to the British Crown, and that all political Connection between them and the State of Great-Britain is, and ought to be, totally dissolved;* and that as FREE AND INDEPENDENT STATES, they have full Power to levy War, conclude Peace, contract Alliances, establish Commerce, and to do all other Acts and Things which INDEPENDENT STATES may of right do.

And for the support of this Declaration, *with a firm Reliance on the Protection of divine Providence*, we mutually pledge to each other our Lives, our Fortunes, and our sacred Honor.

Signed by ORDER *and in* BEHALF *of the* CONGRESS,

JOHN HANCOCK, PRESIDENT.

ATTEST.

CHARLES THOMSON, SECRETARY.

☆ ☆ ☆ ☆ ☆ ☆ ☆ ☆ ☆ ☆ ☆ ☆ ☆

A LETTER FROM
THOMAS JEFFERSON
TO ROGER C. WEIGHTMAN[1]

MONTICELLO, June 24, 1826.

ESPECTED SIR,—The kind invitation I receive from you, on the part of the citizens of the city of Washington, to be present with them at their celebration on the fiftieth anniversary of American Independence, as one of the surviving signers of an instrument pregnant with our own, and the fate of the world, is most flattering to myself, and heightened by the honorable accompaniment proposed for the comfort of such a journey. It adds sensibly to the sufferings of sickness, to be deprived by it of a personal participation in the rejoicings of that day. But acquiescence is a duty, under circumstances not placed among those we are permitted to control. I should, indeed, with peculiar delight, have met and exchanged there congratulations personally with the small band, the remnant of that host of worthies, who joined with us on that day, in the bold and doubtful election we were to make for our country, between submission or the sword; and to have enjoyed with them the consolatory fact, that our fellow citizens, after half a century of experience and prosperity, continue to approve the choice we made.

---

[1] This letter was written less than two weeks before Jefferson's death. It is his last extant letter.

19

May it be to the world, what I believe it will be, (to some parts sooner, to others later, but finally to all,) the signal of arousing men to burst the chains under which monkish ignorance and superstition had persuaded them to bind themselves, and to assume the blessings and security of self-government. That form which we have substituted, restores the free right to the unbounded exercise of reason and freedom of opinion. All eyes are opened, or opening, to the rights of man. The general spread of the light of science has already laid open to every view the palpable truth, that the mass of mankind has not been born with saddles on their backs, nor a favored few booted and spurred, ready to ride them legitimately, by the grace of God. These are grounds of hope for others. For ourselves, let the annual return of this day forever refresh our recollections of these rights, and an undiminished devotion to them.

I will ask permission here to express the pleasure with which I should have met my ancient neighbors of the city of Washington and its vicinities, with whom I passed so many years of a pleasing social intercourse; an intercourse which so much relieved the anxieties of the public cares, and left impressions so deeply engraved in my affections, as never to be forgotten. With my regret that ill health forbids me the gratification of an acceptance, be pleased to receive for yourself, and those for whom you write, the assurance of my highest respect and friendly attachments.

(Signed) Thomas Jefferson.

☆ ☆ ☆ ☆ ☆ ☆ ☆ ☆ ☆ ☆ ☆ ☆ ☆

ARTICLES OF CONFEDERATION
March 1, 1781*

*T*o all to whom these Presents shall come, we the under signed Delegates of the States affixed to our Names, send greeting.

Whereas the Delegates of the United States of America, in Congress assembled, did, on the 15th day of November, in the Year of Our Lord One thousand Seven Hundred and Seventy seven, and in the Second Year of the Independence of America, agree to certain articles of Confederation and perpetual Union between the States of Newhampshire, Massachusetts-bay, Rhodeisland and Providence Plantations, Connecticut, New York, New Jersey, Pennsylvania, Delaware, Maryland, Virginia, North-Carolina, South-Carolina, and Georgia in the words following, viz. "Articles of Confederation and perpetual Union between the states of Newhampshire, Massachusetts-bay, Rhodeisland and Providence Plantations, Connecticut, New-York, New-Jersey, Pennsylvania, Delaware, Maryland, Virginia, North-Carolina, South-Carolina and Georgia."

Article I. The Stile of this confederacy shall be "The United States of America."

* The Articles of Confederation were agreed to by the Congress on November 15, 1777, but did not become fully operable until March 1, 1781. At that time, it appears from the Journals of the Continental Congress, the delegates from Maryland, last of the States to take action, "did in behalf of said State of Maryland, sign and ratify the said Articles by which act the Confederation of the United States of America was completed, each and every of the Thirteen United States, from New Hampshire to Georgia, both included, having adopted and confirmed, by their delegates in Congress, ratified the same."

Article II. Each state retains its sovereignty, freedom, and independence, and every Power, Jurisdiction and right, which is not by this confederation expressly delegated to the United States, in Congress assembled.

Article III. The said states hereby severally enter into a firm league of friendship with each other, for their common defence, the security of their Liberties, and their mutual and general welfare, binding themselves to assist each other, against all force offered to, or attacks made upon them, or any of them, on account of religion, sovereignty, trade, or any other pretence whatever.

Article IV. The better to secure and perpetuate mutual friendship and intercourse among the people of the different states in this union, the free inhabitants of each of these states, paupers, vagabonds and fugitives from justice excepted, shall be entitled to all privileges and immunities of free citizens in the several states; and the people of each state shall have free ingress and regress to and from any other state, and shall enjoy therein all the privileges of trade and commerce, subject to the same duties, impositions and restrictions as the inhabitants thereof respectively, provided that such restriction shall not extend so far as to prevent the removal of property imported into any state, to any other state, of which the Owner is an inhabitant; provided also that no imposition, duties or restriction shall be laid by any state, on the property of the united states, or either of them.

If any Person guilty of, or charged with treason, felony, or other high misdemeanor in any state, shall flee from Justice, and be found in any of the united states, he shall, upon demand of the Governor or executive power, of the state from which he fled, be delivered up and removed to the state having jurisdiction of his offence.

Full faith and credit shall be given in each of these states to the records, acts and judicial proceedings of the courts and magistrates of every other state.

Article V. For the more convenient management of the general interests of the united states, delegates shall be annually appointed in such manner as the legislature of each state shall direct, to meet in Congress on the first Monday in November, in every year, with a power reserved to each state, to recal its delegates, or any of them, at any time within the year, and to send others in their stead, for the remainder of the Year.

No state shall be represented in Congress by less than two, nor by more than seven Members; and no person shall be capable of being a delegate for more than three years in any term of six years; nor shall any person, being a delegate, be capable of holding any office under the united states, for which he, or another for his benefit receives any salary, fees or emolument of any kind.

Each state shall maintain its own delegates in a meeting of the states, and while they act as members of the committee of the states.

In determining questions in the united states in Congress assembled, each state shall have one vote.

Freedom of speech and debate in Congress shall not be impeached or questioned in any Court, or place out of Congress, and the members of congress shall be protected in their persons from arrests and imprisonments, during the time of their going to and from, and attendance on congress, except for treason, felony, or breach of the peace.

Article VI. No state, without the Consent of the united states in congress assembled, shall send any embassy to, or receive any embassy from, or enter into any conference, agreement, alliance or treaty with any King prince or state; nor shall any person holding any office of profit or trust under the united states, or any of them, accept of any present, emolument, office or title of any kind whatever from any king, prince or foreign state; nor shall the united states in congress assembled, or any of them, grant any title of nobility.

No two or more states shall enter into any treaty, confederation or alliance whatever between them, without the consent of the united states in congress assembled, specifying accurately the purposes for which the same is to be entered into, and how long it shall continue.

No state shall lay any imposts or duties, which may interfere with any stipulations in treaties, entered into by the united states in congress assembled, with any king, prince or state, in pursuance of any treaties already proposed by congress, to the courts of France and Spain.

No vessels of war shall be kept up in time of peace by any state, except such number only, as shall be deemed necessary by the united states in congress assembled, for the defence of such state, or its trade; nor shall any body of forces be kept up by any state, in time of peace, except such number only, as in the judgment of the united states, in congress assembled, shall be deemed requisite to garrison the forts necessary for the defence of such state; but every state shall always keep up a well regulated and disciplined militia, sufficiently armed and accoutred, and shall provide and constantly have ready for use, in public stores, a due number of field pieces and tents, and a proper quantity of arms, ammunition and camp equipage.

No state shall engage in any war without the consent of the united states in congress assembled, unless such state be actually invaded by enemies, or shall have received certain advice of a resolution being formed by some nation of Indians to invade such state, and the danger is so imminent as not to admit of a delay till the united states in congress assembled can be consulted: nor shall any state grant commissions to any ships or vessels of war, nor letters of marque or reprisal, except it be after a declaration of war by the united states in congress assembled, and then only against the kingdom or state and the subjects thereof, against which war has been so declared, and under such regulations as shall be established by the united states in congress assembled, unless such state be infested by pirates, in which case vessels of war may be fitted out for that occasion, and kept so long as the danger shall continue, or until the united states in congress assembled, shall determine otherwise.

Article VII. When land-forces are raised by any state for the common defence, all officers of or under the rank of colonel, shall be appointed by the legislature of each state respectively, by whom such forces shall be raised, or in such manner as such state shall direct, and all vacancies shall be filled up by the State which first made the appointment.

Article VIII. All charges of war, and all other expences that shall be incurred for the common defence or general welfare, and allowed by the united states in congress assembled, shall be defrayed out of a common treasury, which shall be supplied by the several states in proportion to the value of all land within each state, granted to or surveyed for any Person, as such land and the buildings and improvements thereon shall be estimated according to such mode as the united states in congress assembled, shall from time to time direct and appoint.

The taxes for paying that proportion shall be laid and levied by the authority and direction of the legislatures of the several states within the time agreed upon by the united states in congress assembled.

Article IX. The united states in congress assembled, shall have the sole and exclusive right and power of determining on peace and war, except in the cases mentioned in the sixth article—of sending and receiving ambassadors—entering into treaties and alliances, provided that no treaty of commerce shall be made whereby the legislative power of the respective states shall be restrained from imposing such imposts and duties on foreigners as their own people are subjected to, or from prohibiting the exportation or importation of any species of goods or commodities, whatsoever—of establishing rules for deciding in all cases, what captures on land or water shall be legal, and in what manner prizes taken by land or naval forces in the service of the united states shall be divided or appropriated—of granting letters of marque and reprisal in times of peace—appointing courts for the trial of piracies and felonies committed on the high seas and establishing courts for receiving and determining finally appeals in all cases of captures, provided that no member of congress shall be appointed a judge of any of the said courts.

The united states in congress assembled shall also be the last resort on appeal in all disputes and differences now subsisting or that hereafter may arise between two or more states concerning boundary, jurisdiction or any other cause whatever; which authority shall always be exercised in the manner following. Whenever the legislative or executive authority or lawful agent of any state in controversy with another shall present a petition to congress stating the matter in question and praying for a hearing, notice thereof shall be given by order of congress to the legislative or executive authority of the other state in controversy, and a day assigned for the appearance of the parties by their lawful agents, who shall then be directed to appoint by joint consent, commissioners or judges to constitute a court for hearing and determining the matter in question: but if they cannot agree, congress shall name three persons out of each of the united states, and from the list of such persons each party shall alternately strike out one, the petitioners beginning, until the number shall be reduced to thirteen; and from that number not less than seven, nor more than nine names as congress shall direct, shall in the presence of congress be drawn out by lot, and the persons whose names shall be so drawn or any five of them, shall be commissioners or judges, to hear and finally determine the controversy, so always as a major part of the judges who shall hear the cause shall agree in the determination: and if either party shall neglect to attend at the day appointed, without showing reasons, which congress shall judge sufficient, or being present shall refuse to strike, the congress shall proceed to nominate three persons out of each state, and the secretary of congress shall strike in behalf of such party absent or refusing; and the judgment and sentence of the court to be appointed, in the manner before prescribed, shall be final and conclusive; and if any of the parties shall refuse to submit to the authority of such court, or to appear or defend their claim or cause, the court shall nevertheless proceed to pronounce sentence, or judgment, which shall in like manner be final and decisive, the judgment or sentence and other proceedings being in either case transmitted to congress, and lodged among the acts of congress for the security of the parties concerned: provided that every commissioner, before he sits in judgment, shall take an oath to be administered by one of the judges of the supreme or superior court of the state, where the cause shall be tried, "well and truly to hear and determine the matter in question, according to the best of his judgment, without favour, affection or hope of reward:" provided also, that no state shall be deprived of territory for the benefit of the united states.

All controversies concerning the private right of soil claimed under different grants of two or more states, whose jurisdictions as they may respect such lands, and the states which passed such grants are adjusted, the said grants or either of them being at the same time claimed to have originated antecedent to such settlement of jurisdiction, shall on the petition of either party to the congress of the united states, be finally determined as near as may be in the same manner as is before prescribed for deciding disputes respecting territorial jurisdiction between different states.

The united states in congress assembled shall also have the sole and exclusive right and power of regulating the alloy and value of coin struck by their own authority, or by that of the respective states—fixing the standard of weights and measures throughout the united states—regulating the trade and managing all affairs with the Indians, not members of any of the states, provided that the legislative right of any state within its own limits be not infringed or violated—establishing or regulating post-offices from one state to another, throughout all the united states, and exacting such postage on the papers passing thro' the same as may be requisite to defray the expences of the said office—appointing all officers of the land forces, in the service of the united states, excepting regimental officers—appointing all the officers of the naval forces, and commissioning all officers whatever in the service of the united states—making rules for the government and regulation of the said land and naval forces, and directing their operations.

The united states in congress assembled shall have authority to appoint a committee, to sit in the recess of congress, to be denominated "A Committee of the States," and to consist of one delegate from each state; and to appoint such other committees and civil officers as may be necessary for managing the general affairs of the united states under their direction—to appoint one of their number to preside, provided that no person be allowed to serve in the office of president more than one year in any term of three years; to ascertain the necessary sums of money to be raised for the service of the united states, and to appropriate and apply the same for defraying the public expences—to borrow money, or emit bills on the credit of the united states, transmitting every half year to the respective states an account of the sums of money so borrowed or emitted,—to build and equip a navy—to agree upon the number of land forces, and to make requisitions from each state for its quota, in proportion to the number of white inhabitants in such state; which requisition shall be binding, and thereupon the legislature of each state shall appoint the regimental officers, raise the men and cloath, arm and equip them in a soldier like manner, at the expence of the united states; and the officers and men so cloathed, armed and equipped shall march to the place appointed, and within the time agreed on by the united states in congress assembled: But if the united states in congress assembled shall, on consideration of circumstances judge proper that any state should not raise men, or should raise a smaller number than its quota, and that any other state should raise a greater number of men than the quota thereof, such extra number shall be raised, officered, cloathed, armed and equipped in the same manner as the quota of such state, unless the legislature of such state shall judge that such extra number cannot be safely spared out of the same, in which case they shall raise officer, cloath, arm and equip as many of such extra number as they judge can be safely spared. And the officers and men so cloathed, armed and equipped, shall march to the place appointed, and within the time agreed on by the united states in congress assembled.

The united states in congress assembled shall never engage in a war, nor grant letters of marque and reprisal in time of peace, nor enter into any treaties or alliances, nor coin money, nor regulate the value thereof, nor ascertain the sums and expences necessary for the defence and welfare of the united states, or any of them, nor emit bills, nor borrow money on the credit of the united states, nor appropriate money, nor agree upon the number of vessels of war, to be built or purchased, or the number of land or sea forces to be raised, nor appoint a commander in chief of the army or navy, unless nine states assent to the same: nor shall a question on any other point, except for adjourning from day to day be determined, unless by the votes of a majority of the united states in congress assembled.

The congress of the united states shall have power to adjourn to any time within the year, and to any place within the united states, so that no period of adjournment be for a longer duration than the space of six Months, and shall publish the Journal of their proceedings monthly, except such parts thereof relating to treaties, alliances or military operations, as in their judgment require secrecy; and the yeas and nays of the delegates of each state on any question shall be entered on the Journal, when it is desired by any delegate; and the delegates of a state, or any of them, at his or their request shall be furnished with a transcript of the said Journal, except such parts as are above excepted, to lay before the legislatures of the several states.

Article X. The committee of the states, or any nine of them, shall be authorized to execute, in the recess of congress, such of the powers of congress as the united states in congress assembled, by the consent of nine states, shall from time to time think expedient to vest them with; provided that no power be delegated to the said committee, for the exercise of which, by the articles of confederation, the voice of nine states in the congress of the united states assembled is requisite.

Article XI. Canada acceding to this confederation, and joining in the measures of the united states, shall be admitted into, and entitled to all the advantages of this union: but no other colony shall be admitted into the same, unless such admission be agreed to by nine states.

Article XII. All bills of credit emitted, monies borrowed and debts contracted by, or under the authority of congress, before the assembling of the united states, in pursuance of the present confederation, shall be deemed and considered as a charge against the united states, for payment and satisfaction whereof the said united states, and the public faith are hereby solemnly pledged.

Article XIII. Every state shall abide by the determinations of the united states in congress assembled, on all questions which by this confederation are submitted to them. And the Articles of this confederation shall be inviolably observed by every state, and the union shall be perpetual; nor shall any alteration at any time hereafter be made in any of them; unless such alteration be agreed to in a congress of the united states, and be afterwards confirmed by the legislatures of every state.

And Whereas it hath pleased the Great Governor of the World to incline the hearts of the legislatures we respectively represent in congress, to approve of, and to authorize us to ratify the said articles of confederation and perpetual union. Know Ye that we the undersigned delegates, by virtue of the power and authority to us given for that purpose, do by these presents, in the name and in behalf of our respective constituents, fully and entirely ratify and confirm each and every of the said articles of confederation and perpetual union, and all and singular the matters and things therein contained: And we do further solemnly plight and engage the faith of our respective constituents, that they shall abide by the determinations of the united states in congress assembled, on all questions, which by the said confederation are submitted to them. And that the articles thereof shall be inviolably observed by the states we respectively represent, and that the union shall be perpetual. In Witness whereof we have hereunto set our hands in Congress. Done at Philadelphia in the state of Pennsylvania the ninth day of July, in the Year of our Lord one Thousand seven Hundred and Seventy-eight, and in the third year of the independence of America.

Josiah Bartlett, John Wentworth, jun' August 8th, 1778,	On the part & behalf of the State of New Hampshire.
John Hancock, Samuel Adams, Elbridge Gerry, Francis Dana, James Lovell, Samuel Holten,	On the part and behalf of the State of Massachusetts Bay.
William Ellery, Henry Marchant, John Collins,	On the part and behalf of the State of Rhode-Island and Providence Plantations.
Roger Sherman, Samuel Huntington, Oliver Wolcott, Titus Hosmer, Andrew Adams,	On the part and behalf of the State of Connecticut.
Ja' Duane, Fra: Lewis, Wm Duer, Gouv' Morris,	On the part and behalf of the State of New York.
Jn° Witherspoon, Nath' Scudder,	On the Part and in Behalf of the State of New Jersey, November 26th, 1778.
Robert Morris, Daniel Roberdeau, Jon. Bayard Smith, William Clingar, Joseph Reed, 22d July, 1778,	On the part and behalf of the State of Pennsylvania.
Tho' McKean, Feb' 22d, 1779, John Dickinson, May 5th, 1779, Nicholas Van Dyke,	On the part & behalf of the State of Delaware.

John Hanson,
    March 1, 1781,   } On the part and behalf of the State of
Daniel Carroll, do   Maryland.

Richard Henry Lee,
John Banister,
Thomas Adams,   } On the Part and Behalf of the State of
Jnº. Harvie,   Virginia.
Francis Lightfoot Lee,

John Penn,
    July 21st, 1778,   } On the part and behalf of the State of
Cornˢ Harnett,   North Carolina.
Jnº. Williams,

Henry Laurens,
William Henry Drayton,
Jnº Mathews,   } On the part and on behalf of the State of
Richᵈ Hutson,   South Carolina.
Thoˢ Heyward, junʳ.

Jnº Walton,
    24th July, 1778,   } On the part and behalf of the State of
Edwᵈ Telfair,   Georgia.[1]
Edwᵈ Langworthy,

---

[1] The proceedings of this day with respect to the signing of the Articles of Confederation, the Articles themselves and the signers are entered in the *Papers of the Continental Congress*, No. 9 (History of the Confederation), but not in the Journal itself. The Articles are printed here from the original roll in the Bureau of Rolls and Library, Department of State.

THE CONSTITUTION
OF THE UNITED STATES
AND AMENDMENTS THERETO

FOREWORD

By Denys P. Myers*

THE Constitution of the United States of America names itself in the Preamble and elsewhere, but the Congress which sent it to the original thirteen States for ratification gave it no caption. It was therefore significant and perhaps natural that in most States it was entitled "A frame of Government" when it was printed for the convenience of ratifying conventions and the information of the people.

It was as a "frame of government" rather than a perfected document that the Constitution came into being by the ratifications of the States. The "United States in Congress assembled," functioning both as the executive and legislative power under the Articles of Confederation, summoned the Federal Convention "for the sole and express purpose of revising the Articles of Confederation and reporting to Congress." The delegates of the States had full powers and in the "Report of the Convention" submitted a document which "is not perhaps to be expected" to meet the full approbation of every State.

Washington's expectation was realized in conventions where the closeness of the vote was in direct proportion to the grass-root character of the delegations. The Constitution was ratified by 1,061 votes to 576 in the conventions of the 13 States, or 64.85 per cent, but the conventions varied so greatly in composition that the total vote means little. From unanimity in Delaware, Georgia

---

* Mr. Myers, now retired from the State Department, where he served both as a historian and as a specialist in international law, for many years handled functions of constitutional amendment within the department. An authority on constitutional texts and revisions, he prepared a monograph, "The Process of Constitutional Amendment," published as a Senate document in 1940.

and New Jersey, the State votes ranged down to 51.5 per cent in Rhode Island. The vote for ratification was 89-79 in Virginia, 30-27 in New York, 187-168 in Massachusetts.

A "frame of government" was all that the States were certain they had. It was good as far as it went, and there was general assent to the conviction that its machinery would work. The debates in the conventions regretted the absence of anything equivalent to the bills of rights embodied in the State constitutions, and in some other respects ideas for improvement of the Constitution were aired in ratifying it. Foremost among these was the insistence of seven States on the amendment that was soon to become the Tenth Amendment.

At the risk of some repetition, it may be useful to take note of the importance attached to this understanding of the structure of the Constitution. Massachusetts placed first among its nine recommendations for alteration, "that it be explicitly declared that all Powers not expressly delegated by the aforesaid Constitution are reserved to the several States to be by them exercised." South Carolina's convention declared "that no Section or paragraph of the said Constitution warrants a Construction that the States do not retain every power not expressly relinquished by them and vested in the General Government of the Union." New Hampshire asked twelve alterations, the first of which was "that it be Explicitly declared that all Powers not expressly & particularly Delegated by the aforesaid Constitution are reserved to the several States to be, by them Exercised." Virginia asked no fewer than twenty amendments. First among these was "that each State in the Union shall respectively retain every power, jurisdiction and right which is not by this Constitution delegated to the Congress of the United States or to the departments of the Federal Government." New York, not to be outdone, demanded thirty-two amendments, and accompanied its grudging resolution of ratification with a long statement of "impressions" and "explanations" regarded as consistent with the Constitution. Among these was a declaration that "every Power, Jurisdiction and right, which is not by the said Constitution clearly delegated to the Congress of the United States, or the departments of the Government thereof, remains to the people of the several States, or to their respective State governments to whom they may have granted the same."

North Carolina put in first place among twenty-six requested amendments a statement "that each State in the Union shall, respectively, retain every power, jurisdiction and right, which is not by this Constitution delegated to the Congress of the United States, or to the departments of the Federal Government." Finally, Rhode Island in the spring of 1790 asked twenty-one amendments, the first of which was that "the United States shall guarantee to each State its sovereignty, freedom and independence, and every power, jurisdiction and right, which is not by this Constitution expressly delegated to the United States."

Confidence in the Constitution increased as the Congress which assembled under it in 1789 filled out the "frame" by creating the institutions it provided for and defined the functions they were assigned within its terms. That accomplishment of the first Congress was a remarkable feat of statesmanship, but it is almost forgotten in the vivid memory of the American people that it also created the Bill of Rights that has done so much to give them national character. Though those 464 words were negotiated in the first six months of Congress, their final text was the 297th proposal to amend or modify the Constitution. So diligent were the Founding Fathers to perfect the Constitution which, in the words of Gladstone, was already "the most wonderful work ever struck off at a given time by the brain and purpose of man."

The Constitution has proved to be a true frame of government. From its basic provisions laws have developed its bare prescriptions into a system of government responsive to the public will, from generation to generation. The genius of the document inheres in its style which, positively or negatively, states what is or is not to be done, without any implication of why. It therefore easily conforms to the conditions of the times, for its meaning is bound only by the philosophy of government that brought it forth. That philosophy recognized change, and the Founding Fathers provided in Article V of the Constitution for its amendment.

The stability of the Constitution is strikingly demonstrated by the fact that, from the ratifications of 1788 through 1960, a total of 5,170 proposals to amend have been made and only 28 have ever been submitted to the States for ratification; and of these 28 proposals, 23 have been ratified. A good many such proposals have been enacted as law. Some ideas have been introduced as proposed amendments 100 or more times. The text of the Constitution itself has been amended, or affected by amendments, only six times by Articles of Amendment XII, XIV, XVI, XVII and XX. All other amendments have added to its content.

The system of amendment set forth in Article V aptly exemplifies the basic principle of the Constitution that the United States has a representative government subject to the eventual will of the people. The article provides for two methods of proposing amendments and two methods of ratifying proposals. The customary method for each procedure is representative. Under one approach, a proposal is approved by an elected Congress and ratified by elected State Legislatures. The other method gives the initiative of proposing amendment to a convention of States and of ratification to State conventions specially chosen. Experience with each method is described below.

PROPOSAL OF AN AMENDMENT

"The Congress, whenever two-thirds of both Houses shall deem it necessary, shall propose amendments"

This procedure has been exclusively followed. Proposals are introduced into both Houses of Congress at the free discretion of members as "joint resolutions," referred usually to the Judiciary Committee, and are subject to hearings and reports. On the first day of the 87th Congress alone, 37 proposals were introduced, and currently in the two years of a Congress nearly 200 proposed amendments may be expected to be introduced in both Houses. A proposal, if reported out, is considered for amendment by majority vote in Committee of the Whole and when perfected is approved by a two-thirds vote. The "joint resolution" embodying a proposed amendment of the Constitution is a complete act of Congress without approval by the President. When President Lincoln approved the proposed 13th Amendment on February 1, 1865, the Senate immediately adopted a resolution declaring that such approval "was unnecessary to give effect to the action of Congress."

From this point on, the amendment procedure is a series of disjunctive duties assigned by Federal or State law to specific officials or agencies. A law of April 20, 1818, directed the Secretary of State to receive the resolution of Congress and to communicate it to the Governors of the States for such action as may be had by the Legislatures; in 1950 the Administrator of General Services succeeded the Secretary of State in these duties. The Governors transmit the proposal to the Legislatures, usually with a message, in accordance with a State law or practice with respect to constitutional amendments. In either case, his action is a federal function and, if the Legislature should not act during a session, the proposal is returned to the Governor for resubmission, and not filed with State bills that die with a legislative session.

"The Congress, . . . on the application of the legislatures of two-thirds of the several States, shall call a convention for proposing amendments"

This provision has not been exercised and no legislation exists concerning its scope or procedures under it. Two reasons for putting it into the Constitution are evident. First, it would enable the Congress to convene the counterpart of the Federal Convention of 1787 which brought forth the Constitution as a revision of the Articles of Confederation. Second, it opens the way for the public opinion of the Nation to initiate proposals in its own right in case Congress is not responsive to demands upon it.

The provision in the original Constitution antedated the stipulation in Article I of the Amendments: "Congress shall make no law . . . abridging . . . the right of the people peaceably . . . to petition the Government for a redress of grievances." In view of this right of petition, Congress and the President both receive great numbers of memorials from Legislatures and petitions from individuals. Congressional hearings and discussion of issues in the press also contribute to the effective expression of public opinion.

No serious movement for a review of the Constitution in convention has occurred, but in the course of time there has been some effort to line up Legislatures in support of amendment proposals. In the early days State legislatures shopped around proposals among themselves, with varying results. The resolution of the Tennessee Legislature, dated November 21, 1811, ratifying the proposed amendment concerning nobility, disapproved three proposals to amend the Constitution emanating from Massachusetts, Pennsylvania and Virginia. Questions such as slavery, woman's suffrage and prohibition produced resolutions calling for conventions as part of the agitation which those questions generated before Congress put forward proposals to amend the Constitution. A conscious effort to get a convention to restrict Federal income and inheritance taxes by resolutions of Legislatures has existed for several years, and a number of such resolutions are filed with Congress, which has also received several repeals of them. If any such proposal approached the mandatory two thirds of legislative applications, Congress would probably put through the identical proposal on its own account as a simpler and less venturesome method of obtaining a decision upon it.

RATIFICATION OF AN AMENDMENT

"amendments ... shall be valid ... when ratified by the legislatures of three-fourths of the several States"

With one exception, all State action has taken place under this provision. A State Legislature acts in a federal capacity under the Constitution, though its own composition, procedure and voting rules remain in effect. In the concept of the Constitution the Legislature acts as representative of the people themselves. Its freedom of judgment is complete and its affirmative decision final. It has been judicially indicated that under the Constitution a proposed amendment is submitted for ratification and that consequently ratification exhausts the Legislature's powers in the premises. The duty of the State Legislature is to exercise its judgment upon whether or not the proposed amendment shall become part of the Constitution. With the exception of a period from 1865 to 1870 each Legislature has been free to reject a proposal at its discretion or fail to act, which may result from lack of consideration or lack of a session during the proposal's pendency, rejection by one house preventing concurrence or failure of either or both houses to act. Both rejection and failure to act have been reversed after the requisite three-fourths of the States have ratified and an amendment has become valid. Whether or not a particular State approves or disapproves, an amendment which has become "valid to all intents and purposes, as a part of this Constitution" is binding upon every State then and subsequently

42

in the Union. No modification of a proposal is acceptable as a ratification.

The form of the instrument of ratification is customarily a joint resolution of the bicameral Legislature. Because the Legislature acts in a federal capacity, its resolution is complete when voted by both houses, and does not require approval by the Governor as would a similar resolution on State matters. By habit, however, Governors in a great number of cases have approved and dated ratifying resolutions. If such a date is not the exact date of completion of the Legislature's action, the record is deficient. A large number of such deficiencies exist on the official records, many of which have had to be adjusted for the purpose of court proceedings or other reasons by revision according to the House and Senate Journals of the States. The correct procedure is for the officers of the two houses of the Legislature to sign the perfected resolution with a notation of the dates of their action; this resolution, certified by the secretary of state of the State, is sent to Washington by the Governor, who is the normal channel of communication between the State and Federal Governments. As a transaction of high level the instrument may well be transmitted under the great seal of the State.

While a proposal is accumulating the requisite ratifications by three-fourths of the States, the dates of their action are not of great importance except as a matter of technical accuracy. But as the number of ratifications approaches three-fourths, the exact dates of action become important. In the case of the 14th Amendment the Secretary of State issued a certificate of adoption, submitted further evidence to Congress and on its instructions issued a second certificate. In the cases of the 20th and 21st Amendments the 36th State was determined by hour and minute timing. Certificates of adoption, which are formally published in Statutes at Large, do not themselves record the date of validity, which can be determined only by consulting the chronological record of ratifications.

It was not until 12 Amendments had been adopted that the United States worked out a method of taking cognizance of their ratification. President Washington himself submitted the first proposal of 1789 to the States, received ratifications and reported them to Congress, which kept the requisite tally. The 11th Amendment, proposed in 1794, was badly reported and on the initiative of Congress President John Adams in 1798 sent word that it had then become valid, though actually ratification had taken place in 1795. The 12th Amendment, proposing a change in the electoral college in anticipation of the election in 1804, was accompanied by a law instructing the Secretary of State to keep track of ratifications so that the provision could apply to that election, which occurred. The proposal on nobility, which failed, was submitted in 1810 and it was 1818 before its failure was known. Uncertainty throughout this period was abetted by the fact that new States were admitted between the time of proposing an amendment and its attainment of the requisite three-fourths ratifications. A law of April 20, 1818, defined duties of the Secretary of State in order to remedy these faults. In those days the Department of State was regarded as the chancery of the Government and the Secretary of State, for the President, was the channel of communication for Federal-State matters. In 1950 this concept was partially abandoned and the duties of the Secretary of State with respect to the Constitution were transferred to the Administrator of General Services, National Archives and Records Service, Federal Register Division. By the law (now 1 U. S. Code, sec. 106b) the duty consists of knowing the number of States which constitutes three-fourths of the whole number, receiving from them "official notice" of ratification of amendment proposals and, when the requisite number has been received, "the Administrator of General Services shall forthwith cause the amendment to be published, with his certificate, specifying the States by which the same may have been adopted, and that the same has become valid, to all intents and purposes, as a part of the Constitution." The official notice of the State is conclusive upon him and he has no discretion to determine the truth of the facts stated, though he may supplement them as a matter of information.

"amendments . . . shall be valid . . . when ratified . . . by conventions in three-fourths of [the several States]."

This procedure of ratification by convention, calculated to reflect closely the public will, was specified to be used in ratification of the 21st Amendment, repealing the 18th Amendment on the subject of prohibition. Especially in the Senate efforts to provide for use of the method had been made since the proposal of the 16th Amendment in 1909. The proposal of the 21st Amendment was made by Congress on February 20, 1933, and was immediately submitted by its own terms for ratification "by conventions in the several States" within seven years. No legislation on the subject of such conventions existed, and 43 States—all except Georgia, Kansas, Louisiana, Mississippi and North Dakota —enacted statutes providing for action upon the proposed amendment between February 18 and August 28, 1933, owing to the fact that the Legislatures were in session that year. The statutes varied in form. Some were general, covering similar future cases; others were limited to the pending proposal. They differed with respect to the method of selecting delegates, their apportionment ("State-wide" or by districts), their number (3 in New Mexico, 329 in Indiana) dates of meeting, instructions from the electors, and other matters. The Department of State was informed by telegraph that the 36th State, Utah, had ratified the proposal in its convention on December 5, 1933, at 3:32½ p.m. Mountain Time (5:32½ p.m., Eastern Standard Time at Washington) and the Acting Secretary of State forthwith issued his certificate of adoption, and the President issued a proclamation repealing the 18th Amendment on that date. The convention in South Carolina rejected the proposal. The North Carolina electorate voted by a large majority against holding a convention. Montana ratified in convention in 1934, but the conventions of Nebraska, Oklahoma and South Dakota, scheduled for 1934, were not held because the Amendment had already been adopted. In the 37 States that ratified in convention the vote was unanimous in 32, the noes negligible in 4 and of significance only in Indiana, 246 ayes to 83 noes. Since 1933 no proposal reported out of committee in either House of Congress has contained a provision for ratification by convention.

THE CONSTITUTION
OF THE UNITED STATES
AND AMENDMENTS THERETO

☆ ☆ ☆ ☆ ☆ ☆ ☆ ☆ ☆ ☆ ☆ ☆ ☆

WE the People of the United States, in order to form a more perfect Union, establish Justice, insure domestic Tranquility, provide for the common Defence, promote the general Welfare, and secure the Blessings of Liberty to ourselves and our Posterity, do ordain and establish this CONSTITUTION for the United States of America.

ARTICLE I.

Sect. 1. ALL legislative powers herein granted shall be vested in a Congress of the United States, which shall consist of a Senate and House of Representatives.

Sect. 2. The House of Representatives shall be composed of members chosen every second year by the people of the several states, and the electors in each state shall have the qualifications requisite for electors of the most numerous branch of the state legislature.

No person shall be a Representative who shall not have attained to the age of twenty-five years, and been seven years a citizen of the United States, and who shall not, when elected, be an inhabitant of that state in which he shall be chosen.

[Representatives and direct taxes shall be apportioned among the several states which may be included within this Union, according to their respective numbers, which shall be determined by adding to the whole number of free persons, including those bound to service for a term of years, and excluding Indians not taxed, three-fifths of all other persons.]¹ The actual enumeration shall be made within three years after the first meeting of the Congress of the United States, and within every subsequent term of ten years, in such manner as they shall by law direct. The number of Representatives shall not exceed one for every thirty-thousand, but each state shall have at least one Representative; and until such enumeration shall be made, the state of New-Hampshire shall be entitled to chuse three, Massachusetts eight, Rhode-Island and Providence Plantations one, Connecticut five, New-York six, New-Jersey four, Pennsylvania eight, Delaware one, Maryland six, Virginia ten, North-Carolina five, South-Carolina five, and Georgia three.

When vacancies happen in the representation from any state, the executive authority thereof shall issue writs of election to fill such vacancies.

The House of Representatives shall chuse their Speaker and other officers; and shall have the sole power of impeachment.

Sect. 3. The Senate of the United States shall be composed of two Senators from each state, chosen [by the legislature thereof]² for six years; and each Senator shall have one vote.

Immediately after they shall be assembled in consequence of the first election, they shall be divided as equally as may be into three classes. The seats of the Senators of the first class shall be vacated at the expiration of the second year, of the second class at the expiration of the fourth year, and of the third class at the expiration of the sixth year, so that one-third may be chosen every second year; [and if vacancies happen by resignation, or otherwise, during the recess of the legisla-

---

¹ The sentence in brackets was repealed by Section 2 of Article of Amendment XIV.

² Paragraph 1 of Article of Amendment XVII was adopted "in lieu of the first paragraph of section three of Article I," according to the joint resolution of Congress proposing the amendment. (37 Stat. 646).

ture of any state, the executive thereof may make temporary appointments until the next meeting of the legislature, which shall then fill such vacancies].[3]

No person shall be a Senator who shall not have attained to the age of thirty years, and been nine years a citizen of the United States, and who shall not when elected, be an inhabitant of that state for which he shall be chosen.

The Vice-President of the United States shall be President of the Senate, but shall have no vote, unless they be equally divided.

The Senate shall chuse their other officers, and also a President *pro tempore*, in the absence of the Vice-President, or when he shall exercise the office of President of the United States.

The Senate shall have the sole power to try all impeachments. When sitting for that purpose, they shall be on oath or affirmation. When the President of the United States is tried, the Chief Justice shall preside: And no person shall be convicted without the concurrence of two-thirds of the members present.

Judgment in cases of impeachment shall not extend further than to removal from office, and disqualification to hold and enjoy any office of honor, trust or profit under the United States; but the party convicted shall nevertheless be liable and subject to indictment, trial, judgment and punishment, according to law.

Sect. 4. The times, places and manner of holding elections for Senators and Representatives, shall be prescribed in each state by the legislature thereof: But the Congress may at any time by law make or alter such regulations, except as to the places of chusing Senators.

---

[3] Paragraph 2 of Article of Amendment XVII was adopted "in lieu of so much of paragraph two of the same article as relates to the filling of vacancies," according to the joint resolution *supra*.

The Congress shall assemble at least once in every year, [and such meeting shall be on the first Monday in December],[4] unless they shall by law appoint a different day.

Sect. 5. Each House shall be the judge of the elections, returns and qualifications of its own members, and a majority of each shall constitute a quorum to do business; but a smaller number may adjourn from day to day, and may be authorised to compel the attendance of absent members, in such manner, and under such penalties as each House may provide.

Each House may determine the rules of its proceedings, punish its members for disorderly behaviour, and, with the concurrence of two-thirds, expel a member.

Each House shall keep a journal of its proceedings, and from time to time publish the same, excepting such parts as may in their judgment require secrecy; and the yeas and nays of the members of either House on any question, shall, at the desire of one-fifth of those present, be entered on the journal.

Neither House, during the session of Congress, shall without the consent of the other, adjourn for more than three days, nor to any other place than that in which the two Houses shall be sitting.

Sect. 6. The Senators and Representatives shall receive a compensation for their services, to be ascertained by law, and paid out of the treasury of the United States. They shall in all cases, except treason, felony and breach of the peace, be privileged from arrest during their attendance at the session of their respective Houses, and in going to and returning from the same; and for any speech or debate in either House, they shall not be questioned in any other place.

No Senator or Representative shall, during the time for which he was elected, be appointed to any civil office under

---

[4] The clause in brackets was changed by section 2 of Article of Amendment XX.

the authority of the United States, which shall have been created, or the emoluments whereof shall have been encreased during such time; and no person holding any office under the United States, shall be a member of either House during his continuance in office.

Sect. 7. All bills for raising revenue shall originate in the House of Representatives; but the Senate may propose or concur with amendments as on other bills.

Every bill which shall have passed the House of Representatives and the Senate, shall, before it become a law, be presented to the President of the United States; if he approve he shall sign it, but if not he shall return it, with his objections to that House in which it shall have originated, who shall enter the objections at large on their journal, and proceed to reconsider it. If after such reconsideration two-thirds of that house shall agree to pass the bill, it shall be sent, together with the objections, to the other House, by which it shall likewise be reconsidered, and if approved by two thirds of that House, it shall become a law. But in all such cases the votes of both Houses shall be determined by yeas and nays, and the names of the persons voting for and against the bill shall be entered on the journal of each House respectively. If any bill shall not be returned by the President within ten days (Sundays excepted) after it shall have been presented to him, the same shall be a law, in like manner as if he had signed it, unless the Congress by their adjournment prevent its return, in which case it shall not be a law.

Every order, resolution or vote to which the concurrence of the Senate and House of Representatives may be necessary (except on a question of adjournment) shall be presented to the President of the United States; and before the same shall take effect, shall be approved by him, or being disapproved by him, shall be re-passed by two-thirds of the Senate and House of Representatives, according to the rules and limitations pre-scribed in the case of a bill.

Sect. 8. The Congress shall have power

To lay and collect taxes, duties, imposts and excises, to pay the debts and provide for the common defence and general welfare of the United States; but all duties, imposts and excises shall be uniform throughout the United States:

To borrow money on the credit of the United States:

To regulate commerce with foreign nations, and among the several states, and with the Indian tribes:

To establish an uniform rule of naturalization, and uniform laws on the subject of bankruptcies throughout the United States:

To coin money, regulate the value thereof, and of foreign coin, and fix the standard of weights and measures:

To provide for the punishment of counterfeiting the securities and current coin of the United States:

To establish post-offices and post-roads:

To promote the progress of science and useful arts, by se-curing for limited times to authors and inventors the exclusive right to their respective writings and discoveries:

To constitute tribunals inferior to the Supreme Court:

To define and punish piracies and felonies committed on the high seas, and offences against the law of nations:

To declare war, grant letters of marque and reprisal, and make rules concerning captures on land and water:

To raise and support armies, but no appropriation of money to that use shall be for a longer term than two years:

To provide and maintain a navy:

To make rules for the government and regulation of the land and naval forces:

To provide for calling forth the militia to execute the laws of the union, suppress insurrections and repel invasions:

To provide for organizing, arming, and disciplining the militia, and for governing such part of them as may be employed in the service of the United States, reserving to the States respectively, the appointment of the officers, and the authority of training the militia according to the discipline prescribed by Congress:

To exercise exclusive legislation in all cases whatsoever, over such district (not exceeding ten miles square) as may by cession of particular states, and the acceptance of Congress, become the seat of the government of the United States, and to exercise like authority over all places purchased by the consent of the legislature of the state in which the same shall be, for the erection of forts, magazines, arsenals, dock-yards, and other needful buildings:—And

To make all laws which shall be necessary and proper for carrying into execution the foregoing powers, and all other powers vested by this constitution in the government of the United States, or in any department or officer thereof.

Sect. 9. The migration or importation of such persons as any of the states now existing shall think proper to admit, shall not be prohibited by the Congress prior to the year one thousand eight hundred and eight, but a tax or duty may be imposed on such importation, not exceeding ten dollars for each person.

The privilege of the writ of *habeas corpus* shall not be suspended, unless when in cases of rebellion or invasion the public safety may require it.

No bill of attainder or *ex post facto* law shall be passed.

No capitation, or other direct tax shall be laid, unless in proportion to the *census* or enumeration herein before directed to be taken.[5]

---

[5] See also Article of Amendment XVI.

No tax or duty shall be laid on articles exported from any state. No preference shall be given by any regulation of commerce or revenue to the ports of one state over those of another; nor shall vessels bound to, or from, one state, be obliged to enter, clear, or pay duties in another.

No money shall be drawn from the treasury, but in consequence of appropriations made by law; and a regular statement and account of the receipts and expenditures of all public money shall be published from time to time.

No title of nobility shall be granted by the United States: And no person holding any office of profit or trust under them, shall, without the consent of the Congress, accept of any present, emolument, office, or title of any kind whatever, from any king, prince or foreign state.

Sect. 10. No state shall enter into any treaty, alliance, or confederation; grant letters of marque and reprisal; coin money; emit bills of credit; make any thing but gold and silver coin a tender in payment of debts; pass any bill of attainder, *ex post facto* law, or law impairing the obligation of contracts, or grant any title of nobility.

No state shall, without the consent of the Congress, lay any imposts or duties on imports or exports, except what may be absolutely necessary for executing its inspection laws; and the net produce of all duties and imposts, laid by any state on imports or exports, shall be for the use of the treasury of the United States; and all such laws shall be subject to the revision and controul of the Congress. No state shall, without the consent of Congress, lay any duty of tonnage, keep troops, or ships of war in time of peace, enter into any agreement or compact with another state, or with a foreign power, or engage in war, unless actually invaded, or in such imminent danger as will not admit of delay.

ARTICLE II.

Sect. 1. The executive power shall be vested in a President of the United States of America. He shall hold his office during the term of four years,[6] and together with the Vice-President, chosen for the same term, be elected as follows:

Each state shall appoint, in such manner as the legislature thereof may direct, a number of electors, equal to the whole number of Senators and Representatives to which the state may be entitled in the Congress: but no Senator or Representative, or person holding an office of trust or profit under the United States, shall be appointed an elector.

[The electors shall meet in their respective states, and vote by ballot for two persons, of whom one at least shall not be an inhabitant of the same state with themselves. And they shall make a list of all the persons voted for, and of the number of votes for each; which list they shall sign and certify, and transmit, sealed to the seat of the government of the United States, directed to the President of the Senate. The President of the Senate shall, in the presence of the Senate and House of Representatives, open all the certificates, and the votes shall then be counted. The person having the greatest number of votes shall be the President, if such number be a majority of the whole number of electors appointed; and if there be more than one who have such majority, and have an equal number of votes, then the House of Representatives shall immediately chuse by ballot one of them for President; and if no person have a majority, then from the five highest on the list the said House shall in like manner chuse the President. But in chusing the President, the votes shall be taken by states,

---

[6] See also Article of Amendment XXII.

the representation from each state having one vote; a quorum for this purpose shall consist of a member or members from two-thirds of the states, and a majority of all the states shall be necessary to a choice. In every case, after the choice of the President, the person having the greatest number of votes of the electors shall be the Vice-President. But if there should remain two or more who have equal votes, the Senate shall chuse from them by ballot the Vice-President.] [7]

The Congress may determine the time of chusing the electors, and the day on which they shall give their votes; which day shall be the same throughout the United States.

No person except a natural born citizen, or a citizen of the United States, at the time of the adoption of this constitution, shall be eligible to the office of President; neither shall any person be eligible to that office who shall not have attained to the age of thirty-five years, and been fourteen years a resident within the United States.

In case of the removal of the President from office, or of his death, resignation, or inability to discharge the powers and duties of the said office, the same shall devolve on the Vice-President, and the Congress may by law provide for the case of removal, death, resignation, or inability, both of the President and Vice-President, declaring what officer shall then act as President, and such officer shall act accordingly, until the disability be removed, or a President shall be elected.

The President shall, at stated times, receive for his services, a compensation, which shall neither be increased nor diminished during the period for which he shall have been elected, and he shall not receive within that period any other emolument from the United States, or any of them.

---

[7] Article of Amendment XII was adopted "in lieu of the third paragraph of the first section of the second article," according to the joint resolution of Congress proposing the amendment. (2 Stat. 306).

Before he enter on the execution of his office, he shall take the following oath or affirmation:

"I do solemnly swear (or affirm) that I will faithfully "execute the office of President of the United States, and will "to the best of my ability, preserve, protect and defend the "constitution of the United States."

Sect. 2. The President shall be commander in chief of the army and navy of the United States, and of the militia of the several states, when called into the actual service of the United States; he may require the opinion, in writing, of the principal officer in each of the executive departments, upon any subject relating to the duties of their respective offices, and he shall have power to grant reprieves and pardons for offences against the United States, except in cases of impeachment.

He shall have power, by and with the advice and consent of the Senate, to make treaties, provided two-thirds of the Senators present concur; and he shall nominate, and by and with the advice and consent of the Senate, shall appoint ambassadors, other public ministers and consuls, judges of the supreme court, and all other officers of the United States, whose appointments are not herein otherwise provided for, and which shall be established by law. But the Congress may by law vest the appointment of such inferior officers, as they think proper, in the President alone, in the courts of law, or in the heads of departments.

The President shall have power to fill up all vacancies that may happen during the recess of the Senate, by granting commissions which shall expire at the end of their next session.

Sect. 3. He shall from time to time give to the Congress information of the state of the union, and recommend to their consideration such measures as he shall judge necessary and expedient; he may on extraordinary occasions, convene both houses, or either of them, and in case of disagreement between them, with respect to the time of adjournment, he may adjourn them to such time as he shall think proper; he shall receive ambassadors and other public ministers; he shall take care that the laws be faithfully executed, and shall commission all the officers of the United States.

Sect. 4. The President, Vice-President and all civil officers of the United States shall be removed from office on impeachment for, and conviction of, treason, bribery, or other high crimes and misdemeanors.

ARTICLE III.

Sect. 1. The judicial power of the United States, shall be vested in one Supreme Court, and in such inferior courts as the Congress may from time to time ordain and establish. The judges, both of the Supreme and Inferior Court, shall hold their offices during good behaviour, and shall, at stated times, receive for their services, a compensation, which shall not be diminished during their continuance in office.

Sect. 2. The judicial power shall extend to all cases, in law and equity, arising under this constitution, the laws of the United States, and treaties made, or which shall be made, under their authority; to all cases affecting ambassadors, other public ministers, and consuls; to all cases of admiralty and maritime jurisdiction; to controversies to which the United States shall be a party; to controversies between two or more states, between a state and citizens of another state, between citizens of different states, between citizens of the same state claiming lands under grants of different states, and between a state, or the citizens thereof, and foreign states, citizens or subjects.

In all cases affecting ambassadors, other public ministers and consuls, and those in which a state shall be a party, the

Supreme Court shall have original jurisdiction. In all the other cases before mentioned, the Supreme Court shall have appellate jurisdiction, both as to law and fact, with such exceptions, and under such regulations as the Congress shall make.

The trial of all crimes, except in cases of impeachment, shall be by jury; and such trial shall be held in the state where the said crimes shall have been committed; but when not committed within any state, the trial shall be at such place or places as the Congress may by law have directed.

Sect. 3. Treason against the United States, shall consist only in levying war against them, or in adhering to their enemies, giving them aid and comfort. No person shall be convicted of treason unless on the testimony of two witnesses to the same overt act, or on confession in open court.

The Congress shall have power to declare the punishment of treason, but no attainder of treason shall work corruption of blood, or forfeiture, except during the life of the person attainted.

ARTICLE IV.

Sect. 1. Full faith and credit shall be given in each state to the public acts, records and judicial proceedings of every other state. And the Congress may by general laws prescribe the manner in which such acts, records and proceedings shall be proved, and the effect thereof.

Sect. 2. The citizens of each state shall be entitled to all privileges and immunities of citizens in the several states.

A person charged in any state with treason, felony, or other crime, who shall flee from justice, and be found in another state, shall, on demand of the executive authority of the state from which he fled, be delivered up, to be removed to the state having jurisdiction of the crime.

No person held to service or labour in one state, under the laws thereof, escaping into another, shall, in consequence of any law or regulation therein, be discharged from such service or labour, but shall be delivered up on claim of the party to whom such service or labour may be due.

Sect. 3. New states may be admitted by the Congress into this union; but no new state shall be formed or erected within the jurisdiction of any other state; nor any state be formed by the junction of two or more states, or parts of states, without the consent of the legislatures of the states concerned as well as of the Congress.

The Congress shall have power to dispose of and make all needful rules and regulations respecting the territory or other property belonging to the United States; and nothing in this constitution shall be so construed as to prejudice any claims of the United States, or of any particular state.

Sect. 4. The United States shall guarantee to every state in this Union a republican form of government, and shall protect each of them against invasion; and on application of the legislature, or of the executive (when the legislature, cannot be convened) against domestic violence.

ARTICLE V.

The Congress, whenever two-thirds of both Houses shall deem it necessary, shall propose amendments to this constitution, or, on the application of the legislatures of two-thirds of the several states, shall call a convention for proposing amendments, which, in either case, shall be valid to all intents and purposes, as part of this constitution, when ratified by the legislatures of three-fourths of the several states, or by Conventions in three-fourths thereof, as the one or the other mode of ratification may be proposed by the Congress: Provided, that no amendment which may be made prior to the year one thousand eight hundred and eight shall in any manner affect the first and fourth clauses in the ninth section of the first article; and that no state, without its consent, shall be deprived of its equal suffrage in the Senate.

ARTICLE VI.

All debts contracted and engagements entered into, before the adoption of this constitution, shall be as valid against the United States under this constitution, as under the confederation.

This constitution, and the laws of the United States which shall be made in pursuance thereof; and all treaties made, or which shall be made, under the authority of the United States, shall be the supreme law of the land; and the judges in every state shall be bound thereby, any thing in the constitution or laws of any state to the contrary notwithstanding.

The senators and representatives before mentioned, and the members of the several state legislatures, and all executive and judicial officers, both of the United States and of the several states, shall be bound by oath or affirmation, to support this constitution; but no religious test shall ever be required as a qualification to any office or public trust under the United States.

ARTICLE VII.

The ratification of the conventions of nine states, shall be sufficient for the establishment of this constitution between the states so ratifying the same.

DONE in Convention, by the unanimous consent of the States present, the seventeenth day of September, in the year of our Lord One Thousand Seven Hundred and Eighty-Seven, and of the independence of the United States of America the Twelfth. In witness whereof we have hereunto subscribed our Names.

GEORGE WASHINGTON, President,

And Deputy from Virginia.

NEW-HAMPSHIRE,	{ John Langdon, Nicholas Gilman,
MASSACHUSETTS,	{ Nathaniel Gorham, Rufus King.
CONNECTICUT,	{ William Samuel Johnson, Roger Sherman.
NEW-YORK,	Alexander Hamilton.
NEW-JERSEY,	{ William Livingston, David Brearly, William Patterson, Jonathan Dayton.
PENNSYLVANIA,	{ Benjamin Franklin, Thomas Mifflin, Robert Morris, George Clymer, Thomas Fitzsimons, Jared Ingersoll, James Wilson, Gouverneur Morris.
DELAWARE,	{ George Read, Gunning Bedford, junior, John Dickinson, Richard Bassett, Jacob Broom.

MARYLAND,	{	James M'Henry,
		Daniel of St. Thomas Jenifer,
		Daniel Carrol.
VIRGINIA,	{	John Blair,
		James Madison, junior.
NORTH-CAROLINA,	{	William Blount,
		Richard Dobbs Spaight,
		Hugh Williamson.
SOUTH-CAROLINA,	{	John Rutledge,
		Charles Cotesworth Pinckney,
		Charles Pinckney,
		Pierce Butler.
GEORGIA,	{	William Few,
		Abraham Baldwin.

Attest. WILLIAM JACKSON, *Secretary.*

MONDAY, *September* 17, 1787.

PRESENT,

The States of New-Hampshire, Massachusetts, Connecticut, Mr. *Hamilton* from New-York, New-Jersey, Pennsylvania, Delaware, Maryland, Virginia, North-Carolina, South-Carolina and Georgia:

RESOLVED,

THAT the preceding Constitution be laid before the United States in Congress assembled, and that it is the opinion of this Convention, that it should afterwards be submitted to a Convention of Delegates, chosen in each state by the people thereof, under the recommendation of its Legislature, for their assent and ratification; and that each Convention assenting to, and ratifying the same, should give notice thereof to the United States in Congress assembled.

Resolved, That it is the opinion of this Convention, that as soon as the Conventions of nine states shall have ratified this Constitution, the United States in Congress assembled should fix a day on which electors should be appointed by the states which shall have ratified the same, and a day on which the electors should assemble to vote for the President, and the time and place for commencing proceedings under this Constitution. That after such publication the electors should be appointed, and the Senators and Representatives elected: That the electors should meet on the day fixed for the election of the President, and should transmit their votes certified, signed, sealed and directed, as the Constitution requires, to the Secretary of the United States in Congress assembled, that the Senators and Representatives should convene at the time and place assigned; that the Senators should appoint a President of the Senate, for the sole purpose of receiving, opening and counting the votes for President; and, that after he shall be chosen, the Congress, together with the President, should, without delay, proceed to execute this Constitution.

By the unanimous Order of the Convention,
GEORGE WASHINGTON, PRESIDENT.
William Jackson, Secretary.

In CONVENTION,

SEPTEMBER 17, 1787.

SIR,

WE have now the honor to submit to the consideration of the United States in Congress assembled, that Constitution which has appeared to us the most adviseable.

The friends of our country have long seen and desired, that the power of making war, peace and treaties, that of levying money and regulating commerce, and the correspondent executive and judicial authorities should be fully and effectually vested in the general government of the Union: But the impropriety of delegating such extensive trust to one body of men is evident—Hence results the necessity of a different organization.

It is obviously impracticable in the federal government of these States, to secure all rights of independent sovereignty to each, and yet provide for the interest and safety of all—Individuals entering into society, must give up a share of liberty to preserve the rest. The magnitude of the sacrifice must depend as well on situation and circumstance, as on the object to be obtained. It is at all times difficult to draw with precision the line between those rights which must be surrendered, and those which may be reserved; and on the present occasion this difficulty was increased by a difference among the several States as to their situation, extent, habits, and particular interests.

In all our deliberations on this subject we kept steadily in our view, that which appears to us the greatest interest of every true American, the consolidation of our Union, in which is involved our prosperity, felicity, safety, perhaps our national existence. This important consideration, seriously and deeply impressed on our minds, led each State in the Convention to be less rigid on points of inferior magnitude, than might have been otherwise expected; and thus the Constitution, which we now present, is the result of a spirit of amity, and of that mutual deference and concession which the peculiarity of our political situation rendered indispensible.

That it will meet the full and entire approbation of every State is not perhaps to be expected; but each will doubtless consider, that had her interest been alone consulted, the consequences might have been particularly disagreeable or injurious to others; that it is liable to as few exceptions as could reasonably have been expected we hope and believe; that it may promote the lasting welfare of that country so dear to us all, and secure her freedom and happiness, is our most ardent wish.

With great respect,

We have the honor to be,

SIR,

Your Excellency's most

Obedient and humble Servants,

GEORGE WASHINGTON, PRESIDENT.

By unanimous Order of the Convention.

His Excellency
The PRESIDENT *of* CONGRESS.

RATIFICATION OF THE CONSTITUTION

The Constitution was ratified by conventions in the several States, in the following order:

State	Ratified	Yeas	Nays
Delaware	Dec. 7, 1787	30	0
Pennsylvania	Dec. 12, 1787	46	23
New Jersey	Dec. 18, 1787	38	0
Georgia	Jan. 2, 1788	26	0
Connecticut	Jan. 9, 1788	128	40
Massachusetts	Feb. 6, 1788	187	168
Maryland	Apr. 28, 1788	63	11
South Carolina	May 23, 1788	149	73
New Hampshire	Jun. 21, 1788	57	46
Virginia	Jun. 25, 1788	89	79
New York	Jul. 26, 1788	30	27
North Carolina	Nov. 21, 1789	184	77
Rhode Island	May 29, 1790	34	32

Delaware, Pennsylvania, New Jersey, Georgia, Connecticut, and Maryland ratified the Constitution in simple resolutions accepting the instrument as it had emerged from the Convention of 1787. Other States, even as they ratified the compact, demanded amendments and alterations, intended, as Massachusetts said, to "remove the fears & quiet the apprehensions of many of the good people of this Commonwealth & more effectually guard against an undue administration of the Federal Government."

The resolutions of Virginia and New York eloquently express the States' anxiety that individual liberties be guaranteed and that State powers be preserved. The following excerpts reflect the spirit of the time:

STATE OF VIRGINIA

Virginia to wit

We the Delegates of the People of Virginia duly elected in

70

pursuance of a recommendation from the General Assembly and now met in Convention having fully and freely investigated and discussed the proceedings of the Fœderal Convention and being prepared as well as the most mature deliberation hath enabled us to decide thereon Do in the name and in behalf of the People of Virginia declare and make known that the powers granted under the Constitution being derived from the People of the United States may be resumed by them whensoever the same shall be perverted to their injury or oppression and that every power not granted thereby remains with them and at their will: that therefore no right of any denomination can be cancelled abridged restrained or modified by the Congress by the Senate or House of Representatives acting in any Capacity by the President or any Department or Officer of the United States except in those instances in which power is given by the Constitution for those purposes: & that among other essential rights the liberty of Conscience and of the Press cannot be cancelled abridged restrained or modified by any authority of the United States. With these impressions with a solemn appeal to the Searcher of hearts for the purity of our intentions and under the conviction that whatsoever imperfections may exist in the Constitution ought rather to be examined in the mode prescribed therein than to bring the Union into danger by a delay with a hope of obtaining Amendments previous to the Ratification, We the said Delegates in the name and in behalf of the People of Virginia do by these presents assent to and ratify the Constitution recommended on the seventeenth day of September one thousand seven hundred and eighty seven by the Fœderal Convention for the Government of the United States hereby announcing to all those whom it may concern that the said Constitution is binding upon the said People according to an authentic Copy hereto annexed in the Words following; . . .

Done in Convention this twenty Sixth day of June
one thousand seven hundred and eighty eight
By Order of the Convention
EDM^D PENDLETON President [SEAL.] . . .

Virginia towit:

Subsequent Amendments agreed to in Convention as necessary to the proposed Constitution of Government for the United States, recommended to the consideration of the Congress which shall first assemble under the said Constitution to be acted upon according to the mode prescribed in the fifth article thereof:

Videlicet;

That there be a Declaration or Bill of Rights asserting and securing from encroachment the essential and unalienable Rights of the People in some such manner as the following;

First, That there are certain natural rights of which men, when they form a social compact cannot deprive or divest their posterity, among which are the enjoyment of life and liberty, with the means of acquiring, possessing and protecting property, and pursuing and obtaining happiness and safety. Second. That all power is naturally vested in and consequently derived from the people; that Magistrates, therefore, are their trustees and agents and at all times amenable to them. Third, That Government ought to be instituted for the common benefit, protection and security of the People; and that the doctrine of non-resistance against arbitrary power and oppression is absurd slavish, and destructive of the good and happiness of mankind. Fourth, That no man or set of Men are entitled to exclusive or seperate public emoluments or privileges from the community, but in Consideration of public services; which not being descendible, neither ought the offices of Magistrate, Legislator or Judge, or any other public office to be hereditary. Fifth, That the legislative, executive, and judiciary powers of Government should be seperate and distinct, and that the members of the two first may be restrained from oppression by feeling and participating the public burthens, they should, at fixt periods be reduced to a private station, return into the mass of the people; and the vacancies be supplied by certain and regular elections; in which all or any part of the former members to be elegible or ineligible, as the rules of the Constitution of Government, and the laws shall direct. Sixth, That elections of representatives in the legislature ought to be free and frequent, and all men having sufficient evidence of permanent common interest with and attachment to the Community ought to have the right of suffrage: and no aid, charge, tax or fee can be set, rated, or levied upon the people without their own consent, or that of their representatives so elected, nor can they be bound by any law to which they have not in like manner assented for the public good. Seventh, That all power of suspending laws or the execution of laws by any authority, without the consent of the representatives of the people in the legislature is injurious to their rights, and ought not to be exercised. Eighth, That in all capital and criminal prosecutions, a man hath a right to demand the cause and nature of his accusation, to be confronted with the accusers and witnesses, to call for evidence and be allowed counsel in his favor, and to a fair and speedy trial by an impartial Jury of his vicinage, without whose unanimous consent he cannot be found guilty, (except in the government of the land and naval forces) nor can he be compelled to give evidence against himself. Ninth. That no freeman ought to be taken, imprisoned, or disseised of his freehold, liberties, privileges or franchises, or outlawed or exiled, or in any manner destroyed or deprived of his life, liberty or property but by the law of the land. Tenth. That every freeman restrained of his liberty is entitled to a remedy to enquire into the lawfulness thereof, and to remove the same, if unlawful, and that such remedy ought not to be denied nor delayed. Eleventh. That in controversies respecting property, and in suits between man and man, the ancient trial by Jury is one of the greatest Securities to the rights of the people, and ought to remain sacred and inviolable. Twelfth. That every freeman ought to find a certain remedy by recourse to the laws for all injuries and wrongs he may receive in his person, property or character. He ought to obtain right and justice freely without sale, compleatly and without denial, promptly and without delay, and that all establishments or regulations contravening these rights, are oppressive and unjust. Thirteenth, That excessive Bail ought not be required, nor excessive fines imposed, nor cruel and unusual punishments inflicted. Fourteenth, That every freeman has a right to be secure from all unreasonable searches and seizures of his person, his papers and his property; all warrants, therefore, to search suspected places, or sieze any freeman, his papers or property, without information upon Oath (or affirmation of a person religiously scrupulous of taking an oath) of legal and sufficient cause, are grievous and oppressive; and all general Warrants to search suspected places, or to apprehend any suspected person, without specially naming or describing the place or person, are dangerous and ought not to be granted. Fifteenth, That the people have a right peaceably to assemble together to consult for the common good, or to instruct their Representatives; and that every freeman has a right to petition or apply to the legislature for redress of grievances. Sixteenth, That the people have a right to freedom of speech, and of writing and publishing their Sentiments; but the freedom of the press is one of the greatest bulwarks of liberty and ought not to be violated. Seventeenth, That the people have a right to keep and bear arms; that a well regulated Militia composed of the body of the people trained to arms is the proper, natural and safe defence of a free State. That standing armies in time of peace are dangerous to liberty, and therefore ought to be avoided, as far as the circumstances and protection of the Community will admit; and that in all cases the military should be under strict subordination to and governed by the Civil power. Eighteenth, That no Soldier in time of peace ought to be quartered in any house without the consent of the owner, and in time of war in such manner only as the laws direct. Nineteenth, That any person religiously scrupulous of bearing arms ought to be exempted upon payment of an equivalent to employ another to bear arms in his stead. Twentieth, That religion or the duty which we owe to our Creator, and the manner of discharging it can be directed only by reason and conviction, not by force or violence, and therefore all men have an equal, natural and unalienable right to the free exercise of religion according to the dictates of conscience, and that no particular religious sect or society ought to be favored or established by Law in preference to others. . . .

Done in Convention this twenty seventh day of June in the year of our Lord one thousand seven hundred and eighty eight.

By order of the Convention.

EDM^D PENDLETON President [SEAL.]

STATE OF NEW YORK*

WE the Delegates of the People of the State of New York,

---

* Reprinted from *Documentary History of the Constitution*, Vol. II (1894), pp. 190-203.

duly elected and Met in Convention, having maturely considered the Constitution for the United States of America, agreed to on the seventeenth day of September, in the year One thousand Seven hundred and Eighty seven, by the Convention then assembled at Philadelphia in the Common-wealth of Pennsylvania (a Copy whereof precedes these presents) and having also seriously and deliberately considered the present situation of the United States, Do declare and make known.

That all Power is originally vested in and consequently derived from the People, and that Government is instituted by them for their common Interest Protection and Security.

That the enjoyment of Life, Liberty and the pursuit of Happiness are essential rights which every Government ought to respect and preserve.

That the Powers of Government may be reassumed by the People, whensoever it shall become necessary to their Happiness; that every Power, Jurisdiction and right, which is not by the said Constitution clearly delegated to the Congress of the United States, or the departments of the Government thereof, remains to the People of the several States, or to their respective State Governments to whom they may have granted the same; And that those Clauses in the said Constitution, which declare, that Congress shall not have or exercise certain Powers, do not imply that Congress is entitled to any Powers not given by the said Constitution; but such Clauses are to be construed either as exceptions to certain specified Powers, or as inserted merely for greater Caution.

That the People have an equal, natural and unalienable right, freely and peaceably to Exercise their Religion according to the dictates of Conscience, and that no Religious Sect or Society ought to be favoured or established by Law in preference of others.

That the People have a right to keep and bear Arms; that a

well regulated Militia, including the body of the People *capable of bearing Arms*, is the proper, natural and safe defence of a free State;

That the Militia should not be subject to Martial Law except in time of War, Rebellion or Insurrection.

That standing Armies in time of Peace are dangerous to Liberty, and ought not to be kept up, except in Cases of necessity; and that at all times, the Military should be under strict Subordination to the civil Power.

That in time of Peace no Soldier ought to be quartered in any House without the consent of the Owner, and in time of War only by the Civil Magistrate in such manner as the Laws may direct.

That no Person ought to be taken imprisoned or disseised of his freehold, or be exiled or deprived of his Privileges, Franchises, Life, Liberty or Property but by due process of Law.

That no Person ought to be put twice in Jeopardy of Life or Limb for one and the same Offence, nor, unless in case of impeachment, be punished more than once for the same Offence.

That every Person restrained of his Liberty is entitled to an enquiry into the lawfulness of such restraint, and to a removal thereof if unlawful, and that such enquiry and removal ought not to be denied or delayed, except when on account of Public Danger the Congress shall suspend the privilege of the Writ of Habeas Corpus.

That excessive Bail ought not to be required; nor excessive Fines imposed; nor Cruel or unusual Punishments inflicted.

That (except in the Government of the Land and Naval Forces, and of the Militia when in actual Service, and in cases of Impeachment) a Presentment or Indictment by a Grand Jury ought to be observed as a necessary preliminary to the trial of all Crimes cognizable by the Judiciary of the United States, and such Trial should be speedy, public, and by an impartial Jury of the County where the Crime was committed; and that no person can be found Guilty without the unanimous consent of such Jury. But in cases of Crimes not committed within any County of any of the United States, and in Cases of Crimes committed within any County in which a general Insurrection may prevail, or which may be in the possession of a foreign Enemy, the enquiry and trial may be in such County as the Congress shall by Law direct; which County in the two Cases last mentioned should be as near as conveniently may be to that County in which the Crime may have been committed. And that in all Criminal Prosecutions, the Accused ought to be informed of the cause and nature of his Accusation, to be confronted with his accusers and the Witnesses against him, to have the means of producing his Witnesses, and the assistance of Council for his defense, and should not be compelled to give Evidence against himself.

That the trial by Jury in the extent that it obtains by the Common Law of England is one of the greatest securities to the rights of a free People, and ought to remain inviolate.

That every Freeman has a right to be secure from all unreasonable searches and seizures of his person his papers or his property, and therefore, that all Warrants to search suspected places or seize any Freeman his papers or property, without information upon Oath or Affirmation of sufficient cause, are grievous and oppressive; and that all general Warrants (or such in which the place or person suspected are not particularly designated) are dangerous and ought not to be granted.

That the People have a right peaceably to assemble together to consult for their common good, or to instruct their Representatives; and that every person has a right to Petition or apply to the Legislature for redress of Grievances. —— That the Freedom of the Press ought not to be violated or restrained.

That there should be once in four years an Election of the President and Vice President, so that no Officer who may be appointed by the Congress to act as President in case of the removal, death, resignation or inability of the President and Vice President can in any case continue to act beyond the termination of the period for which the last President and Vice President were elected.

That nothing contained in the said Constitution is to be construed to prevent the Legislature of any State from passing Laws at its discretion from time to time to divide such State into convenient Districts, and to apportion its Representatives to and amongst such Districts.

That the Prohibition contained in the said Constitution against *ex post facto* Laws, extends only to Laws concerning Crimes.

That all Appeals in Causes determineable according to the course of the common Law, ought to be by Writ of Error and not otherwise.

That the Judicial Power of the United States in cases in which a State may be a party, does not extend to criminal Prosecutions, or to authorize any Suit by any Person against a State.

That the Judicial Power of the United States as to Controversies between Citizens of the same State claiming Lands under Grants of different States is not to be construed to extend to any other Controversies between them except those which relate to such Lands, so claimed under Grants of different States.

That the Jurisdiction of the Supreme Court of the United States, or of any other Court to be instituted by the Congress, is not in any case to be encreased enlarged or extended by any

Fiction Collusion or mere suggestion;—And That no Treaty is to be construed so to operate as to alter the Constitution of any State.

Under these impressions and declaring that the rights aforesaid cannot be abridged or violated, and that the Explanations aforesaid are consistent with the said Constitution, And in confidence that the Amendments which shall have been proposed to the said Constitution will receive an early and mature Consideration: We the said Delegates, in the Name and in the behalf of the People of the State of New York Do by these presents Assent to and Ratify the said Constitution. In full Confidence nevertheless that until a Convention shall be called and convened for proposing Amendments to the said Constitution, the Militia of this State will not be continued in Service out of this State for a longer term than six weeks without the Consent of the Legislature thereof;—that the Congress will not make or alter any Regulation in this State respecting the times places and manner of holding Elections for Senators or Representatives unless the Legislature of this State shall neglect or refuse to make Laws or regulations for the purpose, or from any circumstance be incapable of making the same, and that in those cases such power will only be exercised until the Legislature of this State shall make provision in the Premises; —that no Excise will be imposed on any Article of the Growth production or Manufacture of the United States, or any of them within this State, Ardent Spirits excepted; And that the Congress will not lay direct Taxes within this State, but when the Monies arising from the Impost and Excise shall be insufficient for the public Exigencies, nor then, until Congress shall first have made a Requisition upon this State to assess levy and pay the Amount of such Requisition made agreably to the Census fixed in the said Constitution in such way and manner as the Legislature of this State shall judge best, but that in such case, if the State shall neglect or refuse to pay its proportion pursuant to such Requisition, then the Congress may assess and levy this States proportion together with Interest at the Rate of six per Centum per Annum from the time at which the same was required to be paid.

Done in Convention at Poughkeepsie in the County of Dutchess in the State of New York the twenty sixth day of July in the year of our Lord One thousand Seven hundred and Eighty eight.

By Order of the Convention.

GEO: CLINTON President

Attested

JOHN McKESSON ⎫
AB^M B. BANCKER ⎬ Secretaries—
           ⎭

ARTICLES IN ADDITION TO, AND IN AMENDMENT OF, THE CONSTITUTION OF THE UNITED STATES OF AMERICA

ARTICLE I.

Congress shall make no law respecting an establishment of religion, or prohibiting the free exercise thereof; or abridging the freedom of speech, or of the press; or of the right of the people peaceably to assemble, and to petition the Government for a redress of grievances.

ARTICLE II.

A well regulated Militia, being necessary to the security of a free State, the right of the people to keep and bear Arms, shall not be infringed.

ARTICLE III.

No Soldier shall, in time of peace be quartered in any house, without the consent of the Owner, nor in time of war, but in a manner to be prescribed by law.

ARTICLE IV.

The right of the people to be secure in their persons, houses, papers, and effects, against unreasonable searches and seizures, shall not be violated, and no Warrants shall issue, but upon probable cause, supported by Oath or affirmation, and particularly describing the place to be searched, and the persons or things to be seized.

ARTICLE V.

No person shall be held to answer for a capital, or otherwise infamous crime, unless on a presentment or indictment of a Grand Jury, except in cases arising in the land or naval forces, or in the Militia, when in actual service in time of War or public danger; nor shall any person be subject for the same offence to be twice put in jeopardy of life or limb; nor shall be compelled in any criminal case to be a witness against himself, nor be deprived of life, liberty, or property, without due process of law; nor shall private property be taken for public use, without just compensation.

ARTICLE VI.

In all criminal prosecutions, the accused shall enjoy the right to a speedy and public trial, by an impartial jury of the State and district wherein the crime shall have been committed, which district shall have been previously ascertained by law, and to be informed of the nature and cause of the accusation; to be confronted with the witnesses against him; to have compulsory process for obtaining witnesses in his favor, and to have the Assistance of Counsel for his defence.

ARTICLE VII.

In Suits at common law, where the value in controversy shall exceed twenty dollars, the right of trial by jury shall be preserved, and no fact tried by a jury, shall be otherwise re-examined in any Court of the United States, than according to the rules of the common law.

ARTICLE VIII.

Excessive bail shall not be required, nor excessive fines imposed, nor cruel and unusual punishments inflicted.

ARTICLE IX.

The enumeration in the Constitution, of certain rights, shall not be construed to deny or disparage others retained by the people.

ARTICLE X.

The powers not delegated to the United States by the Constitution, nor prohibited by it to the States, are reserved to the States respectively, or to the people.

The first ten Amendments to the Constitution, along with two others that failed of ratification (see page 62) were proposed by Congress on September 25, 1789, when they passed the Senate, having been approved by the House on the preceding day, both without record votes. The ten successful Amendments were ratified by:

New Jersey	Nov. 20, 1789	New York	Feb. 24, 1790
Maryland	Dec. 19, 1789	Pennsylvania	Mar. 10, 1790
North Carolina	Dec. 22, 1789	Rhode Island	Jun. 7, 1790
South Carolina	Jan. 19, 1790	Vermont	Nov. 3, 1791
New Hampshire	Jan. 25, 1790	Virginia	Dec. 15, 1791
Delaware	Jan. 28, 1790		

Subsequently these ten Amendments were ratified by:

Massachusetts	Mar. 2, 1939	Connecticut	Apr. 19, 1939
Georgia	Mar. 18, 1939		

ARTICLE XI.

The Judicial power of the United States shall not be construed to extend to any suit in law or equity, commenced or prosecuted against one of the United States by Citizens of another State, or by Citizens or Subjects of any Foreign State.

The 11th Amendment was approved by the Senate on January 14, 1794, by a vote of 23 to 2, and proposed to the States with its approval by the House on March 4, 1794, by a vote of 81 to 9. Thereafter it was ratified by:

New York	Mar. 27, 1794	Virginia	Nov. 18, 1794
Rhode Island	Mar. 31, 1794	Georgia	Nov. 29, 1794
Connecticut	May 8, 1794	Kentucky	Dec. 7, 1794
New Hampshire	Jun. 16, 1794	Maryland	Dec. 26, 1794
Massachusetts	Jun. 26, 1794	Delaware	Jan. 23, 1795
Vermont	between Oct. 9 and Nov. 9, 1794	North Carolina	Feb. 7, 1795

Twelve States having ratified the 11th Amendment, it then became a part of the Constitution, though official announcement of ratification was not made by President Adams until January 8, 1798.

South Carolina ratified the Amendment December 4, 1797.

New Jersey, Pennsylvania and Tennessee, which had been admitted to the Union on June 1, 1796, took no action.

ARTICLE XII.

The Electors shall meet in their respective states, and vote by ballot for President and Vice-President, one of whom, at least, shall not be an inhabitant of the same state with themselves; they shall name in their ballots the person voted for as President, and in distinct ballots the person voted for as Vice-President, and they shall make distinct lists of all persons voted for as President, and of all persons voted for as Vice-President, and of the number of votes for each, which lists they shall sign and certify, and transmit sealed to the seat of the government of the United States, directed to the President of the Senate;—The President of the Senate shall, in the presence of the Senate and House of Representatives, open all the certificates and the votes shall then be counted;—The person having the greatest number of votes for President, shall be the President, if such number be a majority of the whole number of Electors appointed; and if no person have such majority, then from the persons having the highest numbers not exceeding three on the list of those voted for as President, the House of Representatives shall choose immediately, by ballot, the President. But in choosing the President, the votes shall be taken by states, the representation from each state having one vote; a quorum for this purpose shall consist of a member or members from two-thirds of the states, and a majority of all the states shall be necessary to a choice. [And if the House of Representatives shall not choose a President whenever the right of choice shall devolve upon them, before the fourth day of March next following, then the Vice-President shall act as President, as in the case of the death or other constitutional disability of the President.] *—The person having the greatest number of votes as Vice-President, shall be the Vice-President, if such number be a majority of the whole number of Electors appointed, and if no person have a majority, then from the two highest numbers on the list, the Senate shall choose the Vice-President; a quorum for the purpose shall consist of two-thirds of the whole number of Senators, and a majority of the whole number shall be necessary to a choice. But no person constitutionally ineligible to the office of Presi-

---

* The sentence in brackets has been superseded by Section 3 of Article of Amendment XX.

dent shall be eligible to that of Vice-President of the United States.

The 12th Amendment was approved by the Senate on December 2, 1803, by a vote of 22 to 10, and by the House on December 9, 1803, by a vote of 83 to 42. Thereafter it was ratified by:

North Carolina	Dec. 21, 1803	New York	Feb. 10, 1804
Maryland	Dec. 24, 1803	New Jersey	Feb. 22, 1804
Kentucky	Dec. 27, 1803	Rhode Island	Mar. 12, 1804
Ohio	Dec. 30, 1803	South Carolina	May 15, 1804
Virginia	between Dec. 20, 1803	Georgia	May 19, 1804
	and Feb. 3, 1804	[New Hampshire	Jun. 15, 1804]
Pennsylvania	Jan. 5, 1804	Tennessee	Jul. 27, 1804
Vermont	Jan. 30, 1804		

Thirteen States having ratified the 12th Amendment, it presumably became a part of the Constitution, there then having been seventeen States in the Union. However, the Governor of New Hampshire vetoed the act of the Legislature on June 20, 1804, and a resolution of ratification failed to pass again by the two-thirds vote then required by the New Hampshire Constitution. Most students of the Constitution believe that approval or disapproval by a Governor has no effect upon the act of a State Legislature in ratifying a Constitutional Amendment. If New Hampshire's ratification be deemed ineffective, the Amendment became operative when it was ratified by Tennessee on July 27, 1804. On September 25, 1804, Secretary of State Madison declared that a sufficient number had ratified the Amendment.

The Amendment was rejected by Delaware on January 18, 1804, and by Connecticut at its session begun May 10, 1804.

There is no record of any action by Massachusetts.

ARTICLE XIII.

Sect. 1. Neither slavery nor involuntary servitude, except as a punishment for crime whereof the party shall have been duly convicted, shall exist within the United States, or any place subject to their jurisdiction.

Sect. 2. Congress shall have power to enforce this article by appropriate legislation.

A resolution in 20 sections was defeated in the Senate in the 38th Congress, 1st Session, and then much amended in Committee of the Whole and passed on April 8, 1864, by a vote of 38 to 6. In the 2d Session the House of Representatives, having rejected it, reconsidered its rejection on January 31, 1865, by a vote of 112 to 57 and agreed to Public Resolution 10 by a vote of 119 to 56.

During its pendency 36 States were members of the Union. The Amendment's validity was established by the following 27 ratifications:

Illinois	Feb. 1, 1865	Nevada	Feb. 16, 1865
Rhode Island	Feb. 2, 1865	Louisiana	Feb. 17, 1865
Michigan	Feb. 2, 1865	Minnesota	Feb. 23, 1865
Maryland	Feb. 3, 1865	Wisconsin	Feb. 24, 1865
New York	Feb. 3, 1865	Vermont	Mar. 9, 1865
Pennsylvania	Feb. 3, 1865	Tennessee	Apr. 7, 1865
West Virginia	Feb. 3, 1865	Arkansas	Apr. 14, 1865
Missouri	Feb. 6, 1865	Connecticut	May 5, 1865
Maine	Feb. 7, 1865	New Hampshire	Jul. 1, 1865
Kansas	Feb. 7, 1865	South Carolina	Nov. 13, 1865
Massachusetts	Feb. 7, 1865	Alabama	Dec. 2, 1865
Virginia	Feb. 9, 1865	North Carolina	Dec. 4, 1865
Ohio	Feb. 10, 1865	Georgia	Dec. 6, 1865
Indiana	Feb. 13, 1865		

The certificate of adoption was issued by the Secretary of State on December 18, 1865.

The following seven ratifications were given after the requisite three-fourths to make the proposal "valid, to all intents and purposes as a part of this Constitution" had been obtained:

Oregon Dec. 8, 1865
California Dec. 19, 1865
Florida Dec. 28, 1865
(joint resolution implying objection to Section 2) ratified outright with 14th Amendment, Jun. 9, 1868
Iowa Jan. 15, 1866
New Jersey Jan. 23, 1866
(after the Assembly, Mar. 1, 1865, voted 30 to 30 and the Senate on Mar. 16, 1865, failed to approve by a vote of 8 to 13)
Texas Feb. 18, 1870
(joint resolution also ratifying the 14th and 15th Amendments)
Delaware Feb. 12, 1901
(rejected by General Assembly Feb. 7, 1865; indefinitely postponed by Senate, Feb. 9, 1865)

The following two States rejected the proposal:

Kentucky   Feb. 24, 1865   State and Federal Relations,
Mississippi   Dec. 4, 1865   adopted by House Nov. 27, 1865,
  (approval by Governor of report   and concurred in by Senate,
  of Joint Standing-Committee on   Dec. 2, 1865)

ARTICLE XIV.

Sect. 1. All persons born or naturalized in the United States, and subject to the jurisdiction thereof, are citizens of the United States and of the State wherein they reside. No State shall make or enforce any law which shall abridge the privileges or immunities of citizens of the United States; nor shall any State deprive any person of life, liberty, or property, without due process of law; nor deny to any person within its jurisdiction the equal protection of the laws.

Sect. 2. Representatives shall be apportioned among the several States according to their respective numbers, counting the whole number of persons in each State, excluding Indians not taxed. But when the right to vote at any election for the choice of electors for President and Vice President of the United States, Representatives in Congress, the Executive and Judicial officers of a State, or the members of the Legislature thereof, is denied to any of the male inhabitants of such State, being twenty-one years of age, and citizens of the United States, or in any way abridged, except for participation in rebellion, or other crime, the basis of representation therein shall be reduced in the proportion which the number of such male citizens shall bear to the whole number of male citizens twenty-one years of age in such State.

Sect. 3. No person shall be a Senator or Representative in Congress, or elector of President and Vice President, or hold any office, civil or military, under the United States, or under any State, who, having previously taken an oath, as a member of Congress, or as an officer of the United States, or as a member of any State legislature, or as an executive or judicial officer of any State, to support the Constitution of the United States, shall have engaged in insurrection or rebellion against the same, or given aid or comfort to the enemies thereof. But Congress may by a vote of two-thirds of each House, remove such disability.

Sect. 4. The validity of the public debt of the United States, authorized by law, including debts incurred for payment of pensions and bounties for services in suppressing insurrection or rebellion, shall not be questioned. But neither the United States nor any State shall assume or pay any debt or obligation incurred in aid of insurrection or rebellion against the United States, or any claim for the loss or emancipation of any slave; but all such debts, obligations and claims shall be held illegal and void.

Sect. 5. The Congress shall have power to enforce, by appropriate legislation, the provisions of this article.

House Resolution 127, 39th Congress, was debated and amendments defeated in the Senate June 6, 1866; amendments to Sections 2, 3 and 4 were adopted June 8 and the resolution passed by a vote of 33 to 11; the Senate amendments were agreed to by the House of Representatives on June 13, 1866, by a vote of 138 to 36. A concurrent resolution requesting the President to transmit the proposal to the Executives of the several States was passed by both houses on June 18, 1866.

Secretary of State William H. Seward on July 20, 1868, issued a proclamation that the 14th Amendment was a part of the Constitution if withdrawals of ratifications by New Jersey and Ohio were ineffective. Congress on July 21, 1868, passed a concurrent resolution declaring the Amendment to be part of the Constitution and directing the Secretary of State to promulgate it as such. On July 28, 1868, Secretary Seward issued an unconditional certificate in which he recapitulated the circumstances, quoted the resolution of Congress and listed, as they then appeared to him, the dates of ratification, rejection or other action of all States, including Alabama and Georgia, which had ratified in the interim. The 28 ratifications which constituted the requisite three-fourths of the whole number included in the proclamation of July 20, 1868, were:

Connecticut Jun. 30, 1866
New Hampshire Jul. 6, 1866
Tennessee Jul. 19, 1866
New Jersey Sep. 11, 1866
(resolution to "rescind" adopted
Feb. 19/20, 1868, and Mar. 5/24,
1868, over Governor's "veto")
Oregon Sep. 19, 1866
(resolution to "rescind" adopted
Oct. 6/15, 1868)
Vermont Oct. 30, 1866
New York Jan. 10, 1867
Ohio Jan. 11, 1867
(resolution to "rescind" adopted
Jan. 13, 1868)
Illinois Jan. 15, 1867
West Virginia Jan. 16, 1867
Michigan Jan. 16, 1867
Minnesota Jan. 16, 1867
Kansas Jan. 17, 1867

Maine Jan. 19, 1867
Nevada Jan. 22, 1867
Indiana Jan. 23, 1867
Missouri Jan. 25, 1867
Pennsylvania Feb. 6, 1867
Rhode Island Feb. 7, 1867
Wisconsin Feb. 13, 1867
Massachusetts Mar. 20, 1867
Nebraska Jun. 15, 1867
Iowa Mar. 16, 1868
Arkansas Apr. 6, 1868
Florida Jun. 9, 1868
(with 13th Amendment)
North Carolina Jul. 4, 1868
(after rejection, Dec. 13/14, 1866)
Louisiana Jul. 9, 1868
(after rejection, Feb. 6, 1867)
South Carolina Jul. 9, 1868
(after rejection, Dec. 19/20, 1866)

The following 7 ratifications were given after the certificate of adoption was issued on July 20, 1868:

Alabama Jul. 13, 1868
Georgia Jul. 21, 1868
(after rejection Nov. 10, 1866);
also Feb. 2, 1870
Virginia Oct. 8, 1869
(after rejection Jan. 9, 1867)
Mississippi Jan. 17, 1870,
(with 15th Amendment)

Texas Feb. 18, 1870
(after rejection Oct. 27, 1866)
with 13th and 15th Amendments.
Delaware Feb. 12, 1901
(after rejection Feb. 6/8, 1867)
Maryland Apr. 4, 1959
(after rejection by Senate Mar.
23, 1867)

The Governor of Kentucky on January 10, 1866, transmitted two copies of a resolution by which the Senate and House rejected the proposal on January 8, 1866.

California made no report of any action.

ARTICLE XV.

Sect. 1. The right of citizens of the United States to vote shall not be denied or abridged by the United States or by any State on account of race, color, or previous condition of servitude—

Sect. 2. The Congress shall have power to enforce this article by appropriate legislation.—

Senate Resolution 8, 40th Congress, after debate was passed by the Senate February 18, 1869, by a vote of 35 to 11; a conference report striking out the words "or hold office" was passed by the House of Representatives February 20, 1869, by a vote of 140 to 37; the conference report was accepted by the Senate February 26, 1869, by a vote of 39 to 13.

This proposal required 28 ratifications from the 37 States to bring it into force. New York, which attempted to "withdraw" its ratification, was included in the list of ratifying States in the certificate of adoption dated March 30, 1870, which listed 30 States which had then ratified. The first 28 ratifications were:

Nevada	Mar. 1, 1869	New Hampshire	Jul. 1, 1869
West Virginia	Mar. 3, 1869	Virginia	Oct. 8, 1869
North Carolina	Mar. 5, 1869	Vermont	Oct. 20, 1869
Illinois	Mar. 5, 1869	Alabama	Nov. 16, 1869
Louisiana	Mar. 5, 1869	Missouri	Jan. 10, 1870
Michigan	Mar. 8, 1869	(also ratified Sec. 1 March 1,	
Wisconsin	Mar. 9, 1869	1869)	
Maine	Mar. 11, 1869	Minnesota	Jan. 13, 1870
Massachusetts	Mar. 12, 1869	Mississippi	Jan. 17, 1870,
Arkansas	Mar. 15, 1869	(with 14th Amendment)	
South Carolina	Mar. 15, 1869	Rhode Island	Jan. 18, 1870
Pennsylvania	Mar. 25, 1869	Kansas	Jan. 19, 1870
New York	Apr. 14, 1869	(also defectively Feb. 27, 1869)	
(resolution to "withdraw" con-		Ohio	Jan. 27, 1870
sent Jan. 5, 1870)		(after rejection Apr. 1/30, 1869)	
Indiana	May 14, 1869	Georgia	Feb. 2, 1870
Connecticut	May 19, 1869	Iowa	Feb. 3, 1870
Florida	Jun. 14, 1869		

Five other ratifications were given, the first two in the following list being included in the certificate of adoption:

Nebraska	Feb. 17, 1870	Delaware	Feb. 12, 1901
Texas	Feb. 18, 1870,	(after rejection Mar. 17/18, 1869)	
(with 13th and 15th Amendments)		Oregon	Feb. 24, 1959
New Jersey	Feb. 15, 1871	(after rejection Oct. 26, 1870)	
(after rejection Mar. 17/18, 1870)			

The following rejections occurred:

California	Jan. 28, 1870	Maryland	Feb. 4/26, 1870
Kentucky	Mar. 11/12, 1869	Tennessee	House, Nov. 16, 1869

ARTICLE XVI.

The Congress shall have power to lay and collect taxes on incomes, from whatever source derived, without apportionment among the several States, and without regard to any census or enumeration.

The 16th Amendment was approved by the Senate, 77 to 0, on July 5, 1909, and by the House, 318 to 14, on July 12, 1909. Thereafter it was ratified by:

Alabama	Aug. 10, 1909	Colorado	Feb. 15, 1911
Kentucky	Feb. 8, 1910	North Dakota	Feb. 17, 1911
South Carolina	Feb. 19, 1910	Kansas	Feb. 18, 1911
Illinois	Mar. 1, 1910	Michigan	Feb. 23, 1911
Mississippi	Mar. 7, 1910	Iowa	Feb. 24, 1911
Oklahoma	Mar. 10, 1910	Missouri	Mar. 16, 1911
Maryland	Apr. 8, 1910	Maine	Mar. 31, 1911
Georgia	Aug. 3, 1910	Tennessee	Apr. 7, 1911
Texas	Aug. 16, 1910	Arkansas	Apr. 22, 1911
Ohio	Jan. 19, 1911	(after rejection Jan. 9, 1911)	
Idaho	Jan. 20, 1911	Wisconsin	May 26, 1911
Oregon	Jan. 23, 1911	New York	Jul. 12, 1911
Washington	Jan. 26, 1911	Arizona	Apr. 6, 1912
Montana	Jan. 30, 1911	Minnesota	Jun. 11, 1912
Indiana	Jan. 30, 1911	Louisiana	Jun. 28, 1912
California	Jan. 31, 1911	West Virginia	Jan. 31, 1913
Nevada	Jan. 31, 1911	Delaware	Feb. 3, 1913
South Dakota	Feb. 3, 1911	Wyoming	Feb. 3, 1913
Nebraska	Feb. 9, 1911	New Mexico	Feb. 3, 1913
North Carolina	Feb. 11, 1911		

More than thirty-six States having ratified the 16th Amendment, it was certified by Secretary of State Philander C. Knox on February 25, 1913, as a part of the Constitution. Thereafter the Amendment was ratified by:

New Jersey	Feb. 4, 1913	Massachusetts	Mar. 4, 1913
Vermont	Feb. 19, 1913	New Hampshire	Mar. 7, 1913
(after rejection Jan. 17, 1911)		(after rejection Mar. 2, 1911)	

Rejections of the proposal were:

Rhode Island	Apr. 29, 1910	Connecticut	Jun. 28, 1911
Utah	Mar. 9, 1911	Florida	May 31, 1913

Failures to complete action were:

Virginia	Senate, 19 to 5, Mar. 9, 1910	Pennsylvania	House, 139 to 4, May 10, 1911

ARTICLE XVII.

The Senate of the United States shall be composed of two Senators from each State, elected by the people thereof, for six years; and each Senator shall have one vote. The electors in each State shall have the qualifications requisite for electors of the most numerous branch of the State legislatures.

When vacancies happen in the representation of any State in the Senate, the executive authority of such State shall issue writs of election to fill such vacancies: *Provided,* That the legislature of any State may empower the executive thereof to make temporary appointments until the people fill the vacancies by election as the legislature may direct.

This amendment shall not be so construed as to affect the election or term of any Senator chosen before it becomes valid as part of the Constitution.

The 17th Amendment was approved in conference report by

the Senate 42 to 36, on April 23, 1912 and by the House, 238 to 39, on May 13, 1912. Thereafter it was ratified by:

Massachusetts	May 22, 1912	Arkansas	Feb. 11, 1913
Arizona	Jun. 3, 1912	Maine	Feb. 11, 1913
Minnesota	Jun. 10, 1912	Illinois	Feb. 13, 1913
New York	Jan. 15, 1913	North Dakota	Feb. 14, 1913
Kansas	Jan. 17, 1913	Wisconsin	Feb. 18, 1913
Oregon	Jan. 23, 1913	Indiana	Feb. 19, 1913
North Carolina	Jan. 24, 1913	New Hampshire	Feb. 19, 1913
California	Jan. 28, 1913	Vermont	Feb. 19, 1913
Michigan	Jan. 28, 1913	South Dakota	Feb. 19, 1913
Iowa	Jan. 30, 1913	Oklahoma	Feb. 24, 1913
Montana	Jan. 30, 1913	Ohio	Feb. 25, 1913
Idaho	Jan. 31, 1913	Missouri	Mar. 7, 1913
West Virginia	Feb. 4, 1913	New Mexico	Mar. 13, 1913
Colorado	Feb. 5, 1913	Nebraska	Mar. 14, 1913
Nevada	Feb. 6, 1913	New Jersey	Mar. 17, 1913
Texas	Feb. 7, 1913	Tennessee	Apr. 1, 1913
Washington	Feb. 7, 1913	Pennsylvania	Apr. 2, 1913
Wyoming	Feb. 8, 1913	Connecticut	Apr. 8, 1913

Thirty-six States having ratified the 17th Amendment, it was certified by Secretary of State William Jennings Bryan on May 31, 1913, as a part of the Constitution. Thereafter, it was ratified by Louisiana on June 11, 1914.

Utah rejected the amendment on February 26, 1913, and Delaware on March 18, 1913.

No action was completed by Alabama, Florida, Georgia, Rhode Island and South Carolina. No legislative sessions were held during the pendency of the proposal in Kentucky, Maryland, Mississippi, and Virginia.

[ARTICLE XVIII.]*

[Sect. 1. After one year from the ratification of this article, the manufacture, sale, or transportation of intoxicating liquors within, the importation thereof into, or the exportation thereof from the United States and all territory subject to the jurisdiction thereof for beverage purposes is hereby prohibited.

---

* Repealed by Section 1 of Article of Amendment XXI.

[*Sect.* 2. The Congress and the several States shall have concurrent power to enforce this article by appropriate legislation.

[*Sect.* 3. This article shall be inoperative unless it shall have been ratified as an amendment to the Constitution by the legislatures of the several States, as provided in the Constitution, within seven years from the date of the submission hereof to the States by the Congress.]

The 18th Amendment was approved by the House of Representatives, 282 to 128, on December 17, 1917, and by the Senate, 65 to 20, on the following day. Thereafter it was ratified by:

Mississippi	Jan. 8, 1918	Maine	Jan. 8, 1919
Virginia	Jan. 11, 1918	West Virginia	Jan. 9, 1919
Kentucky	Jan. 14, 1918	California	Jan. 13, 1919
North Dakota	Jan. 28, 1918	Tennessee	Jan. 13, 1919
South Carolina	Feb. 8, 1918	Washington	Jan. 13, 1919
Maryland	Feb. 13, 1918	Arkansas	Jan. 14, 1919
Montana	Feb. 19, 1918	Kansas	Jan. 14, 1919
Texas	Mar. 4, 1918	Illinois	Jan. 14, 1919
Delaware	Mar. 18, 1918	Indiana	Jan. 14, 1919
South Dakota	Mar. 20, 1918	Alabama	Jan. 15, 1919
Massachusetts	Apr. 2, 1918	Colorado	Jan. 15, 1919
Arizona	May 24, 1918	Iowa	Jan. 15, 1919
Georgia	Jun. 26, 1918	Oregon	Jan. 15, 1919
Louisiana	Aug. 9, 1918	New Hampshire	Jan. 15, 1919
Florida	Dec. 3, 1918	Nebraska	Jan. 16, 1919
Michigan	Jan. 2, 1919	North Carolina	Jan. 16, 1919
Ohio	Jan. 7, 1919	Utah	Jan. 16, 1919
Oklahoma	Jan. 7, 1919	Missouri	Jan. 16, 1919
Idaho	Jan. 8, 1919	Wyoming	Jan. 16, 1919

Acting Secretary of State Frank L. Polk on January 29, 1919, issued a certificate that 36 States, being three-fourths of the whole number of States, had ratified the proposed Amendment, naming the States to which the certificate applied. Of the States in the above chronological list, the certificate omitted the names of Arkansas, Iowa, Missouri and Tennessee, and included those of Minnesota and Wisconsin. It was juridically determined* that the

---

* Dillon v. Gloss, 256 U. S. 368 (1921).

96

Amendment became a part of the Constitution January 16, 1919. It became operative under its own terms January 16, 1920.

Subsequently the Amendment was ratified by:

Minnesota	Jan. 17, 1919	New York	Jan. 29, 1919
Wisconsin	Jan. 17, 1919	Vermont	Jan. 29, 1919
New Mexico	Jan. 20, 1919	Pennsylvania	Feb. 25, 1919
Nevada	Jan. 21, 1919	New Jersey	Mar. 9, 1922

Connecticut failed to act and Rhode Island rejected the proposal.

ARTICLE XIX.

The right of citizens of the United States to vote shall not be denied or abridged by the United States or by any State on account of sex.

Congress shall have power to enforce this article by appropriate legislation.

———

The 19th Amendment was approved by the House of Representatives, 308 to 89, on May 21, 1919, and by the Senate, 56 to 25 on June 4, 1919. Thereafter it was ratified by:

Illinois	Jun. 10, 1919	Maine	Nov. 5, 1919
Michigan	Jun. 10, 1919	North Dakota	Dec. 1, 1919
Wisconsin	Jun. 10, 1919	South Dakota	Dec. 4, 1919
Kansas	Jun. 16, 1919	Colorado	Dec. 15, 1919
New York	Jun. 16, 1919	Kentucky	Jan. 6, 1920
Ohio	Jun. 16, 1919	Rhode Island	Jan. 6, 1920
Pennsylvania	Jun. 24, 1919	Oregon	Jan. 13, 1920
Massachusetts	Jun. 25, 1919	Indiana	Jan. 16, 1920
Texas	Jun. 28, 1919	Wyoming	Jan. 27, 1920
Iowa	Jul. 2, 1919	Nevada	Feb. 7, 1920
Missouri	Jul. 3, 1919	New Jersey	Feb. 9, 1920
Arkansas	Jul. 28, 1919	Idaho	Feb. 11, 1920
Montana	Aug. 2, 1919	Arizona	Feb. 12, 1920
Nebraska	Aug. 2, 1919	New Mexico	Feb. 21, 1920
Minnesota	Sep. 8, 1919	Oklahoma	Feb. 28, 1920
New Hampshire	Sep. 10, 1919	West Virginia	Mar. 10, 1920
Utah	Oct. 2, 1919	Washington	Mar. 22, 1920
California	Nov. 1, 1919	Tennessee	Aug. 18, 1920

Thirty-six States having ratified the 19th Amendment, it was certified on August 26, 1920, by Secretary of State Bainbridge Colby, as a part of the Constitution. Thereafter the Amendment was ratified by:

Connecticut	Sep. 14, 1920	Alabama	Sep. 8, 1953
Vermont	Feb. 8, 1921	(after rejection Sep. 22, 1919)	
Maryland	Mar. 29, 1941		
(after rejection Feb. 24, 1920); certified Feb. 25, 1958			

The amendment was rejected by:

Georgia	Jul. 25, 1919	Mississippi	Mar. 29, 1920
South Carolina	Jan. 28, 1920	Delaware	Jun. 2, 1920
Virginia	Feb. 12, 1920	Louisiana	Jul. 1, 1920

No action appears to have been taken by Florida (not in session) and North Carolina.

ARTICLE XX.

Sect. 1. The terms of the President and Vice President shall end at noon on the 20th day of January, and the terms of Senators and Representatives at noon on the 3d day of January, of the years in which such terms would have ended if this article had not been ratified; and the terms of their successors shall then begin.

Sect. 2. The Congress shall assemble at least once in every year, and such meeting shall begin at noon on the 3d day of January, unless they shall by law appoint a different day.

Sect. 3. If, at the time fixed for the beginning of the term of the President, the President elect shall have died, the Vice President elect shall become President. If a President shall not have been chosen before the time fixed for the beginning of his term, or if the President elect shall have failed to qualify, then the Vice President elect shall act as President until a President shall have qualified; and the Congress may by law provide for the case wherein neither a President elect nor a

Vice President elect shall have qualified, declaring who shall then act as President, or the manner in which one who is to act shall be selected, and such person shall act accordingly until a President or Vice President shall have qualified.

Sect. 4. The Congress may by law provide for the case of the death of any of the persons from whom the House of Representatives may choose a President whenever the right of choice shall have devolved upon them, and for the case of the death of any of the persons from whom the Senate may choose a Vice President whenever the right of choice shall have devolved upon them.

Sect. 5. Sections 1 and 2 shall take effect on the 15th day of October following the ratification of this article.

Sect. 6. This article shall be inoperative unless it shall have been ratified as an amendment to the Constitution by the legislatures of three-fourths of the several States within seven years from the date of its submission.

———————

The 20th Amendment was approved in a conference report by the House of Representatives, without record vote, on March 1, 1932, and by the Senate, 74 to 3, on the following day. It was at once proposed to the States, and thereafter was ratified by:

Virginia	Mar. 4, 1932	Indiana	Aug. 15, 1932
New York	Mar. 11, 1932	Texas	Sep. 7, 1932
Mississippi	Mar. 16, 1932	Alabama	Sep. 13, 1932
Arkansas	Mar. 17, 1932	California	Jan. 4, 1933
Kentucky	Mar. 17, 1932	North Carolina	Jan. 5, 1933
New Jersey	Mar. 21, 1932	North Dakota	Jan. 9, 1933
South Carolina	Mar. 25, 1932	Minnesota	Jan. 12, 1933
Michigan	Mar. 31, 1932	Arizona	Jan. 13, 1933
Maine	Apr. 1, 1932	Montana	Jan. 13, 1933
Rhode Island	Apr. 14, 1932	Nebraska	Jan. 13, 1933
Illinois	Apr. 21, 1932	Oklahoma	Jan. 13, 1933
Louisiana	Jun. 22, 1932	Kansas	Jan. 16, 1933
West Virginia	Jul. 30, 1932	Oregon	Jan. 16, 1933
Pennsylvania	Aug. 11, 1932	Delaware	Jan. 19, 1933

Washington	Jan. 19, 1933	New Mexico	Jan. 21, 1933
Wyoming	Jan. 19, 1933	Georgia	Jan. 23, 1933
Iowa	Jan. 20, 1933	Missouri	Jan. 23, 1933
South Dakota	Jan. 20, 1933	Ohio	Jan. 23, 1933
Tennessee	Jan. 20, 1933	Utah	Jan. 23, 1933
Idaho	Jan. 21, 1933		

More than three-fourths of the States having ratified the 20th Amendment, it was certified by Secretary of State Henry L. Stimson on February 6, 1933, as a part of the Constitution. Section 5 provides that Sections 1 and 2 took effect October 15, 1933; therefore, new terms of Senators and Representatives began January 3, 1934, and the new terms of President and Vice President began January 20, 1937. The above list shows that the Amendment was in effect January 23, 1933.*

All 48 States ratified the Amendment, the others being as follows:

Colorado	Jan. 24, 1933	New Hampshire	Jan. 31, 1933
Massachusetts	Jan. 24, 1933	Vermont	Feb. 2, 1933
Wisconsin	Jan. 24, 1933	Maryland	Mar. 24, 1933
Nevada	Jan. 26, 1933	Florida	Apr. 26, 1933
Connecticut	Jan. 27, 1933		

---

* An amendment to the Constitution comes into force when that State which completes three-fourths of the total number of States ratifies it, and "official notice" of this act is irrevocable, *Chandler* v. *Wise and Moss*, 307 U. S. 474 (1939). The certificate of adoption, issued as promptly as may be after the requisite notices from States are in hand, does not determine that date, but only that the Amendment has then become valid. The date of its effectiveness can only be determined when all the returns are in. The record of the 20th Amendment illustrates the condition confronted by the authority charged with issuing the certificate. The first list of ratifications above records 39 States, where 36 were required. Four of them ratified on January 23, 1933, three more than necessary. The Missouri Legislature completed its action at 10:01 a.m. and Georgia at noon. Notifications of the four were received by the Department of State by February 3 and by February 4 ratifications dated January 24 and 27 were received from Colorado, Massachusetts, Wisconsin and Connecticut, all of which were named in the certificate of adoption issued February 6. The chronological list above includes Iowa, New Mexico, Oregon and Tennessee whose ratifications were given January 16 to 21, prior to the effective date of January 23, but they were not received for record until April. Historically, they constitute part of the three-fourths requirement.

ARTICLE XXI.

Sect. 1. The eighteenth article of amendment to the Constitution of the United States is hereby repealed.

Sect. 2. The transportation or importation into any State, Territory, or possession of the United States for delivery or use therein of intoxicating liquors, in violation of the laws thereof, is hereby prohibited.

Sect. 3. This article shall be inoperative unless it shall have been ratified as an amendment to the Constitution by conventions in the several States, as provided in the Constitution, within seven years from the date of the submission hereof to the States by the Congress.

The 21st Amendment was approved by the Senate, 63 to 23, on February 16, 1933, and by the House of Representatives, 289 to 121, on February 20, 1933. It was immediately proposed to the States, and thereafter was ratified by:

Michigan	Apr. 10, 1933	Tennessee	Aug. 11, 1933
Wisconsin	Apr. 25, 1933	Missouri	Aug. 29, 1933
Rhode Island	May 8, 1933	Arizona	Sep. 5, 1933
Wyoming	May 25, 1933	Nevada	Sep. 5, 1933
New Jersey	Jun. 1, 1933	Vermont	Sep. 23, 1933
Delaware	Jun. 24, 1933	Colorado	Sep. 26, 1933
Indiana	Jun. 26, 1933	Washington	Oct. 3, 1933
Massachusetts	Jun. 26, 1933	Minnesota	Oct. 10, 1933
New York	Jun. 27, 1933	Idaho	Oct. 17, 1933
Illinois	Jul. 10, 1933	Maryland	Oct. 18, 1933
Iowa	Jul. 10, 1933	Virginia	Oct. 25, 1933
Connecticut	Jul. 11, 1933	New Mexico	Nov. 2, 1933
New Hampshire	Jul. 11, 1933	Florida	Nov. 14, 1933
California	Jul. 24, 1933	Texas	Nov. 24, 1933
West Virginia	Jul. 25, 1933	Kentucky	Nov. 27, 1933
Arkansas	Aug. 1, 1933	Ohio	Dec. 5, 1933
Oregon	Aug. 7, 1933	Pennsylvania	Dec. 5, 1933
Alabama	Aug. 8, 1933	Utah	Dec. 5, 1933

Thirty-six States having ratified the 21st Amendment, it was certified on December 5, 1933, by Acting Secretary of State William Phillips, as a part of the Constitution. Thereafter the amendment was ratified by Maine on Dec. 6, 1933, and by Montana on Aug. 6, 1934.

The proposal was rejected by South Carolina on Dec. 4, 1933. The people of North Carolina voted against holding a convention at a referendum conducted Nov. 7, 1933. Nebraska, Oklahoma and South Dakota scheduled conventions in 1934, but did not hold them because the Amendment had been adopted. Georgia, Kansas, Louisiana, Mississippi and North Dakota did not pass laws to provide for conventions.

ARTICLE XXII.

Sect. 1. No person shall be elected to the office of the President more than twice, and no person who has held the office of President, or acted as President, for more than two years of a term to which some other person was elected President shall be elected to the office of the President more than once. But this Article shall not apply to any person holding the office of President when this Article was proposed by the Congress, and shall not prevent any person who may be holding the office of President, or acting as President, during the term within which this Article becomes operative from holding the office of President or acting as President during the remainder of such term.

Sect. 2. This article shall be inoperative unless it shall have been ratified as an amendment to the Constitution by the legislatures of three-fourths of the several States within seven years from the date of its submission to the States by the Congress.

The 22nd Amendment was approved by the Senate, 59 to 23, on March 12, 1947; by the House of Representatives, 285 to 121, on February 6, 1947, and by conference agreement, March 21,

1947. It was formally proposed to the States on March 24, 1947, and thereafter was ratified by:

Maine	Mar. 31, 1947	Virginia	Jan. 28, 1948
Michigan	Mar. 31, 1947	Mississippi	Feb. 12, 1948
Iowa	Apr. 1, 1947	New York	Mar. 9, 1948
Kansas	Apr. 1, 1947	South Dakota	Jan. 21, 1949
New Hampshire	Apr. 1, 1947	North Dakota	Feb. 25, 1949
Delaware	Apr. 2, 1947	Louisiana	May 17, 1950
Illinois	Apr. 3, 1947	Montana	Jan. 25, 1951
Oregon	Apr. 3, 1947	Indiana	Jan. 29, 1951
Colorado	Apr. 12, 1947	Idaho	Jan. 30, 1951
California	Apr. 15, 1947	New Mexico	Feb. 12, 1951
New Jersey	Apr. 15, 1947	Wyoming	Feb. 12, 1951
Vermont	Apr. 15, 1947	Arkansas	Feb. 15, 1951
Ohio	Apr. 16, 1947	Georgia	Feb. 17, 1951
Wisconsin	Apr. 16, 1947	Tennessee	Feb. 20, 1951
Pennsylvania	Apr. 29, 1947	Texas	Feb. 22, 1951
Connecticut	May 21, 1947	Utah	Feb. 26, 1951
Missouri	May 22, 1947	Nevada	Feb. 26, 1951
Nebraska	May 23, 1947	Minnesota	Feb. 27, 1951

Thirty-six States having ratified the 22nd Amendment, it was certified on March 1, 1951, by Jess Larson, Administrator of General Services, as a part of the Constitution. Thereafter the Amendment was ratified by:

North Carolina	Feb. 28, 1951	Florida	Apr. 16, 1951
South Carolina	Mar. 13, 1951	Alabama	May 4, 1951
Maryland	Mar. 14, 1951		

The proposal was rejected by Massachusetts on June 6, 1949 and by Oklahoma in June, 1947 (uncertified). No action was taken by Arizona, Kentucky, Rhode Island, Washington, and West Virginia.

ARTICLE XXIII.

Sect. 1. The District constituting the seat of Government of the United States shall appoint in such manner as the Congress may direct:

A number of electors of President and Vice President equal to the whole number of Senators and Representatives in Congress to which the District would be entitled if it were a State, but in no event more than the least populous State; they shall be in addition to those appointed by the States, but they shall be considered, for the purposes of the election of President and Vice President, to be electors appointed by a State; and they shall meet in the District and perform such duties as provided by the twelfth article of amendment.

Sect. 2. The Congress shall have power to enforce this article by appropriate legislation.

The House Joint Resolution that was to become the 23d Amendment was adopted by voice vote in the House on June 14, 1960. It then was sent to the Senate as a substitute for an earlier version, covering three separate proposals, that had been approved in the Senate February 2, 1960. The Senate accepted the limited House proposal by voice vote on June 16, 1960. In unusually short time (only the 12th and 21st Amendments were ratified more swiftly), the amendment was ratified by:

Hawaii	Jun. 30, 1960	Wyoming	Feb. 17, 1961
Massachusetts	Aug. 22, 1960	Delaware	Feb. 20, 1961
New Jersey	Dec. 19, 1960	Wisconsin	Feb. 21, 1961
New York	Jan. 17, 1961	Pennsylvania	Feb. 28, 1961
California	Jan. 19, 1961	Indiana	Mar. 3, 1961
Oregon	Jan. 27, 1961	North Dakota	Mar. 3, 1961
Maryland	Jan. 30, 1961	Tennessee	Mar. 6, 1961
Idaho	Jan. 31, 1961	Michigan	Mar. 8, 1961
Maine	Jan. 31, 1961	Connecticut	Mar. 9, 1961
Minnesota	Jan. 31, 1961	Arizona	Mar. 10, 1961
New Mexico	Feb. 1, 1961	Illinois	Mar. 14, 1961
Nevada	Feb. 2, 1961	Nebraska	Mar. 15, 1961
Montana	Feb. 2, 1961	Vermont	Mar. 15, 1961
South Dakota	Feb. 6, 1961	Iowa	Mar. 16, 1961
Colorado	Feb. 8, 1961	Missouri	Mar. 20, 1961
Washington	Feb. 9, 1961	Oklahoma	Mar. 21, 1961
West Virginia	Feb. 9, 1961	Rhode Island	Mar. 22, 1961
Alaska	Feb. 10, 1961	New Hampshire	Mar. 29, 1961
Utah	Feb. 16, 1961	Kansas	Mar. 29, 1961

Kansas became the thirty-eighth State to ratify, at 1:14 p.m. on March 29, 1961, thus completing the three-fourths requirement, there being for the first time fifty States in the Union. Ohio ratified 42 minutes later. Arkansas rejected the proposal by a House vote of 59-26 on Jan. 24, 1961. Other States took no action on it. The Administrator of General Services issued a certificate of adoption April 4, 1961.

ARTICLE XXIV.

Sect. 1. The right of citizens of the United States to vote in any primary or other election for President or Vice President, for electors for President or Vice President, or for Senator or Representative in Congress, shall not be denied or abridged by the United States or any State by reason of failure to pay any poll tax or other tax.

Sect. 2. The Congress shall have power to enforce this article by appropriate legislation.

The 24th Amendment won approval in the Senate March 27, 1962, by a vote of 77-16; the resolution passed the House on August 27, 1962, by 295-86. It then was ratified by:

Illinois	Nov. 14, 1962	Idaho	Mar. 8, 1963
New Jersey	Dec. 3, 1962	Washington	Mar. 14, 1963
Oregon	Jan. 25, 1963	Vermont	Mar. 15, 1963
Montana	Jan. 28, 1963	Nevada	Mar. 19, 1963
West Virginia	Feb. 1, 1963	Connecticut	Mar. 20, 1963
New York	Feb. 4, 1963	Tennessee	Mar. 21, 1963
Maryland	Feb. 6, 1963	Pennsylvania	Mar. 25, 1963
California	Feb. 7, 1963	Wisconsin	Mar. 26, 1963
Alaska	Feb. 11, 1963	Kansas	Mar. 28, 1963
Rhode Island	Feb. 14, 1963	Massachusetts	Mar. 28, 1963
Indiana	Feb. 19, 1963	Nebraska	Apr. 4, 1963
Utah	Feb. 20, 1963	Florida	Apr. 18, 1963
Michigan	Feb. 20, 1963	Iowa	Apr. 24, 1963
Colorado	Feb. 21, 1963	Delaware	May 1, 1963
Ohio	Feb. 27, 1963	Missouri	May 13, 1963
Minnesota	Feb. 27, 1963	New Hampshire	Jun. 16, 1963
New Mexico	Mar. 5, 1963	Kentucky	Jun. 27, 1963
Hawaii	Mar. 6, 1963	Maine	Jan. 16, 1964
North Dakota	Mar. 7, 1963	South Dakota	Jan. 23, 1964

Thirty-eight States having ratified the 24th Amendment, its adoption was certified by the Administrator of General Services on Feb. 4, 1964. The proposal was rejected by Mississippi. Other States took no final action on it.

State Action on Amendments

Article and year of validity

State	Date Admitted to Union	1–10 (1791)	11 (1795)	12 (1804)	13 (1865)	14 (1868)	15 (1870)	16 (1913)	17 (1913)	18 (1919)	19 (1920)	20 (1933)	21 (1933)	22 (1951)	23 (1961)	24 (1964)
Alabama	1819	—	—	—	×	+	×	×	⋮	×	+	×	×	+	⋮	⋮
Alaska	1958	—	—	—	—	—	—	—	—	—	—	—	—	—	×	×
Arizona	1912	—	—	—	—	—	—	×	×	×	×	×	×	⋮	×	⋮
Arkansas	1836	—	—	—	×	×	×	×	×	×	×	×	×	×	○	⋮
California	1850	—	—	—	+	⋮	○	×	×	×	×	×	×	×	×	×
Colorado	1876	—	—	—	—	—	—	×	×	×	×	+	×	×	×	×
Connecticut	1787	+	×	○	×	×	×	○	×	⋮	+	+	×	×	×	×
Delaware	1787	×	×	○	+	+	+	×	○	×	○	×	×	×	×	×
Florida	1845	—	—	—	+	×	×	○	⋮	×	⋮	+	×	+	⋮	×
Georgia	1787	+	×	×	×	×	+	×	⋮	×	○	×	⋮	×	⋮	⋮
Hawaii	1959	—	—	—	—	—	—	—	—	—	—	—	—	—	×	×
Idaho	1890	—	—	—	—	—	—	×	×	×	×	×	×	×	×	×
Illinois	1818	—	—	—	×	×	×	×	×	×	×	×	×	×	×	×
Indiana	1816	—	—	—	×	×	×	×	×	×	×	×	×	×	×	×
Iowa	1846	—	—	—	+	×	×	×	×	×	×	×	×	×	×	×
Kansas	1861	—	—	—	×	×	×	×	×	×	×	×	⋮	×	×	×
Kentucky	1792	—	×	×	○	○	○	×	⋮	×	×	×	×	⋮	⋮	×
Louisiana	1812	—	—	—	×	×	×	×	+	×	○	×	⋮	×	⋮	⋮
Maine	1820	—	—	—	×	×	×	×	×	×	×	×	+	×	×	×
Maryland	1787	×	×	×	×	+	○	×	⋮	×	+	×	×	+	×	×
Massachusetts	1787	+	×	⋮	×	×	×	+	×	×	×	+	×	○	×	×
Michigan	1837	—	—	—	×	×	×	×	×	×	×	+	×	×	×	×
Minnesota	1858	—	—	—	×	×	×	×	×	×	×	×	×	×	×	×
Mississippi	1817	—	—	—	○	+	×	×	⋮	+	○	×	⋮	×	⋮	○
Missouri	1821	—	—	—	×	×	×	×	×	×	×	+	×	×	×	×

106

× × × × × × × ┆ × × ┆ × × × ┆ × × ┆ × × ┆ × × × ┆

× × × × × × × ┆ × + × × × × ┆ × × ┆ × × ┆ × × × ×

× × × × × × × + × × ○ × × ┆ + × × × × × × ┆ ┆ × ×

+ ┆ × × × × × ┆ ┆ × ┆ × × × ○ ┆ × × × × × × × × × ×

× × + + × × × × × + × × × × × × × × × + + × × × + ×

× × × × × × × ┆ × × × × × × ○ × × × × + ○ × × × ×

× + + × + + + × × × × × + ○ × × × × × × + × × × + +

× × × × × × × × × × × × × ┆ ┆ × × × ○ × ┆ × × × ×

× × × + + + × × × × × × ┆ ○ × × × × ○ + ○ × × × +

┆ + × × + ┆ ⊕ × ┆ × ┆ + × × × ┆ ○ + ┆ × × ┆ × × ┆

┆ × × × ⊕ ┆ × × ┆ ⊕ ┆ ⊕ × × × ┆ × + ┆ × + ┆ × × ┆

┆ ┆ × × + ┆ × × ┆ × ┆ + × × × ┆ × + ┆ × × ┆ × × ┆

┆ ┆ ┆ × × ┆ × × ┆ × ┆ ┆ × × × ┆ + ┆ ┆ × × ┆ ┆ ┆ ┆

┆ ┆ ┆ × ┆ ┆ × × ┆ ┆ ┆ ┆ ┆ × × ┆ ┆ ┆ ┆ × × ┆ ┆ ┆ ┆

┆ ┆ ┆ × × ┆ × × ┆ ┆ ┆ ┆ × × × ┆ ┆ ┆ ┆ × × ┆ ┆ ┆ ┆

State	Year
Montana	1889
Nebraska	1867
Nevada	1864
New Hampshire	1787
New Jersey	1787
New Mexico	1912
New York	1787
North Carolina	1787
North Dakota	1889
Ohio	1802
Oklahoma	1907
Oregon	1859
Pennsylvania	1787
Rhode Island	1787
South Carolina	1787
South Dakota	1889
Tennessee	1796
Texas	1845
Utah	1896
Vermont	1791
Virginia	1787
Washington	1889
West Virginia	1863
Wisconsin	1848
Wyoming	1890

107

- ┃ Not yet member of the Union
- × Ratified
- + Ratification not counted in certificate of validity
- ⊕ Ratification attempted to be withdrawn
- ○ Rejected
- -- Failure to act

PROPOSALS OF AMENDMENT NOT ADOPTED

Of the 5,300 proposals to amend the Constitution which were introduced in the Congress from 1789 through 1963, only 29 ever were submitted to the States for ratification. Of those 29, 24 have been adopted as articles of amendment. Five proposals submitted to the States for ratification between 1789 and 1924 failed to receive the three-fourths of ratifications by the States requisite for adoption.

The existence of those five incomplete proposals can be disregarded. Theoretically they are still pending, for time limitation on a proposal is, said the Supreme Court in *Coleman* v. *Miller* (1939), an "open one for the consideration of the Congress," which put no limit upon any of them. They are dead in practice, for the reason, as the Court also said, "that the fair inference or implication from Article V [of the Constitution] is that the ratification must be within some reasonable time after the proposal." The Court further quoted an earlier judge

> that an alteration of the Constitution proposed today has relation to the sentiment and the felt needs of today, and that, if not ratified early while that sentiment may be fairly supposed to exist, it ought to be regarded as waived, and not again voted upon, unless a second time proposed by Congress.

Congress itself has followed that advice and since 1917 has limited the life of a proposal to seven years. No adopted article of amendment has required as much as four years to receive the required number of ratifications.

To the following texts of the lost amendments are appended the votes of Congress proposing them, the States which ratified them and an indication of the legal status of their respective subjects.

Apportionment of Representatives, September 25, 1789

The resolution of Congress of September 25, 1789, proposed to the States articles of amendment constituting the Bill of Rights, which were set forth in its Articles III-XII. The Congress thought it desirable also to amplify Article I, Section 2, clause 3, of the Constitution which provided for the enumeration of persons and prescribed that "the number of Representatives shall not exceed one for every thirty thousand." The following article therefore was proposed:

ARTICLE I. After the first enumeration required by the first Article of the Constitution, there shall be one Representative for every thirty thousand, until the number shall amount to one hundred, after which the proportion shall be so regulated by Congress, that there shall be not less than one hundred Representatives, nor less than one Representative for every forty thousand persons, until the number of Representatives shall amount to two hundred, after which the proportion shall be so regulated by Congress, that there shall not be less than two hundred Representatives, nor more than one Representative for every fifty thousand persons.

This proposal was passed by the House of Representatives September 24, 1789, and by the Senate on September 25, 1789, without a record vote. It had been one of the proposed amendments since the House began its debates in June.

Vermont became the 14th State while the resolution was pending, so that 11 ratifications were required to give it validity. The following 10 States ratified:

New Jersey	Nov. 20, 1789	New York	Feb. 24, 1790
Maryland	Dec. 19, 1789	Rhode Island	Jun. 7, 1790
North Carolina	Dec. 22, 1789	Pennsylvania	Sep. 21, 1791
South Carolina	Jan. 19, 1790	Vermont	Nov. 3, 1791
New Hampshire	Jan. 25, 1790	Virginia	Dec. 15, 1791

Delaware postponed action on January 28, 1790.

The Massachusetts General Court considered the original resolution of Congress of 1789, but in its resolution of March 2, 1939 —after a lapse of 150 years—specifically approved the ten Articles of Amendment to the Constitution. The resolutions in Connecticut and Georgia, April 19 and March 18, 1939, respectively, ratified the Articles of Amendment by specific reference.

A statute approved April 13, 1792, reapportioned the House of Representatives at 33,000 persons per representative in consequence of the first census of 1790. Reapportionment has since been effected by statute.

Compensation of Members, September 25, 1789

Article II of the proposal of September 25, 1789, was intended to be an addition to the provision of Article I, Section 6, clause 1, of the Constitution, which stipulates that "Senators and Representatives shall receive a compensation for their services, to be ascertained by law." A law approved September 22, 1789, fixed compensation at $6 per diem of attendance. The proposed amendment was intended to affect both the provision of the Constitution and the law.

> Article II. No law, varying the compensation of the Senators and Representatives, shall take effect, until an election of Representatives shall have intervened.

This proposal was passed by the House of Representatives on September 24, 1789, and by the Senate on September 25, 1789, without a record vote. The proposal was introduced before passage of the law of September 22, 1789.

Vermont became the fourteenth State while the resolution was pending, so that eleven ratifications were required to give it validity. Only the following six States ratified:

Maryland	Dec. 19, 1789	Delaware	Jan. 28, 1790
North Carolina	Dec. 22, 1789	Vermont	Nov. 3, 1791
South Carolina	Jan. 19, 1790	Virginia	Dec. 15, 1791

Other States, alphabetically:

Connecticut	New Jersey
Excluded, Apr. 19, 1939	Excepted, Nov. 20, 1789
Georgia Excluded, Mar. 18, 1939	New York Excepted, Feb. 24, 1790
Massachusetts	Pennsylvania
Omitted, Mar. 2, 1939	Omitted, Mar. 10, 1790
New Hampshire	Rhode Island
Rejected, Jan. 26, 1790	Omitted, Jun. 7, 1790

The compensation at $6 per diem of attendance was confirmed by an act approved March 10, 1796. It has been the practice with respect to increases of compensation to give them effect in the succeeding Congress, that is, after a fresh election of Representatives. The rate of compensation in 1964 is $22,500 per annum, fixed by an act approved March 2, 1955.

Concerning Nobility, May 1, 1810

This proposal amplified Article I, Section 9, clause 8, of the Constitution. It would have denationalized any person accepting, without the consent of Congress, any of the honorifics described in the proposal, which extended the language of the Constitution.

Resolved by the Senate and House of Representatives of the United States of America in Congress assembled (two-thirds of both Houses concurring), That the following section be submitted to the legislatures of the several states, which, when ratified by the legislatures of three fourths of the states, shall be valid and binding, as a part of the constitution of the United States.

If any citizen of the United States shall accept, claim, receive or retain any title of nobility or honour, or shall, without the consent of Congress, accept and retain any present, pension, office or emolument of any kind whatever, from any emperor, king, prince or foreign power, such person shall cease to be a citizen of the United States, and shall be incapable of holding any office of trust or profit under them, or either of them.

The proposal was passed by the Senate on April 27, 1810, by a vote of 19 to 5 and by the House of Representatives on May 1, 1810, by a vote of 87 to 3. At that time no legal procedure existed to control the communication of action by States to the Federal Government, and the status of this proposal was consequently uncertain for some time. Ratification by 13 States was required when the proposal was first submitted to the States. The official file shows 12 ratifications as follows:

Maryland	Dec. 25, 1810	Vermont	Oct. 24, 1811
Kentucky	Jan. 31, 1811	Tennessee	Nov. 21, 1811
Ohio	Jan. 31, 1811	Georgia	Dec. 31, 1811
Delaware	Feb. 2, 1811	North Carolina	Dec. 23, 1811
Pennsylvania	Feb. 6, 1811	Massachusetts	Feb. 27, 1812
New Jersey	Feb. 13, 1811	New Hampshire	Dec. 9, 1812

The official file in the National Archives further shows the following:

Connecticut	rejected, May 13, 1813	Rhode Island	disapproved, Sep. 15, 1814
Louisiana	no action	South Carolina	no action
New York	rejected, Mar. 12, 1812	Virginia	no action

Uncertainty as to the status of this proposal continued for eight years and provoked enactment of the law of April 20, 1818, which prescribed the method for ascertaining ratification of amendments. Secretary of State James Monroe in a circular letter dated March 23, 1813, to Governors inquired concerning its status without result. The House of Representatives by resolution of December 31, 1817, asked President Monroe for that information and on February 27, 1818, he communicated to Congress the record given above. Both the President and Congress were satisfied that the original requirement of 13 ratifications had not been given. Neither of them considered the change in the number of ratifications which had occurred in the interval. The proposal had not been officially submitted to Louisiana, admitted as a State April 30, 1812; to Indiana, admitted December 11, 1816; or to Mississippi, admitted December 10, 1817. On the date of the President's letter to Congress the number of States was 20 and 15 ratifications would have been required to validate the proposal.

Much legislation deals with this subject matter. Naturalized citizens expressly renounce titles or orders of nobility by an act originally passed June 29, 1906. An act of January 31, 1881, defined the consent of Congress for acceptance of a "decoration or other thing." Awarding of such honorific things by other governments cannot be prevented. It is the custom of United States officials who receive such signs of recognition to deposit them with the Department of State. Congress is asked to authorize retired personnel of the Government "to accept and wear such decorations, orders, medals, emblems, presents and other things" (Private Law 85-704, approved August 27, 1958).

Concerning Slavery, March 2[4], 1861

This gesture of compromise was adopted by Congress at the time when Fort Sumter was seized and the War of 1861-65 beginning.

Resolved by the Senate and House of Representatives of the United States of America in Congress assembled, That the following article be proposed to the Legislatures of the several States as an amendment to the Constitution of the United States, which, when ratified by three-fourths of said Legislatures, shall be valid, to all intents and purposes, as part of the said Constitution, viz:

"ARTICLE THIRTEEN
"No amendment shall be made to the Constitution which will authorize or give to Congress the power to abolish or interfere, within any

State, with the domestic institutions thereof, including that of persons held to labor or service by the laws of said State."

As House (Joint) Resolution No. 80, 36th Congress, this proposal passed the House of Representatives on February 28, 1861, by a vote of 133 to 65. The 36th Congress was coming to an end and the Senate continued its "legislative day" of March 2 into the night of March 3/4, during which the Senate passed the proposal by a vote of 24 to 12, and then upheld that vote by another vote of 33 to 1. The date of the resolution is, therefore, legislatively March 2, but March 4 by the calendar.

The document bears this signature: "Approved March 2, 1861. James Buchanan." It was either to give the proposal enhanced standing with the States or by inadvertence that this signature was placed upon it. By Article V "Congress . . . shall propose amendments to this Constitution," so that the President's approval is unnecessary.

Three ratifications were given to the proposal after the outbreak of hostilities, as follows:

| Ohio | May 13, 1861 | Illinois | Feb. 14, 1862 |
| Maryland | Jan. 10, 1862 | (in a constitutional convention) | |

The subject matter of the proposal was covered by the adoption of the 13th Article of Amendment, effective December 6, 1865.

Child Labor, June 2, 1924

This proposal has seen two periods of consideration with respect to ratification. Between 1924 and 1927 it was both ratified and rejected, the subject of child labor being publicly debated at the same time. From 1933 to 1937, active consideration of the proposal was resumed, and several ratifications were recorded. In 1939 the Supreme Court in *Coleman* v. *Miller*, 307 U. S. 433, considered its status, declared that ratification should take place within a reasonable time, the setting of which was a political question for Congress to decide.

Resolved by the Senate and House of Representatives of the United States of America in Congress assembled (two-thirds of each House concurring therein), That the following article is proposed as an amendment to the Constitution of the United States, which, when ratified

113

by the legislatures of three-fourths of the several States, shall be valid to all intents and purposes as a part of the Constitution:

ARTICLE ——

SECTION 1. The Congress shall have power to limit, regulate, and prohibit the labor of persons under 18 years of age.

SECTION 2. The power of the several States is unimpaired by this article except that the operation of State laws shall be suspended to the extent necessary to give effect to legislation enacted by the Congress.

House Joint Resolution 184, 68th Congress, passed the House of Representatives on April 26, 1924, by a vote of 297 to 69, and the Senate on May 31, 1924, by a vote of 62 to 23. In the Senate an amendment to limit the period of ratification to seven years was defeated by a vote of 28 to 55.

It would require ratification by 38 States to bring this proposal into force in 1961, though when it was submitted 36 ratifications were sufficient. The record of ratifications reflects the changing attitude toward the question of child labor, partly by State legislation and partly by public temper, in the number of rejections followed by ratification. The record of the 28 ratifying States is set down in alphabetic order:

Arizona	Jan. 29, 1925	Minnesota	Dec. 14, 1933
Arkansas	Jun. 28, 1924	(rejected Apr. 14, 1925)	
California	Jan. 8, 1925	Montana	Feb. 11, 1927
Colorado	Apr. 28, 1931	Nevada	Jan. 29, 1937
Idaho	Feb. 7, 1935	New Hampshire	May 17, 1933
(adverse vote in House of Representatives, Feb. 7, 1925)		(rejected Mar. 18, 1925)	
		New Jersey	Jun. 12, 1933
		New Mexico	Feb. 12, 1937
Illinois	Jun. 30, 1933	(rejected in 1935)	
Indiana	Feb. 8, 1935	North Dakota	Mar. 4, 1933
(rejected by Senate Feb. 5, 1925, and by House of Representatives Mar. 5, 1925)		(Senate resolved not to ratify Jan. 28, 1925)	
Iowa	Dec. 5, 1933	Ohio	Mar. 22, 1933
(indefinitely postponed by House of Representatives Mar. 11, 1925)		Oklahoma	Jul. 5, 1933
		Oregon	Jan. 31, 1933
Kansas	Feb. 25, 1937	Pennsylvania	Dec. 21, 1933
(rejected Jan. 30, 1925)		(rejected April 16, 1925)	
Kentucky	Jan. 13, 1937	Utah	Feb. 5, 1935
(rejected Mar. 24, 1926)		(rejected Feb. 4, 1925)	
Maine	Dec. 16, 1933	Washington	Feb. 3, 1933
(rejected Apr. 10, 1925)		West Virginia	Dec. 12, 1933
Michigan	May 10, 1933	Wisconsin	Feb. 25, 1925
		Wyoming	Jan. 31, 1935

Rejections that were maintained numbered 15. With the 12 rejections which were followed by ratifications, it appears that the proposal received 27 rejections and 28 ratifications. Details of rejection are given to show whether it was the result of a resolution of the Legislature itself or of one or both houses separately. The following 15 States rejected the proposal:

Connecticut Senate, Feb. 3, 1925 (House of Representatives, Feb. 11, 1925)
Delaware House of Representatives, Jan. 28, 1925 (Senate, Feb. 2, 1925)
Florida Resolution, May 14, 1925
Georgia Resolution, Aug. 6, 1924
Louisiana House of Representatives, Jun. 27, 1924
Maryland Resolution, Mar. 18, 1927
Massachusetts Senate, Feb. 16, 1925 (House of Representatives, Feb. 19, 1925, complying with ballot referendum, Jun. 5, 1924)

Missouri Resolution, Mar. 20, 1925
North Carolina Resolution, Aug. 23, 1924
South Carolina Resolution, Jan. 27, 1925
South Dakota Resolutions rejected Feb. 24, 1925, and Jul. 31, 1933, and failed to pass Legislature, Feb. 11, 1937
Tennessee Resolution, Feb. 4, 1925
Texas Resolution, Feb. 2, 1925
Vermont Resolution, Feb. 26, 1925
Virginia Resolution, Jan. 22, 1926

Of the 48 States, five took no action of record in Washington: Alabama, Mississippi, Nebraska, New York, and Rhode Island.

The CONSTITUTION
OF THE
CONFEDERATE STATES OF AMERICA

CONSTITUTION

OF THE

CONFEDERATE STATES OF AMERICA.

We, the people of the Confederate States, each State acting in its sovereign and independent character, in order to form a permanent federal government, establish justice, insure domestic tranquility, and secure the blessings of liberty to ourselves and our posterity—invoking the favor and guidance of Almighty God—do ordain and establish this Constitution for the Confederate States of America.

ARTICLE I.

SECTION I.

All legislative powers herein delegated shall be vested in a Congress of the Confederate States, which shall consist of a Senate and House of Representatives.

SECTION 2.

1. The House of Representatives shall be composed of members chosen every second year by the people of the several States; and the electors in each State shall be citizens of the Confederate States, and have the qualifications requisite for electors of the most numerous branch of the State Legislature; but no person of foreign birth, not a citizen of the Confederate States, shall be allowed to vote for any officer, civil or political, State or Federal.

2. No person shall be a Representative who shall not have attained the age of twenty-five years, and be a citizen of the Confederate States, and who shall not, when elected, be an inhabitant of that State in which he shall be chosen.

3. Representatives and direct taxes shall be apportioned among the several States, which may be included within this Confederacy, according to their respective numbers, which shall be determined, by adding to the whole number of free persons, including those bound to service for a term of years, and excluding Indians not taxed, three-fifths of all slaves. The actual enumeration shall be made within three years after the first meeting of the Congress of the Confederate States, and within every subsequent term of ten years, in such manner as they shall by law direct. The number of Representatives shall not exceed one for every fifty thousand, but each State shall have at least one Representative; and until such enumeration shall be made, the State of South Carolina shall be entitled to choose six; the State of Georgia ten; the State of Alabama nine; the State of Florida two; the State of Mississippi seven; the State of Louisiana six; and the State of Texas six.

4. When vacancies happen in the representation from any State, the Executive authority thereof shall issue writs of election to fill such vacancies.

5. The House of Representatives shall choose their Speaker and other officers; and shall have the sole power of impeachment; except that any judicial or other Federal officer, resident and acting solely within the limits of any State, may be impeached by a vote of two-thirds of both branches of the Legislature thereof.

SECTION 3.

1. The Senate of the Confederate States shall be composed of two Senators from each State, chosen for six years by the

Legislature thereof, at the regular session next immediately preceding the commencement of the term of service; and each Senator shall have one vote.

2. Immediately after they shall be assembled, in consequence of the first election, they shall be divided as equally as may be into three classes. The seats of the Senators of the first class shall be vacated at the expiration of the second year; of the second class at the expiration of the fourth year; and of the third class at the expiration of the sixth year; so that one-third may be chosen every second year; and if vacancies happen by resignation, or otherwise, during the recess of the Legislature of any State, the Executive thereof may make temporary appointments until the next meeting of the Legislature which shall then fill such vacancies.

3. No person shall be a Senator who shall not have attained the age of thirty years, and be a citizen of the Confederate States; and who shall not, when elected, be an inhabitant of the State for which he shall be chosen.

4. The Vice President of the Confederate States shall be President of the Senate, but shall have no vote unless they be equally divided.

5. The Senate shall choose their other officers; and also a President *pro tempore* in the absence of the Vice President, or when he shall exercise the office of President of the Confederate States.

6. The Senate shall have the sole power to try all impeachments. When sitting for that purpose, they shall be on oath or affirmation. When the President of the Confederate States is tried, the Chief Justice shall preside; and no person shall be convicted without the concurrence of two-thirds of the members present.

7. Judgment in cases of impeachment shall not extend further than to removal from office, and disqualification to hold

and enjoy any office of honor, trust or profit, under the Confederate States; but the party convicted shall, nevertheless, be liable and subject to indictment, trial, judgment and punishment according to law.

1. The times, places and manner of holding elections for Senators and Representatives, shall be prescribed in each State by the Legislature thereof, subject to the provisions of this Constitution; but the Congress may, at any time, by law, make or alter such regulations, except as to the times and places of choosing Senators.

2. The Congress shall assemble at least once in every year; and such meeting shall be on the first Monday in December, unless they shall, by law, appoint a different day.

1. Each House shall be the judge of the elections, returns, and qualifications of its own members, and a majority of each shall constitute a quorum to do business; but a smaller number may adjourn from day to day, and may be authorized to compel the attendance of absent members, in such manner and under such penalties as each House may provide.

2. Each House may determine the rules of its proceedings, punish its members for disorderly behavior, and with the concurrence of two-thirds of the whole number expel a member.

3. Each House shall keep a journal of its proceedings, and from time to time publish the same, excepting such parts as may in their judgment require secrecy; and the yeas and nays of the members of either House, on any question, shall, at the desire of one-fifth of those present, be entered on the journal.

4. Neither House, during the session of Congress, shall, without the consent of the other, adjourn for more than three

days, nor to any other place than that in which the two Houses shall be sitting.

SECTION 6.

1. The Senators and Representatives shall receive a compensation for their services, to be ascertained by law, and paid out of the treasury of the Confederate States. They shall, in all cases, except treason, felony, and breach of the peace, be privileged from arrest during their attendance at the session of their respective Houses, and in going to and returning from the same; and for any speech or debate in either House, they shall not be questioned in any other place.

2. No Senator or Representative shall, during the time for which he was elected, be appointed to any civil office under the authority of the Confederate States, which shall have been created, or the emoluments whereof shall have been increased during such time; and no person holding any office under the Confederate States shall be a member of either House during his continuance in office. But Congress may, by law, grant to the principal officer in each of the Executive Departments a seat upon the floor of either House, with the privilege of discussing any measures appertaining to his department.

SECTION 7.

1. All bills for raising revenue shall originate in the House of Representatives; but the Senate may propose or concur with amendments, as on other bills.

2. Every bill which shall have passed both Houses, shall, before it becomes a law, be presented to the President of the Confederate States; if he approve, he shall sign it; but if not, he shall return it, with his objections, to that House in which it shall have originated, who shall enter the objections at large on their journal, and proceed to reconsider it. If, after such

reconsideration, two-thirds of that House shall agree to pass the bill, it shall be sent, together with the objections, to the other House, by which it shall likewise be reconsidered, and if approved by two-thirds of that House, it shall become a law. But in all such cases, the votes of both Houses shall be determined by yeas and nays, and the names of the persons voting for and against the bill shall be entered on the journal of each House respectively. If any bill shall not be returned by the President within ten days (Sundays excepted) after it shall have been presented to him, the same shall be a law, in like manner as if he had signed it, unless the Congress, by their adjournment, prevent its return; in which case it shall not be a law. The President may approve any appropriation and disapprove any other appropriation in the same bill. In such case he shall, in signing the bill, designate the appropriations disapproved; and shall return a copy of such appropriations, with his objections, to the House in which the bill shall have originated; and the same proceedings shall then be had as in case of other bills disapproved by the President.

3. Every order, resolution or vote, to which the concurrence of both Houses may be necessary, (except on a question of adjournment.) shall be presented to the President of the Confederate States; and before the same shall take effect, shall be approved by him; or being disapproved by him, shall be re-passed by two-thirds of both Houses, according to the rules and limitations prescribed in case of a bill.

SECTION 8.

The Congress shall have power—

1. To lay and collect taxes, duties, imposts, and excises, for revenue necessary to pay the debts, provide for the common defence, and carry on the government of the Confederate States; but no bounties shall be granted from the treasury;

nor shall any duties or taxes on importations from foreign nations be laid to promote or foster any branch of industry; and all duties, imposts, and excises shall be uniform throughout the Confederate States:

2. To borrow money on the credit of the Confederate States:

3. To regulate commerce with foreign nations, and among the several States, and with the Indian tribes; but neither this, nor any other clause contained in the constitution, shall ever be construed to delegate the power to Congress to appropriate money for any internal improvement intended to facilitate commerce; except for the purpose of furnishing lights, beacons, and buoys, and other aids to navigation upon the coasts, and the improvement of harbors and the removing of obstructions in river navigation, in all which cases, such duties shall be laid on the navigation facilitated thereby, as may be necessay to pay the costs and expenses thereof:

4. To establish uniform laws of naturalization, and uniform laws on the subject of bankruptcies, throughout the Confederate States; but no law of Congress shall discharge any debt contracted before the passage of the same:

5. To coin money, regulate the value thereof and of foreign coin, and fix the standard of weights and measures:

6. To provide for the punishment of counterfeiting the securities and current coin of the Confederate States:

7. To establish post-offices and post-routes; but the expenses of the Post-office Department, after the first day of March in the year of our Lord eighteen hundred and sixty-three, shall be paid out of its own revenues:

8. To promote the progress of science and useful arts, by securing for limited times to authors and inventors the exclusive right to their respective writings and discoveries:

9. To constitute tribunals inferior to the Supreme Court:

10. To define and punish piracies and felonies committed on the high seas, and offences against the law of nations:

11. To declare war, grant letters of marque and reprisal, and make rules concerning captures on land and water:

12. To raise and support armies; but no appropriation of money to that use shall be for a longer term than two years:

13. To provide and maintain a navy:

14. To make rules for the government and regulation of the land and naval forces:

15. To provide for calling forth the militia to execute the laws of the Confederate States, suppress insurrections, and repel invasions:

16. To provide for organizing, arming, and disciplining the militia, and for governing such part of them as may be employed in the service of the Confederate States; reserving to the States, respectively, the appointment of the officers, and the authority of training the militia according to the discipline prescribed by Congress:

17. To exercise exclusive legislation, in all cases whatsoever, over such district (not exceeding ten miles square) as may, by cession of one or more States and the acceptance of Congress, become the seat of the government of the Confederate States: and to exercise like authority over all places purchased by the consent of the legislature of the State in which the same shall be, for the erection of forts, magazines, arsenals, dockyards, and other needful buildings: and

18. To make all laws which shall be necessary and proper for carrying into execution the foregoing powers, and all other powers vested by this Constitution in the government of the Confederate States, or in any department or officer thereof.

SECTION 9.

1. The importation of negroes of the African race, from

any foreign country other than the slaveholding States or Territories of the United States of America, is hereby forbidden; and Congress is required to pass such laws as shall effectually prevent the same.

2. Congress shall also have power to prohibit the introduction of slaves from any State not a member of, or Territory not belonging to, this Confederacy.

3. The privilege of the writ of *habeas corpus* shall not be suspended, unless when in cases of rebellion or invasion the public safety may require it.

4. No bill of attainder, *ex post facto* law, or law denying or impairing the right of property in negro slaves shall be passed.

5. No capitation or other direct tax shall be laid, unless in proportion to the census or enumeration hereinbefore directed to be taken.

6. No tax or duty shall be laid on articles exported from any State, except by a vote of two-thirds of both Houses.

7. No preference shall be given by any regulation of commerce or revenue to the ports of one State over those of another.

8. No money shall be drawn from the treasury, but in consequence of appropriations made by law; and a regular statement and account of the receipts and expenditures of all public money shall be published from time to time.

9. Congress shall appropriate no money from the treasury except by a vote of two-thirds of both Houses, taken by yeas and nays, unless it be asked and estimated for by some one of the heads of departments, and submitted to Congress by the President; or for the purpose of paying its own expenses and contingencies; or for the payment of claims against the Confederate States, the justice of which shall have been judicially declared by a tribunal for the investigation of claims against

the government, which it is hereby made the duty of Congress to establish.

10. All bills appropriating money shall specify in federal currency the exact amount of each appropriation and the purposes for which it is made; and Congress shall grant no extra compensation to any public contractor, officer, agent or servant, after such contract shall have been made or such service rendered.

11. No title of nobility shall be granted by the Confederate States; and no person holding any office of profit or trust under them, shall, without the consent of the Congress, accept of any present, emolument, office or title of any kind whatever, from any king, prince, or foreign state.

12. Congress shall make no law respecting an establishment of religion, or prohibiting the free exercise thereof; or abridging the freedom of speech, or of the press; or the right of the people peaceably to assemble and petition the government for a redress of grievances.

13. A well-regulated militia being necessary to the security of a free state, the right of the people to keep and bear arms shall not be infringed.

14. No soldier shall, in time of peace, be quartered in any house, without the consent of the owner; nor in time of war, but in a manner to be prescribed by law.

15. The right of the people to be secure in their persons, houses, papers, and effects, against unreasonable searches and seizures, shall not be violated; and no warrants shall issue but upon probable cause, supported by oath or affirmation, and particularly describing the place to be searched, and the persons or things to be seized.

16. No person shall be held to answer for a capital or otherwise infamous crime, unless on a presentment or indictment of a grand jury, except in cases arising in the land or naval forces,

or in the militia, when in actual service in time of war or public danger; nor shall any person be subject for the same offence to be twice put in jeopardy of life or limb; nor be compelled, in any criminal case, to be a witness against himself; nor be deprived of life, liberty, or property without due process of law; nor shall private property be taken for public use, without just compensation.

17. In all criminal prosecutions, the accused shall enjoy the right to a speedy and public trial, by an impartial jury of the State and district wherein the crime shall have been committed, which district shall have been previously ascertained by law, and to be informed of the nature and cause of the accusation; to be confronted with the witnesses against him; to have compulsory process for obtaining witnesses in his favor; and to have the assistance of counsel for his defence.

18. In suits at common law, where the value in controversy shall exceed twenty dollars, the right of trial by jury shall be preserved; and no fact so tried by a jury shall be otherwise re-examined in any court of the Confederacy, than according to the rules of common law.

19. Excessive bail shall not be required, nor excessive fines imposed, nor cruel and unusual punishments inflicted.

20. Every law, or resolution having the force of law, shall relate to but one subject, and that shall be expressed in the title.

SECTION 10.

1. No State shall enter into any treaty, alliance, or confederation; grant letters of marque and reprisal; coin money; make any thing but gold and silver coin a tender in payment of debts; pass any bill of attainder, or *ex post facto* law, or law impairing the obligation of contracts: or grant any title of nobility.

2. No State shall, without the consent of the Congress, lay any imposts or duties on imports or exports, except what may be absolutely necessary for executing its inspection laws; and the net produce of all duties and imposts, laid by any State on imports or exports, shall be for the use of the Treasury of the Confederate States; and all such laws shall be subject to the revision and control of Congress.

3. No State shall, without the consent of Congress, lay any duty on tonnage, except on sea-going vessels, for the improvement of its rivers and harbors navigated by the said vessels; but such duties shall not conflict with any treaties of the Confederate States with foreign nations; and any surplus revenue, thus derived, shall, after making such improvement, be paid into the common treasury. Nor shall any State keep troops or ships-of-war in time of peace, enter into any agreement or compact with another State, or with a foreign power, or engage in war, unless actually invaded, or in such imminent danger as will not admit of delay. But when any river divides or flows through two or more States, they may enter into compacts with each other to improve the navigation thereof.

ARTICLE II.

SECTION I.

1. The executive power shall be vested in a President of the Confederate States of America. He and the Vice President shall hold their offices for the term of six years; but the President shall not be re-eligible. The President and Vice President shall be elected as follows:

2. Each State shall appoint, in such manner as the legislature thereof may direct, a number of electors equal to the whole number of Senators and Representatives to which the State may be entitled in the Congress; but no Senator or Rep-

resentative or person holding an office of trust or profit under the Confederate States, shall be appointed an elector.

3. The electors shall meet in their respective States and vote by ballot for President and Vice President, one of whom, at least, shall not be an inhabitant of the same State with themselves; they shall name in their ballots the person voted for as President, and in distinct ballots the person voted for as Vice President, and they shall make distinct lists of all persons voted for as President, and of all persons voted for as Vice President, and of the number of votes for each, which lists they shall sign and certify, and transmit, sealed, to the seat of the government of the Confederate States, directed to the President of the Senate; the President of the Senate shall, in the presence of the Senate and House of Representatives, open all the certificates, and the votes shall then be counted; the person having the greatest number of votes for President shall be the President, if such number be a majority of the whole number of electors appointed; and if no person have such majority, then, from the persons having the highest numbers, not exceeding three, on the list of those voted for as President, the House of Representatives shall choose immediately, by ballot, the President. But in choosing the President, the votes shall be taken by States—the representation from each State having one vote; a quorum for this purpose shall consist of a member or members from two-thirds of the States, and a majority of all the States shall be necessary to a choice. And if the House of Representatives shall not choose a President, whenever the right of choice shall devolve upon them, before the fourth day of March next following, then the Vice President shall act as President, as in case of the death, or other constitutional disability of the President.

4. The person having the greatest number of votes as Vice President, shall be the Vice President, if such number be a

majority of the whole number of electors appointed; and if no person have a majority, then, from the two highest numbers on the list, the Senate shall choose the Vice President; a quorum for the purpose shall consist of two-thirds of the whole number of Senators, and a majority of the whole number shall be necessary to a choice.

5. But no person constitutionally ineligible to the office of President shall be eligible to that of Vice President of the Confederate States.

6. The Congress may determine the time of choosing the electors, and the day on which they shall give their votes; which day shall be the same throughout the Confederate States.

7. No person except a natural born citizen of the Confederate States, or a citizen thereof at the time of the adoption of this Constitution, or a citizen thereof born in the United States prior to the 20th of December, 1860, shall be eligible to the office of President; neither shall any person be eligible to that office who shall not have attained the age of thirty-five years, and been fourteen years a resident within the limits of the Confederate States, as they may exist at the time of his election.

8. In case of the removal of the President from office, or of his death, resignation, or inability to discharge the powers and duties of the said office, the same shall devolve on the Vice President; and the Congress may, by law, provide for the case of removal, death, resignation, or inability, both of the President and Vice President, declaring what officer shall then act as President; and such officer shall act accordingly, until the disability be removed or a President shall be elected.

9. The President shall, at stated times, receive for his services a compensation, which shall neither be increased nor diminished during the period for which he shall have been

elected; and he shall not receive within that period any other emolument from the Confederate States, or any of them.

10. Before he enters on the execution of his office, he shall take the following oath or affirmation:

"I do solemnly swear (or affirm) that I will faithfully execute the office of President of the Confederate States, and will, to the best of my ability, preserve, protect, and defend the Constitution thereof."

SECTION 2.

1. The President shall be commander-in-chief of the army and navy of the Confederate States, and of the militia of the several States, when called into the actual service of the Confederate States; he may require the opinion, in writing, of the principal officer in each of the executive departments, upon any subject relating to the duties of their respective offices; and he shall have power to grant reprieves and pardons for offences against the Confederate States, except in cases of impeachment.

2. He shall have power, by and with the advice and consent of the Senate, to make treaties; provided two-thirds of the Senators present concur; and he shall nominate, and by and with the advice and consent of the Senate, shall appoint ambassadors, other public ministers and consuls, judges of the Supreme Court, and all other officers of the Confederate States whose appointments are not herein otherwise provided for, and which shall be established by law; but the Congress may; by law, vest the appointment of such inferior officers, as they think proper, in the President alone, in the courts of law, or in the heads of departments.

3. The principal officer in each of the executive departments, and all persons connected with the diplomatic service, may be removed from office at the pleasure of the President.

All other civil officers of the executive departments may be removed at any time by the President, or other appointing power, when their services are unnecessary, or for dishonesty, incapacity, inefficiency, misconduct, or neglect of duty; and when so removed, the removal shall be reported to the Senate, together with the reasons therefor.

4. The President shall have power to fill all vacancies that may happen during the recess of the Senate, by granting commissions which shall expire at the end of their next session; but no person rejected by the Senate shall be re-appointed to the same office during their ensuing recess.

SECTION 3.

1. The President shall, from time to time, give to the Congress information of the state of the Confederacy, and recommend to their consideration such measures as he shall judge necessary and expedient; he may, on extraordinary occasions, convene both Houses, or either of them; and in case of disagreement between them, with respect to the time of adjournment, he may adjourn them to such time as he shall think proper; he shall receive ambassadors and other public ministers; he shall take care that the laws be faithfully executed, and shall commission all the officers of the Confederate States.

SECTION 4.

1. The President, Vice President, and all civil officers of the Confederate States, shall be removed from office on impeachment, for and conviction of, treason, bribery, or other high crimes and misdemeanors.

ARTICLE III.

SECTION 1.

1. The judicial power of the Confederate States shall be vested in one Supreme Court, and in such inferior courts as

the Congress may, from time to time, ordain and establish. The judges, both of the Supreme and inferior courts, shall hold their offices during good behavior, and shall, at stated times, receive for their services a compensation which shall not be diminished during their continuance in office.

1. The judicial power shall extend to all cases arising under this Constitution, the laws of the Confederate States, and treaties made, or which shall be made, under their authority; to all cases affecting ambassadors, other public ministers and consuls; to all cases of admiralty and maritime jurisdiction; to controversies to which the Confederate States shall be a party; to controversies between two or more States; between a State and citizens of another State, where the State is plaintiff; between citizens claiming lands under grants of different States; and between a State or the citizens thereof, and foreign states, citizens or subjects; but no State shall be sued by a citizen or subject of any foreign state.

2. In all cases affecting ambassadors, other public ministers and consuls, and those in which a State shall be a party, the Supreme Court shall have original jurisdiction. In all the other cases before mentioned, the Supreme Court shall have appellate jurisdiction both as to law and fact, with such exceptions and under such regulations as the Congress shall make.

3. The trial of all crimes, except in cases of impeachment, shall be by jury, and such trial shall be held in the State where the said crimes shall have been committed; but when not committed within any State, the trial shall be at such place or places as the Congress may by law have directed.

1. Treason against the Confederate States shall consist only in levying war against them, or in adhering to their enemies,

giving them aid and comfort. No person shall be convicted of treason unless on the testimony of two witnesses to the same overt act, or on confession in open court.

2. The Congress shall have power to declare the punishment of treason; but no attainder of treason shall work corruption of blood, or forfeiture, except during the life of the person attainted.

ARTICLE IV.

SECTION 1.

1. Full faith and credit shall be given in each State to the public acts, records, and judicial proceedings of every other State. And the Congress may, by general laws, prescribe the manner in which such acts, records, and proceedings shall be proved, and the effect thereof.

SECTION 2.

1. The citizens of each State shall be entitled to all the privileges and immunities of citizens in the several States; and shall have the right of transit and sojourn in any State of this Confederacy, with their slaves and other property; and the right of property in said slaves shall not be thereby impaired.

2. A person charged in any State with treason, felony, or other crime against the laws of such State, who shall flee from justice, and be found in another State, shall, on demand of the executive authority of the State from which he fled, be delivered up, to be removed to the State having jurisdiction of the crime.

3. No slave or other person held to service or labor in any State or Territory of the Confederate States, under the laws thereof, escaping or lawfully carried into another, shall, in consequence of any law or regulation therein, be discharged

from such service or labor: but shall be delivered up on claim of the party to whom such slave belongs, or to whom such service or labor may be due.

1. Other States may be admitted into this Confederacy by a vote of two-thirds of the whole House of Representatives and two-thirds of the Senate, the Senate voting by States; but no new State shall be formed or erected within the jurisdiction of any other State; nor any State be formed by the junction of two or more States, or parts of States, without the consent of the legislatures of the States concerned, as well as of the Congress.

2. The Congress shall have power to dispose of and make all needful rules and regulations concerning the property of the Confederate States, including the lands thereof.

3. The Confederate States may acquire new territory; and Congress shall have power to legislate and provide governments for the inhabitants of all territory belonging to the Confederate States, lying without the limits of the several States; and may permit them, at such times, and in such manner as it may by law provide, to form States to be admitted into the Confederacy. In all such territory, the institution of negro slavery, as it now exists in the Confederate States, shall be recognized and protected by Congress and by the territorial government: and the inhabitants of the several Confederate States and Territories shall have the right to take to such territory any slaves lawfully held by them in any of the States or Territories of the Confederate States.

4. The Confederate States shall guarantee to every State that now is, or hereafter may become, a member of this Confederacy, a republican form of government; and shall protect each of them against invasion; and on application of the legis-

lature, (or of the executive, when the legislature is not in session,) against domestic violence.

ARTICLE V.

SECTION I.

1. Upon the demand of any three States, legally assembled in their several conventions, the Congress shall summon a convention of all the States, to take into consideration such amendments to the Constitution as the said States shall concur in suggesting at the time when the said demand is made; and should any of the proposed amendments to the Constitution be agreed on by the said convention—voting by States—and the same be ratified by the legislatures of two-thirds of the several States, or by conventions in two-thirds thereof—as the one or the other mode of ratification may be proposed by the general convention—they shall thenceforward form a part of this Constitution. But no State shall, without its consent, be deprived of its equal representation in the Senate.

ARTICLE VI.

1. The Government established by this Constitution is the successor of the Provisional Government of the Confederate States of America, and all the laws passed by the latter shall continue in force until the same shall be repealed or modified: and all the officers appointed by the same shall remain in office until their successors are appointed and qualified, or the offices abolished.

2. All debts contracted and engagements entered into before the adoption of this Constitution shall be as valid against the Confederate States under this Constitution, as under the Provisional Government.

3. This Constitution, and the laws of the Confederate States made in pursuance thereof, and all treaties made, or which shall be made, under the authority of the Confederate States, shall be the supreme law of the land; and the judges in every State shall be bound thereby, anything in the constitution or laws of any State to the contrary notwithstanding.

4. The Senators and Representatives before mentioned, and the members of the several State legislatures, and all executive and judicial officers, both of the Confederate States and of the several States, shall be bound by oath or affirmation to support this Constitution; but no religious test shall ever be required as a qualification to any office or public trust under the Confederate States.

5. The enumeration, in the Constitution, of certain rights, shall not be construed to deny or disparage others retained by the people of the several States.

6. The powers not delegated to the Confederate States by the Constitution, nor prohibited by it to the States, are reserved to the States, respectively, or to the people thereof.

ARTICLE VII.

1. The ratification of the conventions of five States shall be sufficient for the establishment of this Constitution between the States so ratifying the same.

2. When five States shall have ratified this Constitution, in the manner before specified, the Congress under the Provisional Constitution shall prescribe the time for holding the election of President and Vice President; and for the meeting of the Electoral College; and for counting the votes, and inaugurating the President. They shall, also, prescribe the time for holding the first election of members of Congress under this Constitution, and the time for assembling the same.

Until the assembling of such Congress, the Congress under the Provisional Constitution shall continue to exercise the legislative powers granted them; not extending beyond the time limited by the Constitution of the Provisional Government.

Adopted unanimously by the Congress of the Confederate States of South Carolina, Georgia, Florida, Alabama, Mississippi, Louisiana and Texas, sitting in Convention at the capitol, in the city of Montgomery, Alabama, on the Eleventh day of March, in the year Eighteen Hundred and Sixty-One.

HOWELL COBB,
President of the Congress.

THE KENTUCKY-VIRGINIA RESOLUTIONS

AND

MR. MADISON'S REPORT OF 1799

THE
KENTUCKY-VIRGINIA
RESOLUTIONS AND
MR. MADISON'S REPORT OF 1799

KENTUCKY LEGISLATURE

in the House of Representatives

November 10th, 1798.

RESOLVED, that the several States composing the United States of America, are not united on the principles of unlimited submission to their General Government; but that by compact under the style and title of a Constitution for the United States and of amendments thereto, they constituted a General Government for special purposes, delegated to that Government certain definite powers, reserving each State to itself, the residuary mass of right to their own self Government; and that whensoever the General Government assumes undelegated powers, its acts are unauthoritative, void, and of no force: That to this compact each State acceded as a State, and is an integral party, its co-States forming as to itself, the other party: That the Government created by this compact was not made the exclusive or final *judge* of the extent of the powers delegated to itself; since that would have made its discretion, and not the Constitution, the measure of its powers; but that as in all other cases of compact among parties having no common Judge, each party has an equal right to judge for itself, as well of infractions as of the mode and measure of redress.

II. Resolved, that the Constitution of the United States having delegated to Congress a power to punish treason, counterfeiting the securities and current coin of the United States, piracies and felonies committed on the High Seas, and offenses against the laws of nations, and no other crimes whatever, and it being true as a general principle, and one of the amendments to the Constitution having also declared, "that the powers not delegated to the United States by the Constitution, nor prohibited by it to the States, are reserved to the States respectively, or to the people," therefore also the same act of Congress passed on the 14th day of July, 1798, and entitled "An act in addition to the act entitled an act for the punishment of certain crimes against the United States," as also the act passed by them on the 27th day of June, 1798, entitled "An act to punish frauds committed on the Bank of the United States" (and all other their acts which assume to create, define, or punish crimes other than those enumerated in the Constitution) are altogether void and of no force, and that the power to create, define, and punish such other crimes is reserved, and of right appertains solely and exclusively to the respective States, each within its own Territory.

III. Resolved, that it is true as a general principle, and is also expressly declared by one of the amendments to the Constitution that "the powers not delegated to the United States by the Constitution, nor prohibited by it to the States, are reserved to the States respectively or to the people;" and that no power over the freedom of religion, freedom of speech, or freedom of the press being delegated to the United States by the Constitution, nor prohibited by it to the States, all lawful powers respecting the same did of right remain, and were reserved to the States, or to the people: That thus was manifested their determination to retain to themselves the right of judging how far the licentiousness of speech and of the press may be abridged without lessening their useful freedom, and how far those abuses which cannot be separated from their use, should be tolerated rather than the use be destroyed; and thus also they guarded against all abridgement by the United States of the freedom of religious opinions and exercises, and retained to themselves the right of protecting the same, as this state by a Law passed on the general demand of its Citizens, had already protected them from all human restraint or inteference: And that in addition to this general principle and express declaration, another and more special provision has been made by one of the amendments to the Constitution which expressly declares, that "Congress shall make no law respecting an Establishment of religion, or prohibiting the free exercise thereof, or abridging the freedom of speech, or the press," thereby guarding in the same sentence, and under the same words, the freedom of religion, of speech, and of the press, insomuch, that whatever violates either, throws down the sanctuary which covers the others, and that libels, falsehoods, and defamation, equally with heresy and false religion, are withheld from the cognizance of federal tribunals. That therefore the act of the Congress of the United States passed on the 14th day of July 1798, entitled "An act in addition to the act for the punishment of certain crimes against the United States," which does abridge the freedom of the press, is not law, but is altogether void and of no effect.

IV. Resolved, that alien friends are under the jurisdiction

and protection of the laws of the State wherein they are; that no power over them has been delegated to the United States, nor prohibited to the individual States distinct from their power over citizens; and it being true as a general principle, and one of the amendments to the Constitution having also declared, that "the powers not delegated to the United States by the Constitution nor prohibited by it to the States are reserved to the States respectively or to the people," the act of the Congress of the United States passed on the 22d day of June, 1798, entitled "An act concerning aliens," which assumes power over alien friends not delegated by the Constitution, is not law, but is altogether void and of no force.

V. Resolved, that in addition to the general principle as well as the express declaration, that powers not delegated are reserved, another and more special provision inserted in the Constitution from abundant caution has declared, "that the *migration* or importation of such persons as any of the States now existing shall think proper to admit, shall not be prohibited by the Congress prior to the year 1808." That this Commonwealth does admit the migration of alien friends described as the subject of the said act concerning aliens; that a provision against prohibiting their migration, is a provision against all acts equivalent thereto, or it would be nugatory; that to remove them when migrated is equivalent to a prohibition of their migration, and is therefore contrary to the said provision of the Constitution and void.

VI. Resolved, that the imprisonment of a person under the protection of the Laws of this Commonwealth on his failure to obey the simple *order* of the President to depart out of the United States, as is undertaken by the said act entitled "An act concerning Aliens," is contrary to the Constitution, one amendment to which has provided, that "no person shall be deprived of liberty without due process of law," and that

146

another having provided "that in all criminal prosecutions, the accused shall enjoy the right to a public trial by an impartial jury, to be informed of the nature and cause of the accusation, to be confronted with the witnesses against him, to have compulsory process for obtaining witnesses in his favour, and to have the assistance of counsel for his defence," the same act undertaking to authorize the President to remove a person out of the United States who is under the protection of the Law, on his own suspicion, without accusation, without jury, without public trial, without confrontation of the witnesses against him, without having witnesses in his favour, without defence, without counsel, is contrary to these provisions also of the Constitution, is therefore not law but utterly void and of no force.

That transferring the power of judging any person who is under the protection of the laws, from the Courts to the President of the United States, as is undertaken by the same act concerning Aliens, is against the article of the Constitution which provides, that "the judicial power of the United States shall be vested in Courts, the Judges of which shall hold their offices during good behaviour," and that the said act is void for that reason also; and it is further to be noted, that this transfer of Judiciary power is to that magistrate of the General Government who already possesses all the Executive, and a qualified negative in all the Legislative powers.

VII. Resolved, that the construction applied by the General Government (as is evinced by sundry of their proceedings) to those parts of the Constitution of the United States which delegate to Congress a power to lay and collect taxes, duties, imposts, and excises; to pay the debts, and provide for the common defence, and general welfare of the United States, and to make all laws which shall be necessary and proper for carrying into execution the powers vested by the Constitution in the Government of the United States, or any department thereof, goes to the destruction of all the limits prescribed to their power by the Constitution—That words meant by that instrument to be subsiduary only to the execution of the limited powers, ought not to be so construed as themselves to give unlimited powers, nor a part so to be taken, as to destroy the whole residue of the instrument: That the proceedings of the General Government under colour of these articles, will be a fit and necessary subject for revisal and correction at a time of greater tranquility, while those specified in the preceding resolutions call for immediate redress.

VIII. Resolved, that the preceeding Resolutions be transmitted to the Senators and Representatives in Congress from this Commonwealth, who are hereby enjoined to present the same to their respective Houses, and to use their best endeavours to procure at the next session of Congress, a repeal of the aforesaid unconstitutional and obnoxious acts.

IX. Resolved lastly, that the Governor of this Commonwealth be, and is hereby authorised and requested to communicate the preceding Resolutions to the Legislatures of the several States, to assure them that this Commonwealth considers Union for specified National purposes, and particularly for those specified in their late Federal Compact, to be friendly to the peace, happiness, and prosperity of all the States: that faithful to that compact, according to the plain intent and meaning in which it was understood and acceded to by the several parties, it is sincerely anxious for its preservation: that it does also believe, that to take from the States all the powers of self government, and transfer them to a general and consolidated Government, without regard to the special delegations and reservations solemnly agreed to in that compact, is not for the peace, happiness, or prosperity of these States: And that therefore, this Commonwealth is determined, as it doubts not its co-States are, tamely to submit to undelegated & consequently unlimited powers in no man or body of men on earth: that if the acts before specified should stand, these conclusions would flow from them; that the General Government may place any act they think proper on the list of crimes & punish it themselves, whether enumerated or not enumerated by the Constitution as cognizable by them: that they may transfer its cognizance to the President or any other person, who may himself be the accuser, counsel, judge, and jury, whose *suspicions* may be the evidence, his order the sentence, his officer the executioner, and his breast the sole record of the transaction: that a very numerous and valuable description of the inhabitants of these States, being by this precedent reduced as outlaws to the absolute dominion of one man and the barrier of the Constitution thus swept away from us all, no rampart now remains against the passions and the power of a majority of Congress, to protect from a like exportation or other more grievous punishment the minority of the same body, the Legislatures, Judges, Governors, & Counsellors of the States, nor their other peaceable inhabitants who may venture to reclaim the constitutional rights & liberties of the States & people, or who for other causes, good or bad, may be obnoxious to the views or marked by the suspicions of the President, or be thought dangerous to his or their elections or other interests public or personal: that the friendless alien has indeed been selected as the safest subject of a first experiment: but the citizen will soon follow, or rather has already followed; for, already has a Sedition Act marked him as its prey: that these and successive acts of the same character, unless arrested on the threshold, may tend to drive these States into revolution and blood, and will furnish new calumnies against Republican Governments, and new pretexts for those who wish it to be believed, that man cannot be governed but by a rod of iron: that it would be a dangerous delusion were a confidence in the men of our choice to silence our fears for the safety of our rights: that confidence is every where the parent of despotism: free government is founded in jealousy and not in confidence; it is jealousy and not confidence which prescribes limited Constitutions to bind down those whom we are obliged to trust with power: that our Constitution has accordingly fixed the limits to which and no further our confidence may go; and let the honest advocate of confidence read the Alien and Sedition Acts, and say if the Constitution has not been wise in fixing limits to the Government it created, and whether we should be wise in destroying those limits? Let him say what the Government is if it be not a tyranny, which the men of our choice have conferred on the President, and the President of our choice has assented to and accepted over the friendly strangers, to whom the mild spirit of our Country and its laws had pledged hospitality and protection: that the men of our choice have more respected the bare suspicions of the President than the solid rights of innocence, the claims of justification, the sacred force of truth, and the forms & substance of law and justice. In questions of power then let no more be heard of confidence in man, but bind him down from mischief by the chains of the Constitution. That this Commonwealth does therefore call on its co-States for an expression of their sentiments on the acts concerning Aliens, and for the punishment of certain crimes herein before specified, plainly declaring whether these acts are or are not authorized by the Federal Compact? And it doubts not that their sense will be so announced as to prove their attachment unaltered to limited Government, whether general or particular, and that the rights and liberties of their co-States will be exposed to no dangers by remaining embarked on a common bottom with their own: That they will concur with this Commonwealth in considering the said acts as so palpably against the Constitution as to amount to an undisguised declaration, that the Compact is not meant to be the measure of the powers of the General Government, but that it will proceed in the exercise over these States of all powers whatsoever: That they will view this as seizing the rights of the States and consolidating them in the hands of the General Government with a power assumed to bind the States (not merely in cases made federal) but in all cases whatsoever, by laws made, not with their consent, but by others against their consent: That this would be to surrender the form of Government we have chosen, and to live under one deriving its powers from its own will, and not from our authority; and that the co-States recurring to their natural right in cases not made federal, will concur in declaring these acts void and of no force, and will each unite with this Commonwealth in requesting their repeal at the next session of Congress.

EDMUND BULLOCK, S. H. R.
JOHN CAMPBELL, S. S. P. T.

Passed the House of Representatives, Nov. 10th, 1798.
Attest,

THOMAS TODD, C. H. R.

In SENATE, *November 13th, 1798, unanimously*
concurred in,
Attest, B. THRUSTON, *Clk. Sen.*

Approved November 16th, 1798.

JAMES GARRARD, G. K.

By THE GOVERNOR,

HARRY TOULMIN,
Secretary of State.

151

Friday, December 21, 1798.

RESOLVED, That the General Assembly of Virginia, doth unequivocally express a firm resolution to maintain and defend the Constitution of the United States, and the Constitution of this State, against every aggression either foreign or domestic, and that they will support the government of the United States in all measures warranted by the former.

That this Assembly most solemnly declares a warm attachment to the Union of the States, to maintain which it pledges all its powers; and that for this end, it is their duty to watch over and oppose every infraction of those principles which constitute the only basis of that Union, because a faithful observance of them, can alone secure its existence and the public happiness.

That this Assembly doth explicitly and peremptorily declare, that it views the powers of the federal government, as resulting from the compact, to which the States are parties; as limited by the plain sense and intention of the instrument constituting that compact; as no further valid than they are authorized by the grants enumerated in that compact; and that in case of a deliberate, palpable, and dangerous exercise of other powers, not granted by the said compact, the States who are parties thereto, have the right, and are in duty bound, to interpose for arresting the progress of the evil, and for maintaining within their respective limits, the authorities, rights and liberties appertaining to them.

That the General Assembly doth also express its deep regret, that a spirit has in sundry instances, been manifested by the federal government, to enlarge its powers by forced constructions of the constitutional charter which defines them; and that indications have appeared of a design to expound certain general phrases (which having been copied from the very limited grant of powers in the former articles of confederation were the less liable to be misconstrued) so as to destroy the meaning and effect, of the particular enumeration which necessarily explains and limits the general phrases; and so as to consolidate the States by degrees, into one sovereignty, the obvious tendency and inevitable consequence of which would be, to transform the present republican system of the United States, into an absolute, or at best a mixed monarchy.

That the General Assembly doth particularly protest against the palpable and alarming infractions of the Constitution, in the two late cases of the "Alien and Sedition Acts" passed at the last session of Congress; the first of which exercises a power nowhere delegated to the federal government, and which by uniting legislative and judicial powers to those of executive, subverts the general principles of free government, as well as the particular organization, and positive provisions of the federal Constitution; and the other of which acts, exercises in like manner, a power not delegated by the Constitution, but on the contrary, expressly and positively forbidden by one of the amendments thereto;—a power, which more than any other, ought to produce universal alarm, because it is leveled against that right of freely examining public characters and measures, and of free communication among the people thereon, which has ever been justly deemed, the only effectual guardian of every other right.

That this State having by its Convention, which ratified the Federal Constitution, expressly declared, that among other essential rights, "the Liberty of Conscience and of the Press cannot be cancelled, abridged, restrained, or modified by any authority of the United States," and from its extreme anxiety to guard these rights from every possible attack of sophistry or ambition, having with other States, recommended an amendment for that purpose, which amendment was, in due time, annexed to the Constitution; it would mark a reproachful inconsistency, and criminal degeneracy, if an indifference were now shewn, to the most palpable violation of one of the Rights, thus declared and secured; and to the establishment of a precedent which may be fatal to the other.

That the good people of this Commonwealth, having ever felt, and continuing to feel, the most sincere affection for their brethren of the other States; the truest anxiety for establishing and perpetuating the union of all; and the most scrupulous fidelity to that Constitution, which is the pledge of mutual friendship, and the instrument of mutual happiness, the General Assembly doth solemnly appeal to the like dispositions of the other States, in confidence that they will concur with this Commonwealth in declaring, as it does hereby declare, that the acts aforesaid, are unconstitutional; and that the necessary and proper measures will be taken by each, for cooperating with this State, in maintaining the Authorities, Rights, and Liberties, reserved to the States respectively, or to the People.

That the Governor be desired, to transmit a copy of the foregoing Resolutions to the executive authority of each of the other States, with a request that the same may be communicated to the Legislature thereof; and that a copy be furnished to each of the Senators and Representatives representing this State in the Congress of the United States.

Agreed to by the Senate, December 24, 1798.

KENTUCKY LEGISLATURE

in the House of Representatives

November 14th, 1799.

RESOLVED, That this Commonwealth considers the federal Union, upon the terms and for the purposes specified in the late compact, conducive to the liberty and happiness of the several States: That it does now unequivocally declare its attachment to the Union, and to that compact, agreeably to its obvious and real intention, and will be among the last to seek its dissolution: That, if those who administer the General Government be permitted to transgress the limits fixed by that compact, by a total disregard to the special delegations of power therein contained, an annihilation of the State Governments, and the creation upon their ruins, of a General Consolidated Government, will be the inevitable consequence: That the principle and construction contended for by sundry of the State legislatures, that the General Government is the exclusive judge of the extent of the powers delegated to it, stop nothing short of *despotism*—since the discretion of those who administer the government, and not the *Constitution*, would be the measure of their powers: That the several States who formed that instrument being sovereign and independent, have the unquestionable right to judge of the infraction; and *That a Nullification by those sovereignties, of all unauthorized acts done under color of that instrument is the rightful remedy:* That this Commonwealth does, under the most deliberate reconsideration, declare, that the said Alien and Sedition Laws are, in their opinion, palpable violations of the said Constitution: and, however cheerfully it may be disposed to surrender its opinion to a majority of its sister States, in matters of ordinary or doubtful policy, yet, in momentous regulations like the present, which so vitally wound the best rights of the citizen, it would consider a silent acquiescence as highly criminal: That, although this Commonwealth, as a party to the federal compact, will bow to the laws of the Union, yet, it does, at the same time declare, that it will not now, or ever hereafter, cease to oppose in a constitutional manner, every attempt at what quarter soever offered, to violate that compact. And, finally, in order that no pretext or arguments may be drawn from a supposed acquiescence, on the part of this Commonwealth in the constitutionality of these laws, and be thereby used as precedents for similar future violations of the federal compact—this Commonwealth does now enter against them its solemn PROTEST.

Attest,

THOMAS TODD, C.H.R.

In SENATE, *Nov. 22, 1799.*
Attest,

B. THRUSTON, C.S.

THE GENERAL ASSEMBLY OF VIRGINIA

in the House of Delegates

Tuesday, January 7, 1800.

HE House according to the order of the day, resolved itself into a committee of the whole House, on the report of the committee to whom was committed the proceedings of sundry of the other States in answer to the resolutions of the General Assembly of the 21st day of December, 1798, and after some time spent therein, Mr. Speaker resumed the chair, and Mr. Mercer reported, that the committee of the whole House had, according to order, had the said report under their consideration, and had made an amendment thereto, which he read in his place, and then delivered in at the clerk's table where the same was again twice read, and agreed to by the House.

The said report as amended, is as follows:

Whatever room might be found in the proceedings of some of the States, who have disapproved of the resolutions of the General Assembly of this Commonwealth, passed on the 21st day of December, 1798, for painful remarks on the spirit and manner of those proceedings, it appears to the committee, most consistent with the duty, as well as dignity of the General Assembly, to hasten an oblivion of every circumstance, which might be construed into a diminution of mutual respect, confidence and affection, among the members of the union.

The committee have deemed it a more useful task, to revise

157

with a critical eye, the resolutions which have met with this disapprobation; to examine fully the several objections and arguments which have appeared against them; and to enquire, whether there be any errors of fact, of principle, or of reasoning, which the candour of the General Assembly ought to acknowledge and correct.

The first of the resolutions is in the words following:

Resolved, that the General Assembly of Virginia, doth unequivocally express a firm resolution to maintain and defend the Constitution of the United States, and the Constitution of this State, against every aggression either foreign or domestic, and that they will support the government of the United States in all measures warranted by the former.

No unfavorable comment can have been made on the sentiments here expressed. To maintain and defend the Constitution of the United States, and of their own State, against every aggression both foreign and domestic, and to support the government of the United States in all measures warranted by their constitution, are duties, which the General Assembly ought always to feel, and to which on such an occasion, it was evidently proper to express their sincere and firm adherence.

In their next resolution—*The General Assembly most solemnly declares a warm attachment to the union of the States, to maintain which, it pledges all its powers; and that for this end, it is their duty to watch over and oppose every infraction of those principles, which constitute the only basis of that union, because a faithful observance of them, can alone secure its existence and the public happiness.*

The observation just made is equally applicable to this solemn declaration, of warm attachment to the union, and this solemn pledge to maintain it: nor can any question arise among enlightened friends of the union, as to the duty of watching over and opposing every infraction of those principles which constitute its basis, and a faithful observance of which, can alone secure its existence, and the public happiness thereon depending.

The third resolution is in the words following:

That this Assembly doth explicitly and peremptorily declare, that it views the powers of the Federal Government, as resulting from the compact, to which the States are parties, as limited by the plain sense and intention of the instrument constituting that compact; as no farther valid than they are authorized by the grants enumerated in that compact; and that in case of a deliberate, palpable *and* dangerous *exercise of other powers, not granted by the said compact, the states who are parties thereto, have the right, and are in duty bound, to interpose, for arresting the progress of the evil, and for maintaining within their respective limits, the authorities, rights and liberties appertaining to them.*

On this resolution, the committee have bestowed all the attention which its importance merits: They have scanned it not merely with a strict, but with a severe eye; and they feel confidence in pronouncing, that in its just and fair construction, it is unexceptionably true in its several positions, as well as constitutional and conclusive in its inferences.

The resolution declares, *first,* that "it views the powers of the Federal Government, as resulting from the compact to which the States are parties," in other words, that the federal powers are derived from the Constitution, and that the Constitution is a compact to which the states are parties.

Clear as the position must seem, that the federal powers are derived from the Constitution, and from that alone, the committee are not unapprized of a late doctrine which opens another source of federal powers, not less extensive and important, than it is new and unexpected. The examination of this doctrine will be most conveniently connected with a review of a succeeding resolution. The committee satisfy themselves here with briefly remarking, that in all the co-temporary discussions and comments, which the Constitution underwent, it was constantly justified and recommended on the ground, that the powers not given to the government, were withheld from it; and that if any doubt could have existed on this subject, under the original text of the Constitution, it is removed as far as words could remove it, by the [TENTH] Amendment, now a part of the Constitution, which expressly declares, "that the powers not delegated to the United States, "by the Constitution, nor prohibited by it to the States, are "reserved to the States respectively, or to the people."

The other position involved in this branch of the resolution, namely, "that the States are parties to the Constitution or compact," is in the judgment of the committee, equally free from objection. It is indeed true that the term "States," is sometimes used in a vague sense, and sometimes in different senses, according to the subject to which it is applied. Thus it sometimes means the separate sections of territory occupied by the political societies within each; sometimes the particular governments, established by those societies; sometimes those societies as organized into those particular governments; and lastly, it means the people composing those political societies, in their highest sovereign capacity. Although it might be wished that the perfection of language admitted less diversity in the signification of the same words, yet little inconveniency is produced by it, where the true sense can be collected with certainty from the different applications. In the present instance whatever different constructions of the term "States," in the resolution may have been entertained, all will at least concur in that last mentioned; because in that sense, the Con-

160

stitution was submitted to the "States:" In that sense the "States" ratified it; and in that sense of the term "States," they are consequently parties to the compact from which the powers of the Federal government result.

The next position is, that the General Assembly views the powers of the Federal government, "as limited by the plain sense and intention of the instrument constituting that compact," and "as no farther valid than they are authorized by the grants therein enumerated." It does not seem possible that any just objection can lie against either of these clauses. The first amounts merely to a declaration that the compact ought to have the interpretation, plainly intended by the parties to it; the other, to a declaration, that it ought to have the execution and effect intended by them. If the powers granted, be valid, it is solely because they are granted; and if the granted powers are valid, because granted, all other powers not granted, must not be valid.

The resolution having taken this view of the federal compact, proceeds to infer, "that in case of a deliberate, palpable, and dangerous exercise of other powers not granted by the said compact, the States who are parties thereto, have the right, and are in duty bound to interpose for arresting the progress of the evil, and for maintaining within their respective limits, the authorities, rights and liberties appertaining to them."

It appears to your committee to be a plain principle, founded in common sense, illustrated by common practice, and essential to the nature of compacts; that where resort can be had to no tribunal superior to the authority of the parties, the parties themselves must be the rightful judges in the last resort, whether the bargain made, has been pursued or violated. The Constitution of the United States was formed by the sanction of the States, given by each in its sovereign capacity. It adds to the stability and dignity, as well as to the authority of the Constitution, that it rests on this legitimate and solid foundation. The States then being the parties to the constitutional compact, and in their sovereign capacity, it follows of necessity, that there can be no tribunal above their authority, to decide in the last resort, whether the compact made by them be violated; and consequently that as the parties to it, they must themselves decide in the last resort, such questions as may be of sufficient magnitude to require their interposition.

It does not follow, however, that because the States as sovereign parties to their constitutional compact, must ultimately decide whether it has been violated, that such a decision ought to be interposed either in a hasty manner, or on doubtful and inferior occasions. Even in the case of ordinary conventions between different nations, where, by the strict rule of interpretation, a breach of a part may be deemed a breach of the whole; every part being deemed a condition of every other part, and of the whole, it is always laid down that the breach must be both wilful and material to justify an application of the rule. But in the case of an intimate and constitutional union, like that of the United States, it is evident that the interposition of the parties, in their sovereign capacity, can be called for by occasions only, deeply and essentially affecting the vital principles of their political system.

The resolution has accordingly guarded against any misapprehension of its object, by expressly requiring for such an interposition "the case of a *deliberate, palpable* and *dangerous* breach of the Constitution, by the exercise of *powers not granted* by it. It must be a case, not of a light and transient nature, but of a nature *dangerous* to the great purposes for which the Constitution was established. It must be a case moreover not obscure or doubtful in its construction, but plain and *palpable*. Lastly, it must be a case not resulting from a partial consideration, or hasty determination; but a case stampt with a final consideration and *deliberate* adherence. It is not necessary because the resolution does not require, that the question should be discussed, how far the exercise of any particular power, ungranted by the Constitution, would justify the interposition of the parties to it. As cases might easily be stated, which none would contend, ought to fall within that description: Cases, on the other hand, might, with equal ease, be stated, so flagrant and so fatal as to unite every opinion in placing them within the description.

But the resolution has done more than guard against misconstruction, by expressly referring to cases of a *deliberate, palpable* and *dangerous* nature. It specifies the object of the interposition which it contemplates, to be solely that of arresting the progress of the *evil* of usurpation, and of maintaining the authorities, rights and liberties appertaining to the States, as parties to the Constitution.

From this view of the resolution, it would seem inconceivable that it can incur any just disapprobation from those, who laying aside all momentary impressions, and recollecting the genuine source and object of the Federal Constitution, shall candidly and accurately interpret the meaning of the General Assembly. If the deliberate exercise, of dangerous powers, palpably withheld by the Constitution, could not justify the parties to it, in interposing even so far as to arrest the progress of the evil, and thereby to preserve the Constitution itself as well as to provide for the safety of the parties to it; there would be an end to all relief from usurped power, and a direct subversion of the rights specified or recognized under all the State constitutions, as well as a plain denial of the fundamental principle on which our independence itself was declared.

But it is objected that the judicial authority is to be regarded as the sole expositor of the Constitution, in the last resort; and it may be asked for what reason, the declaration by the General Assembly, supposing it to be theoretically true, could be required at the present day and in so solemn a manner.

On this objection it might be observed *first*, that there may be instances of usurped power, which the forms of the Constitution would never draw within the control of the Judicial Department: secondly, that if the decision of the judiciary be raised above the authority of the sovereign parties to the Constitution, the decisions of the other departments, not carried by the forms of the Constitution before the judiciary, must be equally authoritative and final with the decisions of that department. But the proper answer to the objection is, that the resolution of the General Assembly relates to those great and extraordinary cases, in which all the forms of the Constitution may prove ineffectual against infractions dangerous to the essential rights of the parties to it. The resolution supposes that dangerous powers not delegated, may not only be usurped and executed by the other departments, but that the Judicial Department also may exercise or sanction dangerous powers beyond the grant of the Constitution; and consequently that the ultimate right of the parties to the Constitution, to judge whether the compact has been dangerously violated, must extend to violations by one delegated authority, as well as by another; by the judiciary, as well as by the executive, or the legislature.

However true therefore it may be that the Judicial Department, is, in all questions submitted to it by the forms of the Constitution, to decide in the last resort, this resort must necessarily be deemed the last in relation to the authorities of the other departments of the government; not in relation to the rights of the parties to the constitutional compact, from which the judicial as well as the other departments hold their delegated trusts. On any other hypothesis, the delegation of judicial power, would annul the authority delegating it; and the concurrence of this department with the others in usurped powers, might subvert forever, and beyond the possible reach of any rightful remedy, the very Constitution, which all were instituted to preserve.

The truth declared in the resolution being established, the expediency of making the declaration at the present day, may safely be left to the temperate consideration and candid judgment of the American public. It will be remembered that a frequent recurrence to fundamental principles is solemnly enjoined by most of the State constitutions, and particularly by our own, as a necessary safeguard against the danger of degeneracy to which republics are liable, as well as other governments, though in a less degree than others. And a fair comparison of the political doctrines not unfrequent at the present day, with those which characterized the epoch of our revolution, and which form the basis of our republican constitutions, will best determine whether the declaratory recurrence here made to those principles ought to be viewed as unseasonable and improper, or as a vigilant discharge of an important duty. The authority of constitutions over governments, and of the sovereignty of the people over constitutions, are truths which are at all times necessary to be kept in mind; and at no time perhaps more necessary than at the present.

The fourth resolution stands as follows:—

That the General Assembly doth also express its deep regret, that a spirit has in sundry instances, been manifested by the Federal Government, to enlarge its powers by forced constructions of the Constitutional charter which defines them; and that indications have appeared of a design to expound cer-

165

tain general phrases, (which, having been copied from the very limited grant of powers in the former articles of confederation were the less liable to be misconstrued) so as to destroy the meaning and effect, of the particular enumeration which necessarily explains, and limits the general phrases; and so as to consolidate the States by degrees, into one sovereignty, the obvious tendency and inevitable result of which would be, to transform the present republican system of the United States, into an absolute, or at best a mixed monarchy.

The *first* question here to be considered is, whether a spirit has in sundry instances been manifested by the Federal government to enlarge its powers by forced constructions of the constitutional charter.

The General Assembly having declared their opinion merely by regretting in general terms that forced constructions for enlarging the Federal powers have taken place, it does not appear to the committee necessary to go into a specification of every instance to which the resolution may allude. The Alien and Sedition Acts being particularly named in a succeeding resolution are of course to be understood as included in the allusion. Omitting others which have less occupied public attention, or been less extensively regarded as unconstitutional, the resolution may be presumed to refer particularly to the bank law, which from the circumstances of its passage as well as the latitude of construction on which it is founded, strikes the attention with singular force; and the carriage tax, distinguished also by circumstances in its history having a similar tendency. Those instances alone, if resulting from forced construction and calculated to enlarge the powers of the Federal government, as the committee cannot but conceive to be the case, sufficiently warrant this part of the resolution. The committee have not thought it incumbent on them to extend their attention to laws which have been objected to, rather as varying the constitutional distribution of powers in the Federal government, than as an absolute enlargement of them; because instances of this sort however important in their principles and tendencies, do not appear to fall strictly within the text under review.

The other questions presenting themselves, are—1. Whether indications have appeared of a design to expound certain general phrases copied from the "articles of confederation," so as to destroy the effect of the particular enumeration explaining and limiting their meaning. 2. Whether this exposition would by degrees consolidate the States into one sovereignty. 3. Whether the tendency and result of this consolidation would be to transform the republican system of the United States into a monarchy.

1. The general phrases here meant must be those "of providing for the common defence and general welfare."

In the "articles of confederation" the phrases are used as follows, in article VIII. "All charges of war, and all other expences that shall be incurred *for the common defence and general welfare*, and allowed by the United States in Congress assembled, shall be defrayed out of a common treasury, which shall be supplied by the several States, in proportion to the value of all land within each State, granted to or surveyed for any person, as such land and the buildings and improvements thereon shall be estimated, according to such mode as the United States in Congress assembled, shall from time to time direct and appoint."

In the existing Constitution, they make the following part of section 8. "The Congress shall have power, to lay and collect taxes, duties, imposts and excises to pay the debts, and provide for the common defence and general welfare of the United States."

This similarity in the use of these phrases in the two great federal charters, might well be considered, as rendering their meaning less liable to be misconstrued in the latter; because it will scarcely be said that in the former they were ever understood to be either a general grant of power, or to authorize the requisition or application of money by the old Congress to the common defence and general welfare, except in the cases afterwards enumerated which explained and limited their meaning; and if such was the limited meaning attached to these phrases in the very instrument revised and remodeled by the present Constitution, it can never be supposed that when copied into this Constitution, a different meaning ought to be attached to them.

That notwithstanding this remarkable security against misconstruction, a design has been indicated to expound these phrases in the Constitution so as to destroy the effect of the particular enumeration of powers by which it explains and limits them, must have fallen under the observation of those who have attended to the course of public transactions. Not to multiply proofs on this subject, it will suffice to refer to the debates of the Federal Legislature in which arguments have on different occasions been drawn, with apparent effect from these phrases in their indefinite meaning.

To these indications might be added without looking farther, the official report on manufactures by the late Secretary of the Treasury, made on the 5th of December, 1791; and the report of a committee of Congress in January, 1797, on the promotion of agriculture. In the first of these it is expressly contended to belong "to the discretion of the National "legislature to pronounce upon the objects which concern "the *general welfare*, and for which under that description, "an appropriation of money is requisite and proper. And there "seems to be no room for a doubt that whatever concerns the

"general interests of LEARNING, of AGRICULTURE, of MANUFAC-
"TURES, and of COMMERCE, are within the sphere of the na-
"tional councils, *as far as regards an application of money.*"
The latter report assumes the same latitude of power in the
national councils and applies it to the encouragement of agriculture, by means of a society to be established at the seat of
government. Although neither of these reports may have received the sanction of a law carrying it into effect; yet, on the
other hand, the extraordinary doctrine contained in both, has
passed without the slightest positive mark of disapprobation
from the authority to which it was addressed.

Now whether the phrases in question be construed to authorize every measure relating to the common defence and
general welfare, as contended by some; or every measure only
in which there might be an application of money, as suggested
by the caution of others, the effect must substantially be the
same, in destroying the import and force of the particular
enumeration of powers, which follow these general phrases in
the Constitution. For it is evident that there is not a single
power whatever, which may not have some reference to the
common defence, or the general welfare; nor a power of any
magnitude which in its exercise does not involve or admit
an application of money. The government therefore which
possesses power in either one or other of these extents, is a
government without the limitations formed by a particular
enumeration of powers; and consequently the meaning and
effect of this particular enumeration, is destroyed by the exposition given to these general phrases.

This conclusion will not be affected by an attempt to qualify the power over the "general welfare," by referring it to
cases where the *general welfare* is beyond the reach of *separate* provisions by the *individual States;* and leaving to these
their jurisdictions in cases, to which their separate provisions

may be competent. For as the authority of the individual States must in all cases be incompetent to general regulations operating through the whole, the authority of the United States would be extended to every object relating to the general welfare, which might by any possibility be provided for by the general authority. This qualifying construction therefore would have little, if any tendency, to circumscribe the power claimed under the latitude of the terms "general welfare."

The true and fair construction of this expression, both in the original and existing Federal compacts appears to the committee too obvious to be mistaken. In both, the Congress is authorized to provide money for the common defence and *general welfare*. In both, is subjoined to this authority, an enumeration of the cases, to which their powers shall extend. Money cannot be applied to the *general welfare*, otherwise than by an application of it to some *particular* measure conducive to the general welfare. Whenever therefore, money has been raised by the general authority, and is to be applied to a particular measure, a question arises, whether the particular measure be within the enumerated authorities vested in Congress. If it be, the money requisite for it may be applied to it; if it be not, no such application can be made. This fair and obvious interpretation coincides with, and is enforced by, the clause in the Constitution which declares that "no money shall be drawn from the treasury, but in consequence of appropriations by law." An appropriation of money to the general welfare, would be deemed rather a mockery than an observance of this constitutional injunction.

2. Whether the exposition of the general phrases here combated, would not, by degrees consolidate the States into one sovereignty, is a question concerning which, the committee can perceive little room for difference of opinion. To consoli-

date the States into one sovereignty, nothing more can be wanted, than to supercede their respective sovereignties in the cases reserved to them, by extending the sovereignty of the United States to all cases of the "general welfare," that is to say, to *all cases whatever.*

3. That the obvious tendency and inevitable result of a consolidation of the States into one sovereignty, would be, to transform the republican system of the United States into a monarchy, is a point which seems to have been sufficiently decided by the general sentiment of America. In almost every instance of discussion, relating to the consolidation in question, its certain tendency to pave the way to monarchy, seems not to have been contested. The prospect of such a consolidation has formed the only topic of controversy. It would be unnecessary therefore, for the committee to dwell long on the reasons which support the position of the General Assembly. It may not be improper however to remark two consequences evidently flowing from an extension of the Federal powers to every subject falling within the idea of the "general welfare."

One consequence must be, to enlarge the sphere of discretion allotted to the executive magistrate. Even within the legislative limits properly defined by the Constitution, the difficulty of accomodating legal regulations to a country so great in extent, and so various in its circumstances, has been much felt; and has led to occasional investments of power in the executive, which involve perhaps as large a portion of discretion, as can be deemed consistent with the nature of the executive trust. In proportion as the objects of legislative care might be multiplied, would the time allowed for each be diminished, and the difficulty of providing uniform and particular regulations for all, be increased. From these sources would necessarily ensue, a greater latitude to the agency of that department which is always in existence, and which could best mould regulations of a general nature, so as to suit them to the diversity of particular situations. And it is in this latitude, as a supplement to the deficiency of the laws, that the degree of executive prerogative materially consists.

The other consequence would be, that of an excessive augmentation of the offices, honors, and emoluments depending on the executive will. Add to the present legitimate stock, all those of every description which a consolidation of the States would take from them, and turn over to the federal government, and the patronage of the executive would necessarily be as much swelled in this case, as its prerogative would be in the other.

This disproportionate increase of prerogative and patronage must, evidently, either enable the chief magistrate of the union, by quiet means, to secure his re-election from time to time, and finally, to regulate the succession as he might please; or, by giving so transcendent an importance to the office, would render the elections to it so violent and corrupt, that the public voice itself might call for an hereditary, in place of an elective succession. Which ever of these events might follow, the transformation of the Republican system of the United States into a monarchy, anticipated by the General Assembly from a consolidation of the States into one sovereignty, would be equally accomplished; and whether it would be into a mixt or an absolute monarchy, might depend on too many contingencies to admit of any certain foresight.

The resolution next in order, is contained in the following terms:

That the General Assembly doth particularly protest against the palpable, and alarming infractions of the Constitution, in the two late cases of the "Alien and Sedition acts," passed at the last session of Congress; the first of which, exercises a power no where delegated to the Federal government; and which by uniting legislative and judicial powers to those of executive, subverts the general principles of a free government, as well as the particular organization, and positive provisions of the Federal Constitution; and the other of which acts, exercises in like manner, a power not delegated by the Constitution, but on the contrary, expressly and positively forbidden by one of the amendments thereto;—a power, which more than any other, ought to produce universal alarm; because it is leveled against that right of freely examining public characters and measures, and of free communication among the people thereon, which has ever been justly deemed the only effectual guardian of every other right.

The subject of this resolution having, it is presumed, more particularly led the General Assembly into the proceedings which they communicated to the other States, and being in itself of peculiar importance; it deserves the most critical and faithful investigation; for the length of which no other apology will be necessary.

The subject divides itself into *first*, "The Alien Act," *secondly*, "The Sedition Act."

Of the "Alien Act," it is affirmed by the resolution, 1st. That it exercises a power no where delegated to the federal government. 2d. That it unites legislative and judicial powers to those of the executive. 3d. That this union of power, subverts the general principles of free government. 4th. That it subverts the particular organization and positive provisions of the Federal Constitution.

In order to clear the way for a correct view of the first position, several observations will be premised.

In the first place, it is to be borne in mind, that it being a characteristic feature of the Federal Constitution, as it was originally ratified, and an amendment thereto having precisely declared, "That the powers not delegated to the United States by the Constitution, nor prohibited by it to the States, are reserved to the States respectively, or to the people;" it is incumbent in this, as in every other exercise of power by the Federal government, to prove from the Constitution, that it grants the particular power exercised.

The next observation to be made, is, that much confusion and fallacy have been thrown into the question, by blending the two cases of *aliens, members of a hostile nation;* and *aliens, members of friendly nations.* These two cases are so obviously, and so essentially distinct, that it occasions no little surprise that the distinction should have been disregarded: and the surprise is so much the greater, as it appears that the two cases are actually distinguished by two separate acts of Congress, passed at the same session, and comprised in the same publication; the one providing for the case of "alien enemies;" the other "concerning aliens" indiscriminately; and consequently extending to aliens of every nation in peace and amity with the United States. With respect to alien enemies, no doubt has been intimated as to the federal authority over them; the Constitution having expressly delegated to Congress the power to declare war against any nation, and of course to treat it and all its members as enemies. With respect to aliens, who are not enemies, but members of nations in peace and amity with the United States, the power assumed by the act of Congress, is denied to be constitutional; and it is accordingly against this act, that the protest of the General Assembly is expressly and exclusively directed.

A third observation is, that were it admitted as is contended, that the "act concerning aliens," has for its object, not a *penal,* but a *preventive* justice; it would still remain to

174

be proved that it comes within the constitutional power of the Federal legislature, and if within its power, that the legislature has exercised it in a constitutional manner.

In the administration of preventive justice, the following principles have been held sacred; that some probable ground of suspicion be exhibited before some judicial authority; that it be supported by oath or affirmation; that the party may avoid being thrown into confinement, by finding pledges or sureties for his legal conduct sufficient in the judgment of some judicial authority; that he may have the benefit of a writ of habeas corpus, and thus obtain his release, if wrongfully confined; and that he may at any time be discharged from his recognizance, or his confinement, and restored to his former liberty and rights, on the order of the proper judicial authority; if it shall see sufficient cause.

All these principles of the only preventive justice known to American jurisprudence, are violated by the Alien Act. The ground of suspicion is to be judged of, not by any judicial authority, but by the executive magistrate alone; no oath or affirmation is required; if the suspicion be held reasonable by the President, he may order the suspected alien to depart the territory of the United States, without the opportunity of avoiding the sentence, by finding pledges for his future good conduct; as the President may limit the time of departure as he pleases, the benefit of the writ of habeas corpus, may be suspended with respect to the party, although the Constitution ordains, that it shall not be suspended, unless when the public safety may require it in case of rebellion or invasion, neither of which existed at the passage of the act: And the party being, under the sentence of the President, either removed from the United States, or being punished by imprisonment, or disqualification ever to become a citizen on conviction of not obeying the order of removal, he cannot be discharged from the proceedings against him, and restored to the benefits of his former situation, although the *highest judicial authority* should see the most sufficient cause for it.

But, in the last place, it can never be admitted, that the removal of aliens, authorized by the act, is to be considered, not as punishment for an offence; but as a measure of precaution and prevention. If the banishment of an alien from a country into which he has been invited, as the asylum most auspicious to his happiness; a country, where he may have formed the most tender of connections, where he may have vested his entire property, and acquired property of the real and permanent, as well as the moveable and temporary kind; where he enjoys under the laws, a greater share of the blessings of personal security and personal liberty, than he can elsewhere hope for, and where he may have nearly compleated his probationary title to citizenship; if moreover, in the execution of the sentence against him, he is to be exposed, not only to the ordinary dangers of the sea, but to the peculiar casualties incident to a crisis of war, and of unusual licentiousness on that element, and possibly to vindictive purposes which his emigration itself may have provoked; if a banishment of this sort be not a punishment, and among the severest of punishments, it will be difficult to imagine a doom to which the name can be applied. And if it be a punishment, it will remain to be enquired, whether it can be constitutionally inflicted, on mere suspicion, by the single will of the executive magistrate, on persons convicted of no personal offence against the laws of the land, nor involved in any offence against the law of nations, charged on the foreign state of which they are members.

One argument offered in justification of this power exercised over aliens, is, that the admission of them into the country being of favor not of right, the favor is at all times revokable.

To this argument it might be answered, that allowing the truth of the inference, it would be no proof of what is required. A question would still occur, whether the Constitution had vested the discretionary power of admitting aliens in the federal government or in the State governments.

But it can not be a true inference, that because the admission of an alien is a favor, the favor may be revoked at pleasure. A grant of land to an individual, may be of favor not of right; but the moment the grant is made, the favor becomes a right, and must be forfeited before it can be taken away. To pardon a malefactor may be a favor, but the pardon is not, on that account, the less irrevocable. To admit an alien to naturalization, is as much a favor, as to admit him to reside in the country; yet it cannot be pretended, that a person naturalized can be deprived of the benefit, any more than a native citizen can be disfranchised.

Again it is said, that aliens not being parties to the Constitution, the rights and privileges which it secures, cannot be at all claimed by them.

To this reasoning also, it might be answered, that although aliens are not parties to the Constitution, it does not follow that the Constitution has vested in Congress an absolute power over them. The parties to the Constitution may have granted, or retained, or modified the power over aliens, without regard to that particular consideration.

But a more direct reply is, that it does not follow, because aliens are not parties to the Constitution, as citizens are parties to it, that whilst they actually conform to it, they have no right to its protection. Aliens are not more parties to the laws, than they are parties to the Constitution; yet it will not be disputed, that as they owe on one hand, a temporary obedience, they are entitled in return, to their protection and advantage.

If aliens had no rights under the constitution, they might not only be banished, but even capitally punished, without a jury or the other incidents to a fair trial. But so far has a contrary principle been carried, in every part of the United States, that except on charges of treason, an alien has, besides all the common privileges, the special one of being tried by a jury, of which one half may be also aliens.

It is said, further, that by the law and practice of nations, aliens may be removed at discretion, for offences against the law of nations; that Congress are authorized to define and punish such offences; and that to be dangerous to the peace of society is, in aliens, one of those offences.

The distinction between alien enemies and alien friends, is a clear and conclusive answer to this argument. Alien enemies are under the law of nations, and liable to be punished for offences against it. Alien friends, except in the single case of public ministers, are under the municipal law, and must be tried and punished according to that law only.

This argument also, by referring the Alien Act, to the power of Congress to define and *punish* offences against the law of nations, yields the point that the act is of a *penal*, not merely of a preventive operation. It must, in truth be so considered. And if it be a penal act, the punishment it inflicts, must be justified by some offence that deserves it.

Offenses for which aliens within the jurisdiction of a country, are punishable, are first, offences committed by the nation of which they make a part, and in whose offences they are involved: Secondly, offences committed by themselves alone, without any charge against the nation to which they belong. The first is the case of alien enemies; the second the case of alien friends. In the first case, the offending nation can no otherwise be punished than by war, one of the laws which authorizes the expulsion of such of its members, as may be found within the country, against which the offence has been committed. In the second case, the offence being committed by the individual, not by his nation, and against the municipal law, not against the law of nations; the individual only, and not the nation is punishable; and the punishment must be conducted according to the municipal law, not according to the law of nations. Under this view of the subject, the act of Congress, for the removal of alien enemies, being conformable to the law of nations, is justified by the Constitution: and the act, for the removal of alien friends, being repugnant to the constitutional principles of municipal law, is unjustifiable.

Nor is the act of Congress, for the removal of alien friends, more agreeable to the general practice of nations, than it is within the purview of the law of nations. The general practice of nations, distinguishes between alien friends and alien enemies. The latter it has proceeded against, according to the law of nations, by expelling them as enemies. The former it has considered as under a local and temporary allegiance, and entitled to a correspondent protection. If contrary instances are to be found in barbarous countries, under undefined prerogatives, or amid revolutionary dangers; they will not be deemed fit precedents for the government of the United States, even, if not beyond its constitutional authority.

It is said, that Congress may grant letters of marque and reprisal; that reprisals may be made on persons, as well as property; and that the removal of aliens may be considered as the exercise in an inferior degree, of the general power of reprisal on persons.

Without entering minutely into a question that does not seem to require it; it may be remarked, that reprisal is a seizure of foreign persons or property, with a view to obtain that justice for injuries done by one state or its members, to another state or its members; for which a refusal of the aggressor requires such a resort to force under the law of nations. It must be considered as an abuse of words to call the removal of persons from a country, a seizure or reprisal on them; nor is the distinction to be overlooked between reprisals on persons within the country and under the faith of its laws, and on persons out of the country. But, laying aside these considerations; it is evidently impossible to bring the Alien Act within the power of granting reprisals; since it does not allege or imply any injury received from any particular nation, for which this proceeding against its members was intended as a reparation. The proceeding is authorized against aliens *of every nation*; of nations charged neither with any similar proceeding against American citizens, nor with any injuries for which justice might be sought, in the mode prescribed by the act. Were it true therefore, that good causes existed for reprisals against one or more foreign nations, and that neither the persons nor property of its members under the faith of our laws, could plead an exemption; the operation of the act ought to have been limited to the aliens among us, belonging to such nations. To license reprisals against all nations, for aggressions charged on one only, would be a measure as contrary to every principle of justice and public law, as to a wise policy, and the universal practice of nations.

It is said, that the right of removing aliens is an incident to the power of war, vested in Congress by the Constitution.

This is a former argument in a new shape only; and is answered by repeating, that the removal of alien enemies is an incident to the power of war; that the removal of alien friends, is not an incident to the power of war.

It is said, that Congress, is, by the Constitution, to protect each State against invasion; and that the means of *preventing* invasion, are included in the power of protection against it.

The power of war in general, having been before granted by the Constitution, this clause must either be a mere specification for greater caution and certainty, of which there are other examples in the instrument; or be the injunction of a duty, superadded to a grant of the power. Under either explanation, it cannot enlarge the powers of Congress on the subject. The power and the duty to protect each state against an invading enemy, would be the same under the general power, if this regard to greater caution had been omitted.

Invasion is an operation of war. To protect against invasion is an exercise of the power of war. A power therefore not incident to war, cannot be incident to a particular modification of war. And as the removal of alien friends has appeared to be no incident to a general state of war, it cannot be incident to a partial state, or a particular modification of war.

Nor can it ever be granted, that a power to act on a case when it actually occurs, includes a power over all the means that may *tend to prevent* the occurrence of the case. Such a latitude of construction would render unavailing, every practicable definition of particular and limited powers. Under the idea of preventing war in general, as well as invasion in particular, not only an indiscriminate removal of all aliens, might be enforced; but a thousand other things still more remote from the operations and precautions appurtenant to war, might take place. A bigoted or tyrannical nation might threaten us with war, unless certain religious or political regulations were adopted by us; yet it never could be inferred, if the regulations which would prevent war, were such as Congress had otherwise no power to make, that the power to make them would grow out of the purpose they were to answer. Congress have power to suppress insurrections, yet it would not be allowed to follow, that they might employ all the means tending to prevent them; of which a system of

181

moral instruction for the ignorant, and of provident support for the poor, might be regarded as among the most efficacious.

One argument for the power of the General Government to remove aliens would have been passed in silence, if it had appeared under any authority inferior to that of a report, made during the last session of Congress, to the House of Representatives by a committee, and approved by the House. The doctrine on which this argument is founded, is of so new and so extraordinary a character, and strikes so radically at the political system of America, that it is proper to state it in the very words of the report.

"The act [concerning aliens] is said to be unconstitutional, "because to remove aliens, is a direct breach of the Consti- "tution which provides, by the 9th section of the 1st article: "that the migration or importation of such persons as any of "the states shall think proper to admit, shall not be prohibited "by the Congress, prior to the year 1808."

Among the answers given to this objection to the constitutionality of the act, the following very remarkable one is extracted.

"Thirdly, that as the Constitution has *given to the States*, "no power to remove aliens, during the period of the limita- "tion under consideration, in the meantime, on the construc- "tion assumed, there would be no authority in the country, "empowered to send away dangerous aliens which cannot be "admitted."

The reasoning here used, would not in any view, be conclusive; because there are powers exercised by most other governments, which, in the United States are withheld by the people, both from the general government and from the State governments. Of this sort are many of the powers prohibited by the Declarations of right prefixed to the Constitutions, or by the clauses in the Constitutions, in the nature of such Declarations. Nay, so far is the political system of the United States distinguishable from that of other countries, by the caution with which powers are delegated and defined; that in one very important case, even of commercial regulation and revenue, the power is absolutely locked up against the hands of both governments. A tax on exports can be laid by no constitutional authority whatever. Under a system thus peculiarly guarded, there could surely be no absurdity in supposing, that alien friends, who if guilty of treasonable machinations may be punished, or if suspected on probable grounds, may be secured by pledges or imprisonment, in like manner with permanent citizens, were never meant to be subjected to banishment by any arbitrary and unusual process, either under the one government or the other.

But it is not the inconclusiveness of the general reasoning in this passage, which chiefly calls the attention to it. It is the principle assumed by it, that the powers held by the States, are given to them by the Constitution of the United States; and the inference from this principle, that the powers supposed to be necessary which are not so given to the State governments, must reside in the government of the United States.

The respect which is felt for every portion of the constituted authorities, forbids some of the reflections which this singular paragraph might excite; and they are the more readily suppressed, as it may be presumed, with justice perhaps, as well as candour, that inadvertence may have had its share in the error. It would be an unjustifiable delicacy nevertheless, to pass by so portentous a claim, proceeding from so high an authority, without a monitory notice of the fatal tendencies with which it would be pregnant.

Lastly, it is said, that a law on the same subject with the Alien Act, passed by this State originally in 1785, and re-enacted in 1792, is a proof that a summary removal of suspected aliens, was not heretofore regarded by the Virginia Legislature as liable to the objections now urged against such a measure.

This charge against Virginia, vanishes before the simple remark, that the law of Virginia relates to "suspicious persons, "being the subjects of any foreign power or state, who shall "have *made a declaration of war*, or actually *commenced hos-* "*tilities*, or from whom the President shall apprehend *hostile* "*designs*;" whereas the act of Congress relates to aliens, being the subjects of foreign powers and states, who have *neither declared war, nor commenced hostilities, nor from whom hostile designs are apprehended.*

II. It is next affirmed of the Alien Act, that it unites legislative, judicial and executive powers in the hands of the President.

However difficult it may be to mark, in every case, with clearness and certainty, the line which divides legislative power, from the other departments of power; all will agree, that the powers referred to these departments may be so general and undefined, as to be of a legislative, not of an executive or judicial nature; and may for that reason be unconstitutional. Details, to a certain degree, are essential to the nature and character of a law; and, on criminal subjects, it is proper, that details should leave as little as possible to the discretion of those who are to apply and to execute the law. If nothing more were required, in exercising a legislative trust, than a general conveyance of authority, without laying down any precise rules, by which the authority conveyed, should be carried into effect; it would follow, that the whole power of legislation might be transferred by the legislature from itself, and proclamations might become substitutes for laws. A delegation of power in this latitude, would not be denied to be a union of the different powers.

To determine then, whether the appropriate powers of the distinct departments are united by the act authorizing the executive to remove aliens, it must be enquired whether it contains such details, definitions, and rules, as appertain to the true character of a law; especially, a law by which personal liberty is invaded, property deprived of its value to the owner, and life itself indirectly exposed to danger.

The Alien Act, declares, "that it shall be lawful for the President to order all such aliens as he shall judge *dangerous* to the peace and safety of the United States, or shall have reasonable grounds to *suspect*, are concerned in any treasonable, *or secret machinations*, against the government thereof, to depart," &c.

Could a power be well given in terms less definite, less particular, and less precise? To be *dangerous to the public safety;* to be *suspected of secret machinations* against the government: these can never be mistaken for legal rules or certain definitions. They leave every thing to the President. His will is the law.

But it is not a legislative power only that is given to the President. He is to stand in the place of the judiciary also. His suspicion is the only evidence which is to convict: his order the only judgment which is to be executed.

Thus it is the President whose will is to designate the offensive conduct; it is his will that is to ascertain the individuals on whom it is charged; and it is his will, that is to cause the sentence to be executed. It is rightly affirmed therefore, that the act unites legislative and judicial powers to those of the executive.

III. It is affirmed that this union of powers subverts the general principles of free government.

It has become an axiom in the science of government, that a separation of the legislative, executive and judicial departments, is necessary to the preservation of public liberty. No where has this axiom been better understood in theory, or more carefully pursued in practice, than in the United States.

IV. It is affirmed that such a union of power subverts the particular organization and positive provisions of the Federal Constitution.

According to the particular organization of the Constitution, its legislative powers are vested in the Congress; its executive powers in the President, and its judicial powers, in a supreme and inferior tribunals. The union of any two of these powers, and still more of all three, in any one of these departments, as has been shewn to be done by the Alien Act, must consequently subvert the constitutional organization of them.

That positive provisions in the Constitution, securing to individuals the benefits of fair trial, are also violated by the union of powers in the Alien Act, necessarily results from the two facts, that the act relates to alien friends, and that alien friends being under the municipal law only, are entitled to its protection.

The *second* object against which the resolution protests is the Sedition Act.

Of this act it is affirmed 1. That it exercises in like manner a power not delegated by the Constitution. 2d. That the power, on the contrary, is expressly and positively forbidden by one of the amendments to the Constitution. 3d. That this is a power, which more than any other ought to produce universal alarm; because it is leveled against that right of freely examining public characters and measures, and of free communication thereon; which has ever been justly deemed the only effectual guardian of every other right.

I. That it exercises a power not delegated by the Constitution.

Here, again it will be proper to recollect, that the Federal

Government being composed of powers specifically granted, with a reservation of all others to the States or to the people, the positive authority under which the Sedition Act could be passed must be produced by those who assert its constitutionality. In what part of the Constitution then is this authority to be found?

Several attempts have been made to answer this question, which will be examined in their order. The committee will begin with one, which has filled them with equal astonishment and apprehension; and which, they cannot but persuade themselves, must have the same effect on all, who will consider it with coolness and impartiality, and with a reverence for our Constitution, in the true character in which it issued from the sovereign authority of the people. The committee refer to the doctrine lately advanced as a sanction to the Sedition Act: "that the common or unwritten law," a law of vast extent and complexity, and embracing almost every possible subject of legislation, both civil and criminal, "makes a part of the law of these States; in their united and national capacity."

The novelty, and in the judgment of the committee, the extravagance of this pretension, would have consigned it to the silence, in which they have passed by other arguments, which an extraordinary zeal for the act has drawn into the discussion. But the auspices, under which this innovation presents itself, have constrained the committee to bestow on it an attention, which other considerations might have forbidden.

In executing the task, it may be of use, to look back to the colonial state of this country, prior to the revolution; to trace the effect of the revolution which converted the colonies into independent States; to enquire into the import of the articles of confederation, the first instrument by which the union of the States was regularly established; and finally to consult the

Constitution of 1788, which is the oracle that must decide the important question.

In the State prior to the revolution, it is certain that the common law under different limitations, made a part of the colonial codes. But whether it be understood that the original colonists brought the law with them, or made it their law by adoption; it is equally certain that it was the separate law of each colony within its respective limits, and was unknown to them, as a law pervading and operating through the whole, as one society.

It could not possibly be otherwise. The common law was not the same in any two of the colonies; in some, the modifications were materially and extensively different. There was no common legislature, by which a common will, could be expressed in the form of a law; nor any common magistracy, by which such a law could be carried into practice. The will of each colony alone and separately, had its organs for these purposes.

This stage of our political history, furnishes no foothold for the patrons of this new doctrine.

Did then, the principle or operation of the great event which made the colonies, independent states, imply or introduce the common law, as a law of the union?

The fundamental principle of the revolution was, that the colonies were co-ordinate members with each other, and with Great Britain; of an Empire, united by a common Executive Sovereign, but not united by any common Legislative Sovereign. The Legislative power was maintained to be as complete in each American Parliament, as in the British Parliament. And the royal prerogative was in force in each colony, by virtue of its acknowledging the King for its Executive Magistrate, as it was in Great Britain, by virtue of a like acknowledgement there. A denial of these principles by Great Britain, and

188

the assertion of them by America, produced the revolution. There was a time indeed, when an exception to the Legislative separation of the several component and co-equal parts of the Empire, obtained a degree of acquiescence. The British Parliament was allowed to regulate the trade with foreign nations, and between the different parts of the Empire. This was however mere practice without right, and contrary to the true theory of the constitution. The conveniency of some regulations in both those cases, was apparent; and as there was no Legislature with power over the whole, nor any constitutional pre-eminence among the Legislatures of the several parts; it was natural for the Legislature of that particular part which was the eldest and the largest, to assume this function, and for the others to acquiesce in it. This tacit arrangement was the less criticised, as the regulations established by the British Parliament, operated in favor of that part of the Empire, which seemed to bear the principal share of the public burdens, and were regarded as an indemnification of its advances for the other parts. As long as this regulating power was confined to two objects of conveniency and equity, it was not complained of, nor much enquired into. But no sooner was it perverted to the selfish views of the party assuming it, than the injured parties began to feel and to reflect; and the moment the claim to a direct and indefinite power was ingrafted on the precedent of the regulating power, the whole charm was dissolved, and every eye opened to the usurpation. The assertion by G. B. of a power to make laws for the other members of the Empire *in all cases whatsoever*, ended in the discovery, that she had a right to make laws for them, *in no cases whatsoever.*

Such being the ground of our revolution, no support nor colour can be drawn from it, for the doctrine that the common law is binding on these States as one society. The doctrine on the contrary, is evidently repugnant to the fundamental principle of the revolution.

The articles of confederation, are the next source of information on this subject.

In the interval between the commencement of the revolution, and the final ratification of these articles, the nature and extent of the union was determined by the circumstances of the crisis, rather than by any accurate delineation of the general authority. It will not be alleged that the "common law," could have had any legitimate birth as a law of the United States, during that state of things. If it came as such, into existence at all, the charter of confederation must have been its parent.

Here again, however, its pretensions are absolutely destitute of foundation. This instrument does not contain a sentence or syllable, that can be tortured into a countenance of the idea, that the parties to it were with respect to the objects of the common law, to form one community. No such law is named or implied, or alluded to, as being in force, or as brought into force by that compact. No provision is made by which such a law could be carried into operation; whilst on the other hand, every such inference or pretext is abolutely precluded, by article 2d, which declares, "that each State retains its sovereignity, freedom and independence, and every power, jurisdiction and right, which is not by this confederation expressly delegated to the United States, in Congress assembled."

Thus far it appears, that not a vestige of this extraordinary doctrine can be found, in the origin or progress of American institutions. The evidence against it, has, on the contrary, grown stronger at every step; till it has amounted to a formal and positive exclusion, by written articles of compact among the parties concerned.

Is this exclusion revoked, and the common law introduced as a national law, by the present Constitution of the United States? This is the final question to be examined.

It is readily admitted, that particular parts of the common law, may have a sanction from the Constitution, so far as they are necessarily comprehended in the technical phrases which express the powers delegated to the government; and so far also, as such other parts may be adopted as necessary and proper, for carrying into execution the powers expressly delegated. But the question does not relate to either of these portions of the common law. It relates to the common law, beyond these limitations.

The only part of the Constitution which seems to have been relied on in this case, is the 2d sect. of art. III. The judicial power shall extend to all cases, *in law and equity*, arising *under this Constitution*, the "laws of the United States, and treaties made or which shall be made under their authority."

It has been asked what cases distinct from those arising under the laws and treaties of the United States, can arise under the Constitution, other than those arising under the common law; and it is inferred, that the common law is accordingly adopted or recognized by the Constitution.

Never perhaps was so broad a construction applied to a text so clearly unsusceptible of it. If any colour for the inference could be found, it must be in the impossibility of finding any other cases in law and equity, within the provision of the Constitution, to satisfy the expression; and rather than resort to a construction affecting so essentially the whole character of the government, it would perhaps be more rational to consider the expression as a mere pleonasm or inadvertence. But it is not necessary to decide on such a dilemma. The expression is fully satisfied, and its accuracy justified, by two descriptions of cases, to which the judicial authority is extended, and

191

neither of which implies that the common law is the law of the United States. One of these descriptions comprehends the cases growing out of the restrictions on the legislative power of the States. For example, it is provided that "no State shall emit bills of credit," or "make any thing but gold and silver coin a tender in payment of debts." Should this prohibition be violated, and a suit *between citizens of the same State* be the consequence, this would be a case arising under the constitution before the judicial power of the United States. A second description comprehends suits between citizens and foreigners, or citizens of different States, to be decided according to the State or foreign laws; but submitted by the Constitution to the judicial power of the United States; the judicial power being, in several instances, extended beyond the legislative power of the United States.

To this explanation of the text, the following observations may be added.

The expression, cases in law and equity, is manifestly confined to cases of a civil nature; and would exclude cases of criminal jurisdiction. Criminal cases in law and equity, would be a language unknown to the law.

The succeeding paragraph of the same section, is in harmony with this construction. It is in these words—"In all cases affecting ambassadors, other public ministers and consuls, and those in which a State shall be party, the Supreme Court shall have original jurisdiction. *In all* the other cases [including cases in law and equity arising under the Constitution] the Supreme Court shall have *appellate* jurisdiction both as to law and *fact;* with such exceptions, and under such regulations as Congress shall make."

This paragraph, by expressly giving an *appellate* jurisdiction, in cases of law and equity arising under the Constitution, to *fact,* as well as to law, clearly excludes criminal cases, where the trial by jury is secured; because the fact, in such cases, is not a subject of appeal. And although the appeal is liable to such *exceptions* and regulations as Congress may adopt; yet it is not to be supposed that an exception of all criminal cases could be contemplated; as well because a discretion in Congress to make or omit the exception would be improper; as because it would have been unnecessary. The exception could as easily have been made by the Constitution itself, as referred to the Congress.

Once more, the amendment last added to the Constitution, deserves attention, as throwing light on this subject. "This judicial power of the United States shall not be construed to extend to any suit in law or equity, commenced or prosecuted against one of the United States, by citizens of another State, or by citizens or subjects of any foreign power." As it will not be pretended that any criminal proceeding could take place against a State, the terms *law* or *equity*, must be understood as appropriate to *civil* in exclusion of *criminal* cases.

From these considerations, it is evident, that this part of the Constitution, even if it could be applied at all, to the purpose for which it has been cited, would not include any cases whatever of a criminal nature; and consequently, would not authorise the inference from it, that the judicial authority extends to offences against the common law, as offences arising under the Constitution.

It is further to be considered, that even if this part of the Constitution could be strained into an application to every common law case, criminal as well as civil, it could have no effect in justifying the Sedition Act; which is an exercise of legislative, and not of judicial power: and it is the judicial power only of which the extent is defined in this part of the Constitution.

There are two passages in the Constitution, in which a description of the law of the United States, is found—The first is contained in article III. sect. 2, in the words following: "This Constitution, the laws of the United States, and treaties made, or which shall be made under their authority." The second is contained in the 2d paragraph of art. VI. as follows: "This Constitution and the laws of the United States which shall be made in pursuance thereof, and all treaties made, or which shall be made under the authority of the United States, shall be the supreme law of the land." The first of these descriptions was meant as a guide to the judges of the United States; the second as a guide to the judges in the several States. Both of them consist of an enumeration, which was evidently meant to be precise and compleat. If the common law had been understood to be a law of the United States, it is not possible to assign a satisfactory reason why it was not expressed in the enumeration.

In aid of these objections, the difficulties and confusion inseparable from a constructive introduction of the common law, would afford powerful reasons against it.

Is it to be the common law with, or without the British statutes?

If without the statutory amendments, the vices of the code would be insupportable?

If with these amendments, what period is to be fixed for limiting the British authority over our laws?

Is it to be the date of the eldest or the youngest of the colonies?

Or are the dates to be thrown together, and a medium deduced?

Or is our independence to be taken for the date?

Is, again, regard to be had to the various changes in the common law made by the local codes of America?

Is regard to be had to such changes, subsequent, as well as prior, to the establishment of the Constitution?

Is regard to be had to future, as well as past changes?

Is the law to be different in every State, as differently modified by its code; or are the modifications of any particular State, to be applied to all?

And on the latter supposition, which among the State codes would form the standard?

Questions of this sort might be multiplied with as much case, as there would be difficulty in answering them.

The consequences flowing from the proposed contruction, furnish other objections equally conclusive; unless the text were peremptory in its meaning, and consistent with other parts of the instrument.

These consequences may be in relation; to the legislative authority of the United States; to the executive authority; to the judicial authority, and to the governments of the several States.

If it be understood that the common law is established by the Constitution, it follows that no part of the law can be altered by the legislature; such of the statutes already passed as may be repugnant thereto, would be nullified, particularly the "Sedition Act" itself which boasts of being a melioration of the common law; and the whole code with all its incongruities, barbarisms, and bloody maxims would be inviolably saddled on the good people of the United States.

Should this consequence be rejected, and the common law be held, like other laws, liable to revision and alteration, by the authority of Congress; it then follows, that the authority of Congress is co-extensive with the objects of common law; that is to say, with every object of legislation: For to every such object, does some branch or other of the common law extend. The authority of Congress would therefore be no longer under the limitations, marked out in the Constitution. They would be authorized to legislate in all cases whatsoever.

In the next place, as the President possesses the executive powers of the Constitution, and is to see that the laws be faithfully executed, his authority also must be co-extensive with every branch of the common law. The additions which this would make to his power, though not readily to be estimated, claims the most serious attention.

This is not all; it will merit the most profound consideration, how far an indefinite admission of the common law, with a latitude in construing it, equal to the construction by which it is deduced from the Constitution, might draw after it the various prerogatives making part of the unwritten law of England. The English constitution itself is nothing more than a composition of unwritten laws and maxims.

In the third place, whether the common law be admitted as of legal or of constitutional obligation, it would confer on the judicial department a discretion little short of a legislative power.

On the supposition of its having a constitutional obligation, this power in the judges would be permanent and irremediable by the legislature. On the other supposition, the power would not expire, until the legislature should have introduced a full system of statutory provisions. Let it be observed too, that besides all the uncertainties above enumerated, and which present an immense field for judicial discretion, it would remain with the same department to decide what parts of the common law would, and what would not, be properly applicable to the circumstances of the United States.

A discretion of this sort, has always been lamented as incongruous and dangerous, even in the colonial and State courts; although so much narrowed by positive provisions in the local codes on all the principal subjects embraced by the common law. Under the United States, where so few laws exist on those subjects, and where so great a lapse of time must happen before the vast chasm could be supplied, it is manifest that the power of the judges over the law would, in fact, erect them into legislators; and that for a long time, it would be impossible for the citizens to conjecture, either what was, or would be law.

In the last place, the consequence of admitting the common law as the law of the United States, on the authority of the individual States, is as obvious as it would be fatal. As this law relates to every subject of legislation, and would be paramount to the constitutions and laws of the States, the admission of it would overwhelm the residuary sovereignty of the States, and by one constructive operation new model the whole political fabric of the country.

From the review thus taken of the situation of the American colonies prior to their independence; of the effect of this event on their situation; of the nature and import of the articles of confederation; of the true meaning of the passage in the existing Constitution from which the common law has been deduced; of the difficulties and uncertainties incident to the doctrine; and of its vast consequences in extending the powers of the federal government, and in superceding the authorities of the State governments; the committee feel the utmost confidence in concluding that the common law never was, nor by any fair construction, ever can be, deemed a law for the American people as one community; and they indulge the strongest expectation that the same conclusion will finally be drawn, by all candid and accurate enquirers into the subject. It is indeed distressing to reflect, that it ever should have been made a question, whether the Constitution, on the whole face of which is seen so much labour to enumerate and define the several objects of federal power, could intend to introduce in the lump, in an indirect manner, and by a forced construction of a few phrases, the vast and multifarious jurisdiction involved in the common law; a law filling so many ample volumes; a law overspreading the entire field of legislation; and a law that would sap the foundation of the Constitution as a system of limited and specified powers. A severer reproach could not in the opinion of the committee be thrown on the Constitution, on those who framed, or on those who established it, than such a supposition would throw on them.

The argument then drawn from the common law, on the ground of its being adopted or recognized by the Constitution, being inapplicable to the Sedition Act, the committee will proceed to examine the other arguments which have been founded on the Constitution.

They will waste but little time on the attempt to cover the act by the preamble to the Constitution; it being contrary to every acknowledged rule of construction, to set up this part of an instrument, in opposition to the plain meaning, expressed in the body of the instrument. A preamble usually contains the general motives or reasons, for the particular regulations or measures which follow it; and is always understood to be explained and limited by them. In the present instance, a contrary interpretation would have the inadmissable effect, of rendering nugatory or improper, every part of the Constitution which succeeded the preamble.

The paragraph in art. 1, sect. 8, which contains the power to lay and collect taxes, duties, imposts, and excises, to pay the debts, and provide for the common defence and general welfare, having been already examined, will also require no particular attention in this place. It will have been seen that in its fair and consistent meaning, it cannot enlarge the enumerated powers vested in Congress.

The part of the Constitution which seems most to be recurred to, in defence of the "Sedition Act," is the last clause of the above section, empowering Congress "to make all laws which shall be necessary and proper for carrying into execution the foregoing powers, and all other powers vested by this Constitution in the government of the United States, or in any department or officer thereof."

The plain import of this clause is, that Congress shall have all the incidental or instrumental powers, necessary and proper for carrying into execution all the express powers; whether they be vested in the government of the United States, more collectively, or in the several departments, or officers thereof. It is not a grant of new powers to Congress, but merely a declaration, for the removal of all uncertainty, that the means of carrying into execution, those otherwise granted, are included in the grant.

Whenever, therefore a question arises concerning the constitutionality of a particular power; the first question is, whether the power be expressed in the Constitution. If it be, the question is decided. If it be not expressed; the next enquiry must be, whether it is properly an incident to an express power, and necessary to its execution. If it be, it may be exercised by Congress. If it be not; Congress cannot exercise it.

Let the question be asked, then, whether the power over the press exercised in the "Sedition Act," be found among the powers expressly vested in the Congress? This is not pretended.

Is there any express power, for executing which, it is necessary and proper power?

The power which has been selected, as least remote, in answer to this question, is that of "suppressing insurrections;" which is said to imply a power to *prevent* insurrections, by punishing whatever may *lead* or *tend* to them. But it surely cannot, with the least plausibility, be said, that a regulation of the press, and a punishment of libels, are exercises of a power to suppress insurrections. The most that could be said, would be, that the punishment of libels, if it had the tendency ascribed to it, might prevent the occasion, of passing or executing laws, necessary and proper for the suppression of insurrections.

Has the federal government no power, then, to prevent as well as to punish resistance to the laws;

They have the power which the Constitution deemed most proper in their hands for the purpose. The Congress has power, before it happens, to pass laws for punishing it; and the Executive and Judiciary have power to enforce those laws when it does happen.

It must be recollected by many, and could be shewn to the satisfaction of all, that the construction here put on the terms "necessary and proper" is precisely the construction which prevailed during the discussions and ratifications of the Constitution. It may be added, and cannot too often be repeated, that it is a construction absolutely necessary to maintain their consistency with the peculiar character of the government, as possessed of particular and defined powers only; not of the general and indefinite powers vested in ordinary governments. For if the power to *suppress insurrections*, includes a power to *punish libels;* or if the power to *punish*, includes a power to *prevent*, by all the means that may have that *tendency;* such is the relation and influence among the most remote subjects of legislations, that a power over a very few, would carry with it a power over all. And it must be wholly immaterial, whether unlimited powers be exercised under the name of unlimited powers, or be exercised under the name of unlimited means of carrying into execution, limited powers.

This branch of the subject will be closed with a reflection which must have weight with all; but more especially with those who place peculiar reliance on the judicial exposition of the Constitution, as the bulwark provided against undue extensions of the legislative power. If it be understood that the powers implied in the specified powers, have an immediate and appropriate relation to them, as means, necessary and proper for carrying them into execution, questions on the constitutionality of laws passed for this purpose, will be of a nature sufficiently precise and determinate for judicial cognizance and control. If, on the other hand, Congress are not limited in the choice of means by any such appropriate relation of them to the specified powers; but may employ all such means as they may deem fitted to *prevent* as well as to *punish*, crimes subjected to their authority; such as may have a *tendency* only to *promote* an object for which they are authorized to provide; every one must perceive that questions relating to means of this sort, must be questions of mere policy and expediency; on which legislative discretion alone can decide, and from which the judicial interposition and controul are completely excluded.

II. The next point which the resolution requires to be proved, is, that the power over the press exercised by the Sedition Act, is positively forbidden by one of the amendments to the Constitution.

The amendment stands in these words—"Congress shall make no law respecting an establishment of religion, or prohibiting the free exercise thereof, *or abridging the freedom of speech or of the press*; or the right of the people peaceably to assemble, and to petition the government for a redress of grievances."

In the attempts to vindicate the "Sedition Act," it has been contended, 1. That the "freedom of the press" is to be determined by the meaning of these terms in the common law. 2. That the article supposes the power over the press to be in Congress, and prohibits them only from *abridging* the freedom allowed to it by the common law.

Although it will be shewn, in examining the second of these positions, that the amendment is a denial to Congress of all power over the press; it may not be useless to make the following observations on the first of them.

It is deemed to be a sound opinion, that the Sedition Act, in its definition of some of the crimes created, is an abridgment of the freedom of publication, recognized by principles of the common law in England.

The freedom of the press under the common law, is, in the defences of the Sedition Act, made to consist in an exemption from all *previous* restraint on printed publications, by persons authorized to inspect and prohibit them. It appears to the committee, that this idea of the freedom of the press, can never be admitted to be the American idea of it: since a law inflicting penalties on printed publications, would have a familiar effect with a law authorizing a previous restraint on them. It would seem a mockery to say, that no law should be passed, preventing publications from being made, but that laws might be passed for punishing them in case they should be made.

The essential difference between the British government, and the American Constitution, will place this subject in the clearest light.

In the British government, the danger of encroachments on the rights of the people, is understood to be confined to the executive magistrate. The representatives of the people in the legislature, are not only exempt themselves, from distrust, but are considered as sufficient guardians of the rights of their constituents against the danger from the executive. Hence it is a principle, that the parliament is unlimited in its powers; or in their own language, is omnipotent. Hence too, all the ramparts for protecting the rights of the people, such as their magna charta, their bill of rights, &c. are not reared against the parliament, but against the royal prerogative. They are merely legislative precautions, against executive usurpations. Under such a government as this, an exemption of the press from previous restraint by licensers appointed by the king, is all the freedom that can be secured to it.

In the United States, the case is altogether different. The people, not the government, possess the absolute sovereignty. The legislature, no less than the executive, is under limitations of power. Encroachments are regarded as possible from the one, as well as from the other. Hence in the United States, the great and essential rights of the people are secured against legislative, as well as against executive ambition. They are secured, not by laws paramount to prerogative; but by constitutions paramount to laws. This security of the freedom of the press, requires that it should be exempt, not only from previous restraint by the executive, as in Great Britain; but from legislative restraint also; and this exemption, to be effectual, must be an exemption, not only from the previous inspection of licensers, but from the subsequent penalty of laws.

The state of the press, therefore, under the common law, can not in this point of view, be the standard of its freedom in the United States.

But there is another view, under which it may be necessary to consider this subject. It may be alleged, that although the security for the freedom of the press, be different in Great Britain and in this country; being a legal security only in the former, and a constitutional security in the latter; and although there may be a further difference, in an extension of the freedom of the press, here, beyond an exemption from previous restraint, to an exemption from subsequent penalties also; yet that the actual legal freedom of the press, under the common law, must determine the degee of freedom, which is meant by the terms and which is constitutionally secured against both previous and subsequent restraints.

The committee are not aware of the difficulty of all general questions which, may turn on the proper boundary between the liberty and licentiousness of the press. They will leave it therefore for consideration only, how far the difference between the nature of the British government, and the nature of the American governments, and the practice under the latter, may shew the degree of rigor in the former, to be inapplicable to, and not obligatory in, the latter.

The nature of government elective, limited and responsible, in all their branches, may well be supposed to require a greater freedom of animadversion, than might be tolerated by the genuis of such a government as that of Great Britain. In the latter, it is a maxim, that the king, an hereditary, not a responsible magistrate, can do no wrong; and that the legislature, which in two thirds of its composition, is also hereditary, not responsible, can do what it pleases. In the United States, the executive magistrates are not held to be infallible, nor the legislatures to be omnipotent; and both being elective, are both responsible. Is it not natural and necessary, under such different circumstances, that a different degree of freedom, in the use of the press, should be contemplated?

Is not such an inference favored by what is observable in Great Britain itself? Notwithstanding the general doctrine of the common law, on the subject of the press, and the occasional punishment of those, who use it with a freedom offensive to the government; it is well known, that with respect to the responsible members of the government, where the reasons operating here, become applicable there; the freedom exercised by the press, and protected by the public opinion, far exceeds the limits prescribed by the ordinary rules of law. The ministry, who are responsible to impeachment, are at all times, animadverted on, by the press, with peculiar freedom; and during the elections for the House of Commons, the other responsible part of the government, the press is employed with as little reserve towards the candidates.

The practice in America must be entitled to much more respect. In every state, probably, in the union, the press has exerted a freedom in canvassing the merits and measures of public men, of every description, which has not been confined to the strict limits of the common law.—On this footing, the freedom of the press has stood; on this footing it yet stands. And it will not be a breach, either of truth or of candour, to say, that no persons or presses are in the habit of more unrestrained animadversions on the proceedings and functionaries of the State governments, than the persons and presses most zealous, in vindicating the act of Congress for punishing similar animadversions on the government of the United States.

The last remark will not be understood, as claiming for the State governments, an immunity greater than they have heretofore enjoyed. Some degree of abuse is inseparable from the proper use of every thing; and in no instance is this more true, than in that of the press. It has accordingly been decided by the practice of the States, that it is better to leave a few of its noxious branches, to their luxuriant growth, than by pruning them away, to injure the vigor of those yielding the proper fruits. And can the wisdom of this policy be doubted by any who reflect, that to the press alone, chequered as it is with abuses, the world is indebted for all the triumphs which have been gained by reason and humanity, over error and oppression; who reflect that to the same beneficent source, the United States owe much of the lights which conducted them to the rank of a free and independent nation; and which have improved their political system, into a shape so auspicious to their happiness. Had "sedition acts," fobidding every publication that might bring the constituted agents into contempt or disrepute, or that might excite the hatred of the people against the authors of unjust or pernicious measures, been uniformly enforced against the press; might not the United States have been languishing at this day, under the infirmities of a sickly confederation? Might they not possibly be miserable colonies, groaning under a foreign yoke?

To these observations one fact will be added, which demonstrates that the common law cannot be admitted as the *universal* expositor of American terms, which may be the same with those contained in that law. The freedom of conscience, and of religion, are found in the same instruments, which assert the freedom of the press. It will never be admitted, that the meaning of the former, in the common law of England, is to limit their meaning in the United States.

Whatever weight may be allowed to these considerations, the committee do not, however, by any means, intend to rest the question on them. They contend that the article of amendment, instead of supposing in Congress, a power that might be exercised over the press, provided its freedom be not abridged, was meant as a positive denial to Congress, of any power whatever on the subject.

To demonstrate that this was the true object of the article, it will be sufficient to recall the circumstances which led to it, and to refer to the explanation accompanying the article.

When the Constitution was under the discussions which preceded its ratification, it is well known, that great apprehensions were expressed by many, lest the omission of some positive exception from the powers delegated, of certain rights, and of the freedom of the press particularly, might expose them to the danger of being drawn by construction within some of the powers vested in Congress; more especially of the power to make all laws necessary and proper, for carrying their other powers into execution. In reply to this objection, it was invariably urged to be a fundamental and characteristic principle of the Constitution that all powers not given by it, were reserved; that no powers were given beyond those enumerated in the Constitution, and such as were fairly incident to them; that the power over the rights in question, and particularly over the press, was neither among the enumerated powers, nor incident to any of them; and consequently that an exercise of any such power, would be a manifest usurpation. It is painful to remark, how much the arguments now employed in behalf of the Sedition Act are at variance with the reasoning which then justified the Constitution, and invited its ratification.

From this posture of the subject, resulted the interesting question in so many of the conventions, whether the doubts and dangers ascribed to the Constitution should be removed by any amendments previous to the ratification, or be postponed, in confidence that as far as they might be proper, they would be introduced in the form provided by the Constitution. The latter course was adopted, and in most of the States, the ratifications were followed by propositions and instructions for rendering the Constitution more explicit, and more safe to the rights, not meant to be delegated by it. Among those rights, the freedom of the press, in most instances, is particularly and emphatically mentioned. The firm and very pointed manner, in which it is asserted in the proceedings of the convention of this State will be hereafter seen.

In pursuance of the wishes thus expressed, the first Congress that assembled under the constitution, proposed certain amendments which have since, by the necessary ratifications, been made a part of it; among which amendments is the article containing, among other prohibitions on the Congress, an express declaration that they should make no law abridging the freedom of the press.

Without tracing farther the evidence on this subject, it would seem scarcely possible to doubt, that no power whatever over the press, was supposed to be delegated by the Constitution, as it originally stood; and that the amendment was intended as a positive and absolute reservation of it.

But the evidence is still stronger. The proposition of amendments made by Congress, is introduced in the following terms: *"The Convention of a number of the States having at the time of their adopting the Constitution, expressed a desire, in order to prevent misconstructions or abuse of its powers, that further declaratory and restrictive clauses should be added; and as extending the ground of public confidence in the government, will best ensure the beneficent ends of its institutions."*

Here is the most satisfactory and authentic proof, that the several amendments proposed, were to be considered as either declaratory or restrictive; and whether the one or the other, as corresponding with the desire expressed by a number of the States, and as extending the ground of public confidence in the government.

Under any other construction of the amendment relating to the press, than that it declared the press to be wholly exempt from the power of Congress, the amendment could neither be said to correspond with the desire expressed by a number of the States, nor be calculated to extend the ground of public confidence in the government.

Nay more; the construction employed to justify the "Sedition Act," would exhibit a phenomenon, without a parallel in the political world. It would exhibit a number of respectable States, as denying first that any power over the press was delegated by the Constitution; as proposing next, that an amendment to it, should explicitly declare that no such power was delegated; and finally, as concurring in an amendment actually recognizing or delegating such a power.

Is then the Federal government, it will be asked, destitute of every authority for restraining the licentiousness of the press, and for shielding itself against the libellous attacks which may be made on those who administer it? The Constitution alone can answer this question. If no such power be expressly delegated, and it be not both necessary and proper to carry into execution an express power; above all, if it be expressly forbidden by a declaratory amendment to the Constitution, the answer must be, that the Federal government is destitute of all such authority.

And might it not be asked in turn, whether it is not more probable, under all the circumstances which have been reviewed, that the authority should be withheld by the Constitution, than that it should be left to a vague and violent construction: whilst so much pains were bestowed in enumerating other powers, and so many less important powers are included in the enumeration.

Might it not be likewise asked, whether the anxious circumspection which dictated so many *peculiar* limitations on the general authority, would be unlikely to exempt the press altogether from that authority? The peculiar magnitude of some of the powers necessarily committed to the Federal government; the peculiar duration required for the functions of some of its departments; the peculiar distance of the seat of its proceedings from the great body of its constituents; and the peculiar difficulty of circulating an adequate knowledge of them through any other channel; will not these considerations, some or other of which produced other exceptions from the powers of ordinary governments, all together, account for the policy of binding the hand of the Federal government, from touching the channel which alone can give efficacy to its responsibility to its constituents; and of leaving those who administer it, to a remedy for injured reputations, under the same laws, and in the same tribunals, which protect their lives, their liberties, and their properties.

But the question does not turn either on the wisdom of the Constitution, or on the policy which gave rise to its particular organization. It turns on the actual meaning of the instrument; by which it has appeared, that a power over the press is clearly excluded, from the number of powers delegated to the Federal government.

III. And in the opinion of the committee well may it be said, as the resolution concludes with saying, that the unconstitutional power exercised over the press by the "Sedition Act," ought "more than anyother, to produce universal alarm; "because it is leveled against that right of freely examining "public characters and measures, and of free communication "among the people thereon, which has ever been justly deemed the only effectual guardian of every other right."

Without scrutinizing minutely into all the provisions of the "Sedition Act," it will be sufficient to cite so much of section 2. as follows: "And be it further enacted, that if any "person shall write, print, utter or publish, or shall cause or "procure to be written, printed, uttered or published, or shall "knowingly and willingly assist or aid in writing, printing, "uttering or publishing any false, scandalous, and malicious "writing or writings against the government of the United "States, or either house of the Congress of the United States, "or the President of the United States, *with an intent to de-* "*fame the said government, or either house of the said Con-* "*gress, or the President, or to bring them, or either of them,* "*into contempt or disrepute; or to excite against them, or ei-* "*ther, or any of them, the hatred of the good people of the* "*United States, &c. Then such person being thereof convicted* "*before any court of the United States, having jurisdiction*

"*thereof, shall be punished by a fine not exceeding two thou-*
"*sand dollars, and by imprisonment not exceeding two years.*"
On this part of the act the following observations present
themselves.

1. The Constitution supposes that the President, the Congress, and each of its houses, may not discharge their trusts,
either from defect of judgment, or other causes. Hence, they
are all made responsible to their constituents, at the returning periods of election; and the President, who is singly entrusted with very great powers, is, as a further guard, subjected to an intermediate impeachment.

2. Should it happen, as the Constitution supposes it may
happen, that either of these branches of the government, may
not have duly discharged its trust; it is natural and proper,
that according to the cause and degree of their faults, they
should be brought into contempt or disrepute, and incur the
hatred of the people.

3. Whether it has, in any case, happened that the proceedings of either, or all of those branches, evinces such a violation
of duty as to justify a contempt, a disrepute or hatred among
the people, can only be determined by a free examination
thereof, and a free communication among the people thereon.

4. Whenever it may have actually happened, that proceedings of this sort are chargeable on all or either of the branches
of the government, it is the duty as well as right of intelligent
and faithful citizens, to discuss and promulgate them freely, as
well to controul them by the censorship of the public opinion,
as to promote a remedy according to the rules of the Constitution. And it cannot be avoided, that those who are to apply
the remedy must feel, in some degree, a contempt or hatred
against the transgressing party.

5. As the act was passed on July 14, 1798, and is to be in
force until March 3, 1801, it was of course, that during its

continuance, two elections of the entire House of Representatives, an election of a part of the Senate, and an election of a President, were to take place.

6. That consequently, during all these elections, intended by the Constitution to preserve the purity, or to purge the faults of the administration, the great remedial rights of the people were to be exercised, and the responsibility of their public agents to be screened, under the penalities of this act.

May it not be asked of every intelligent friend to the liberties of his country whether, the power exercised in such an act as this, ought not to produce great and universal alarm? Whether a rigid execution of such an act, in time past, would not have repressed that information and communication among the people, which is indispensable to the just exercise of their electoral rights? And whether such an act, if made perpetual, and enforced with rigor, would not, in time to come, either destroy our free system of government, or prepare a convulsion that might prove equally fatal to it.

In answer to such questions, it has been pleaded that the writings and publications forbidden by the act, are those only which are false and malicious, and intended to defame; and merit is claimed for the privilege allowed to authors to justify, by proving the truth of their publications, and for the limitations to which the sentence of fine and imprisonment is subjected.

To those who concurred in the act, under the extraordinary belief, that the option lay between the passing of such an act, and leaving in force the common law of libels, which punishes truth equally with falsehood, and submits the fine and imprisonment to the indefinite discretion of the court, the merit of good intentions ought surely not to be refused. A like merit may perhaps be due for the discontinuance of the *corporal punishment* which the common law also leaves to the discretion of the court.—This merit of *intention*, however, would have been greater, if the several mitigations had not been limited to so short a period; and the apparent inconsistency would have been avoided, between justifying the act at one time, by contrasting it with the rigors of the common law, otherwise in force; and at another time by appealing to the nature of the crisis, as requiring the temporary rigor exerted by the act.

But whatever may have been the meritorious intentions of all or any who contributed to the Sedition Act, a very few reflections will prove, that its baneful tendency is little diminished by the privilege of giving in evidence the truth of the matter contained in political writings.

In the first place, where simple and naked facts alone are in question, there is sufficient difficulty in some cases, and sufficient trouble and vexation in all, of meeting a prosecution from the government, with the full and formal proof, necessary in a court of law.

But in the next place, it must be obvious to the plainest minds; that opinions, and inferences, and conjectural observations, are not only in many cases inseparable from the facts, but may often be more the objects of the prosecution than the facts themselves; or may even be altogether abstracted from particular facts; and that opinions and inferences, and conjectural observations, cannot be subjects of that kind of proof which appertains to facts, before a court of law.

Again, it is no less obvious, that the *intent* to defame or bring into contempt or disrepute, or hatred, which is made a condition of the offence created by the act; cannot prevent its pernicious influence, on the freedom of the press. For omitting the enquiry, how far the malice of the intent is an inference of the law from the mere publication; it is manifestly impossible to punish the intent to bring those who administer the government into disrepute or contempt, without striking at the right of freely discussing public characters and measures: because those who engage in such discussions, must expect and *intend* to excite these unfavorable sentiments, so far as they may be thought to be deserved. To prohibit therefore the intent to excite those unfavorable sentiments against those who administer the government, is equivalent to a prohibition of the actual excitement of them; and to prohibit the actual excitement of them, is equivalent to a prohibition of discussions having that tendency and effect; which, again, is equivalent to a protection of those who administer the government, if they should at any time deserve the contempt or hatred of the people, against being exposed to it, by free animadversions on their characters and conduct. Nor can there be a doubt, if those in public trust be shielded by penal laws from such strictures of the press, as may expose them to contempt or disrepute, or hatred, where they may deserve it, that in exact proportion as they may deserve to be exposed, will be the certainty and criminality of the intent to expose them, and the vigilance of prosecuting and punishing it; nor a doubt, that a government thus intrenched in penal statutes, against the just and natural effects of a culpable administration, will easily evade the responsibility, which is essential to a faithful discharge of its duty.

Let it be recollected, lastly, that the right of electing the members of the government, constitutes more particularly the essence of a free and responsible government. The value and efficacy of this right, depends on the knowledge of the comparative merits and demerits of the candidates for public trust; and on the equal freedom, consequently, of examining and discussing these merits and demerits of the candidates respectively. It has been seen that a number of important elections will take place whilst the act is in force; although it should not be continued beyond the term to which it is limited. Should there happen, then, as is extremely probable in relation to some or other of the branches of the government, to be competition between those who are, and those who are not, members of the government; what will be the situations of the competitors? Not equal; because the characters of the former will be covered by the "Sedition Act" from animadversions exposing them to disrepute among the people; whilst the latter may be exposed to the contempt and hatred of the people, without a violation of the act? What will be the situation of the people? Not free; because they will be compelled to make their election between competitors, whose pretensions they are not permitted by the act, equally to examine, to discuss, and to ascertain. And from both these situations, will not those in power derive an undue advantage for continuing themselves in it; which by impairing the right of election, endangers the blessings of the government founded on it.

It is with justice, therefore, that the General Assembly hath affirmed in the resolution, as well that the right of freely examining public characters and measures, and of free communication thereon, is the only effectual guardian of every other right; as that this particular right is leveled at, by the power exercised in the "Sedition Act."

The resolution next in order is as follows:

That this State having by its Convention, which ratified the Federal Constitution, expressly declared, that among other essential rights, "the liberty of conscience and of the press cannot be cancelled, abridged, restrained or modified by any authority of the United States," and from its extreme anxiety to guard these rights from every possible attack of sophistry and ambition, having with other States, recommended an amendment for that purpose, which amendment was, in due, time, annexed to the Constitution; it would mark a reproachful inconsistency, and criminal degeneracy, if an indifference were not shewn, to the most palpable violation of one of the rights, thus declared and secured; and to the establishment of a precedent, which may be fatal to the other.

To place this resolution in its just light, it will be necessary to recur to the act of ratification by Virginia which stands in the ensuing form.

We, the Delegates of the people of Virginia, duly elected in pursuance of a recommendation from the General Assembly, and now met in Convention, having fully and freely investigated and discussed the proceedings of the federal convention, and being prepared as well as the most mature deliberation hath enabled us, to decide thereon; DO, in the name and in behalf of the people of Virginia, declare and make known, that the powers granted under the Constitution, being derived from the people of the United States, may be resumed by them, whensoever the same shall be perverted to their injury or oppression; and that every power not granted thereby, remains with them, and at their will. That therefore, no right of any denomination can be cancelled, abridged, restrained or modified, by the Congress, by the Senate or House of Representatives acting in any capacity, by the President, or any department or officer of the United States, except in those instances in which power is given by the Constitution for those purposes; and, that among other essential rights, the liberty of conscience and of the press, cannot be cancelled, abridged, restrained or modified by any authority of the United States.

Here is an express and solemn declaration by the convention of the State, that they ratified the Constitution in the sense, that no right of any denomination can be cancelled, abridged, restrained or modified by the government of the United States or any part of it; except in those instances in which power is given by the Constitution; and in the sense

216

particularly, "that among other essential rights, the liberty of conscience and freedom of the press cannot be cancelled, abridged, restrained or modified, by any authority of the United States."

Words could not well express, in a fuller or more forcible manner, the understanding of the convention, that the liberty of conscience and the freedom of the press, were *equally* and *completely* exempted from all authority whatever of the United States.

Under an anxiety to guard more effectually these rights against every possible danger, the convention, after ratifying the Constitution, proceeded to prefix to certain amendments proposed by them, a declaration of rights, in which are two articles providing, the one for the liberty of conscience, the other for the freedom of speech and of the press.

Similar recommendations having proceeded from a number of other States; and Congress, as has been seen, having in consequence thereof, and with a view to extend the ground of public confidence, proposed among other declaratory and restrictive clauses, a clause expressly securing the liberty of conscience and of the press; and Virginia having concurred in the ratifications which made them a part of the Constitution; it will remain with a candid public to decide, whether it would not mark an inconsistency and degeneracy, if an indifference were now shewn to a palpable violation of one of those rights, the freedom of the press; and to a precedent therein, which may be fatal to the other, the free exercise of religion.

That the precedent established by the violation of the former of these rights, may, as is affirmed by the resolution, be fatal to the latter, appears to be demonstrable, by a comparison of the grounds on which they respectively rest; and from the scope of reasoning, by which the power over the former has been vindicated.

First. Both of these rights, the liberty of conscience and of the press, rest equally on the original ground of not being delegated by the Constitution, and consequently withheld from the government. Any construction therefore, that would attack this original security for the one must have the like effect on the other.

Secondly. They are both equally secured by the supplement to the Constitution; being both included in the same amendment, made at the same time, and by the same authority. Any construction or argument then which would turn the amendment into a grant or acknowledgment of power with respect to the press, might be equally applied to the freedom of religion.

Thirdly. If it be admitted that the extent of the freedom of the press secured by the amendment, is to be measured by the common law on this subject; the same authority may be resorted to, for the standard which is to fix the extent of the "free exercise of religion." It cannot be necessary to say what this standard would be; whether the common law be taken solely as the unwritten, or as varied by the written, law of England.

Fourthly. If the words and phrases in the amendment, are to be considered as chosen with a studied discrimination, which yields an argument for a power over the press, under the limitation that its freedom be not abridged; the same argument results from the same consideration, for a power over the exercise of religion, under the limitation that its freedom be not prohibited.

For if Congress may regulate the freedom of the press, provided they do not abridge it: because it is said only, "they shall not abridge it;" and is not said, "they shall make no law respecting it:" the analogy of reasoning is conclusive, that Congress may *regulate* and even *abridge* the free exercise of religion; provided they do not *prohibit* it; because it is said only "they shall not prohibit it;" and is *not* said "they shall make no law *respecting* or no law *abridging* it."

The General Assembly were governed by the clearest reason, then, in considering the "Sedition Act," which legislates on the freedom of the press, as establishing a precedent that may be fatal to the liberty of conscience and it will be the duty of all, in proportion as they value the security of the latter, to take the alarm at every encroachment on the former.

The two concluding resolutions only remain to be examined. They are in the words following.

"That the good people of this commonwealth, having ever "felt, and continuing to feel the most sincere affection for "their brethren of the other States; the truest anxiety for estab- "lishing and perpetuating the union of all; and the most "scrupulous fidelity to that Constitution, which is the pledge "of mutual friendship, and the instrument of mutual happi- "ness; the General Assembly doth solemnly appeal to the like "dispositions in the other States, in confidence that they will "concur with this commonwealth in declaring, as it does "hereby declare, that the acts aforesaid, are unconstitutional; "and, that the necessary and proper measures will be taken "by each, for co-operating with this State, in maintaining un- "impaired, the authorities, rights, and liberties, reserved to the "States respectively, or to the People."

"That the Governor be desired, to transmit a copy of the "foregoing resolutions to the executive authority of each of "the other States, with a request that the same may be com- "municated to the Legislature thereof; and that a copy be fur- "nished to each of the Senators and Representatives represent- "ing this State in the Congress of the United States."

The fairness and regularity of the course of proceeding,

here pursued, have not protected it, against objections even from sources too respectable to be disregarded.

It has been said that it belongs to the judiciary of the United States, and not to the State legislatures, to declare the meaning of the Federal Constitution.

But a declaration that proceedings of the Federal government are not warranted by the Constitution, is a novelty neither among the citizens, nor among the legislatures of the States; nor are the citizens or the legislature of Virginia, singular in the example of it.

Nor can the declarations of either, whether affirming or denying the constitutionality of measures of the Federal government; or whether made before or after judicial decisions thereon, be deemed, in any point of view, an assumption of the office of the judge. The declarations in such cases, are expressions of opinion, unaccompanied with any other effect, than what they may produce on opinion, by exciting reflection. The expositions of the judiciary, on the other hand, are carried into immediate effect by force. The former may lead to a change in the legislative expression of the general will; possibly to a change in the opinion of the judiciary: the latter enforces the general will, whilst that will and that opinion continue unchanged.

And if there be no impropriety in declaring the unconstitutionality of proceedings in the Federal government; where can be the impropriety of communicating the declaration to other States, and inviting their concurrence in a like declaration? What is allowable for one, must be allowable for all; and a free communication among the States, where the Constitution imposes no restraint, is as allowable among the State governments, as among other public bodies, or private citizens. This consideration derives a weight, that cannot be denied to it, from the relation of the state legislatures, to the federal legislature, as the immediate constituents of one of its branches.

The legislatures of the States have a right also, to originate amendments to the Constitution, by a concurrence of two thirds of the whole number, in applications to Congress for the purpose. When new States are to be formed by a junction of two or more States, or parts of States, the legislatures of the States concerned, are, as well as Congress, to concur in the measure. The States have a right also, to enter into agreements, or compacts, with the consent of Congress. On all such cases, a communication among them, results from the object which is common to them.

It is lastly to be seen, whether the confidence expressed by the resolution, that the *necessary and proper measures*, would be taken by the other States, for co-operating with Virginia, in maintaining the rights reserved to the States, or to the people, be in any degree liable to the objections which have been raised against it.

If it be liable to objection, it must be, because either the object, or the means, are objectionable.

The object being to maintain what the Constitution has ordained, is in itself a laudable object.

The means are expressed in the terms "the necessary and proper measures." A proper object was to be pursued, by means both necessary and proper.

To find an objection then, it must be shewn, that some meaning was annexed to these general terms, which was not proper; and for this purpose, either that the means used by the General Assembly, were an example of improper means, or that there were no proper means to which the terms could refer.

In the example given by the State, of declaring the Alien and Sedition Acts to be unconstitutional, and of communicating the declaration to the other States, no trace of improper means has appeared. And if the other States had concurred in making a like declaration, supported too by the numerous applications flowing immediately from the people, it can scarcely be doubted, that these simple means would have been as sufficient, as they are unexceptionable.

It is no less certain, that other means might have been employed, which are strictly within the limits of the Constitution. The legislatures of the States might have made a direct representation to Congress, with a view to obtain a rescinding of the two offensive acts; or they might have represented to their respective senators in Congress, their wish, that two thirds thereof would propose an explanatory amendment to the Constitution; or two thirds of themselves, if such had been their option, might, by an application to Congress, have obtained a convention for the same object.

These several means, though not equally eligible in themselves, nor probably, to the States, were all constitutionally open for consideration. And if the General Assembly, after declaring the two acts to be unconstitutional, the first and most obvious proceeding on the subject, did not undertake to point out to the other States, a choice among the farther measures that might become necessary and proper, the reserve will not be misconstrued by liberal minds, into any culpable imputation.

These observations appear to form a satisfactory reply, to every objection which is not founded on a misconception of the terms, employed in the resolutions. There is one other however, which may be of too much importance not to be added. It cannot be forgotten, that among the arguments addressed to those, who apprehended danger to liberty, from the establishment of the general government over so great a country; the appeal was emphatically made to the intermediate existence of the State governments, between the people and that government, to the vigilance with which they would descry the first symptoms of usurpation, and to the promptitude with which they would sound the alarm to the public. This argument was probably not without its effect; and if it was a proper one, then, to recommend the establishment of the Constitution; it must be a proper one now, to assist in its interpretation.

The only part of the two concluding resolutions, that remain to be noticed, is the repetition in the first, of that warm affection to the union and its members, and of that scrupulous fidelity to the Constitution which have been invaribly felt by the people of this State. As the proceedings were introduced with these sentiments, they could not be more properly closed, than in the same manner. Should there be any so far misled, as to call in question the sincerity of these professions, whatever regret may be excited by the error, the General Assembly cannot descend into a discussion of it. Those who have listened to the suggestion, can only be left to their own recollection, of the part which this State has borne in the establishment of our national independence; in the establishment of our national Constitution; and in maintaining under it, the authority and laws of the union, without a single exception of internal resistance or commotion. By recurring to these facts, they will be able to convince themselves, that the representatives of the people of Virginia must be above the necessity of opposing any other shield to attacks on their national patriotism, than their own consciousness and the justice of an enlightened public; who will perceive in the resolutions themselves, the strongest evidence of attachment both to the Constitution and to the union, since it is only by maintaining the different governments and departments within their respective limits, that the blessings of either can be perpetuated.

The extensive view of the subject thus taken by the committee, has led them to report to the house, as the result of the whole, the following resolution.

Resolved, That the General Assembly, having carefully and respectfully attended to the proceedings of a number of the States, in answer to their resolutions of December 21, 1798, and having accurately and fully re-examined and re-considered the latter, find it to be their indispensable duty to adhere to the same, as founded in truth, as consonant with the Constitution, and as conducive to its preservation; and more especially to be their duty, to renew, as they do hereby renew, their protest against "the Alien and Sedition Acts," as palpable and alarming infractions of the Constitution.

☆   ☆   ☆

A motion was then made, and the question being put, that the House do agree to the report of the committee?

It passed in the affirmative.

"On the state of the commonwealth;" being read,

Ordered, that the same be put off until to-morrow.

And then the House adjourned 'till to-morrow morning ten o'clock.

THOMAS JEFFERSON
ON CONSTITUTIONAL
ISSUES

☆ ☆ ☆ ☆ ☆ ☆ ☆ ☆ ☆ ☆ ☆ ☆ ☆

THOMAS JEFFERSON ON CONSTITUTIONAL ISSUES

INTRODUCTION

THE writings of Thomas Jefferson offer an important historical commentary on the problems of limited, constitutional government. They present the views of a man who was well versed in political theory and practical politics and active in the national government during the formative years of the American republic. They also provide the reflections of an elder statesman who after he had retired from the political arena never withdrew his interest nor his attention from the problems of the new nation.

The selections here presented from Jefferson's extensive published papers have been chosen in an effort to group in a short publication some of the basic statements and significant reflections which Jefferson made on constitutional issues at various periods of his life. These writings reflect but one segment of Jefferson's total political philosophy and should be read with the knowledge that Jefferson's emphasis on limited government was firmly rooted in his devotion to the principle—not shared by all of his contemporaries—that the people had the right and the capacity to govern themselves.

Jefferson's faith in the American experiment was great. He considered his efforts in its behalf as labors "in the holy cause of freedom"; and he told his neighbors in Albemarle County shortly before assuming the office of Secretary of State in 1790: "It rests now with ourselves alone to enjoy in peace and concord the blessings of self-government, so long denied to mankind: to shew by example the sufficiency of human reason for the care of human affairs and that the will of the majority, the Natural law of every society, is the only sure guardian of the rights of man."

227

Jefferson had no part in the writing of the Constitution, nor did he participate in the contest attending its ratification. As American minister to France, the author of the Declaration of Independence was in Paris from 1784 to late 1789, the years during which the movement for a new constitution took form and the Constitution was written and adopted. Being thus removed from the immediate scene, Jefferson's reaction to the Constitution was unusually free from the involvements of domestic politics. The best summary of Jefferson's views on the Constitution at the time when ratification was pending is found in a famous letter to James Madison, December 20, 1787 (Document I). The Constitution was, he concluded in a subsequent letter, "a good canvas, on which some strokes only want retouching." Much of the retouching which Jefferson wanted was soon accomplished by the first ten amendments.

As Secretary of State under President Washington, Jefferson was directly involved in the implementation of the new instrument of government, and he early displayed a strict-constructionist position. Jefferson's opinion on the constitutionality of a national bank (Document II) advanced a rigid interpretation of the Constitution. His reasoning failed, however, to convince Washington, who accepted Alexander Hamilton's arguments in support of implied powers and signed the bill creating the Bank of the United States.

As the presidential campaign of 1800 approached, Candidate Jefferson expounded his constitutional and political views to numerous correspondents. His concept of limited government was clearly emphasized, although he did not go so far in stressing the powers of the States in his letters as he had gone in the Kentucky Resolutions of 1798, which he had secretly authored. Jefferson's letter to Massachusetts' politically prominent Elbridge Gerry (Document III) contains one of Jefferson's best statements on his basic political and constitutional creed and foreshadows his first inaugural address of 1801. He expanded further on the theory of the federal form of government and the dangers of centralization in a letter to Connecticut Jeffersonian Republican leader Gideon Granger in 1800 (Document IV).

During his Presidency, Jefferson was faced with a major constitutional question in 1803 in regard to the power of the national government to acquire the Louisiana territory. The President clearly favored a constitutional amendment to authorize the transaction, but he was persuaded to proceed without such action by the exigencies of the moment—particularly the danger that Napoleon might withdraw his offer if closing of the agreement were delayed by the slow process of amendment. Congress in ratifying the act, Jefferson concluded, must "throw themselves on their country for doing for them unauthorized what we know they would have done for themselves had they been in a situation to do it." The President's struggle with this issue is vividly revealed in a letter to Senator Wilson Cary Nicholas of Virginia (Document V).

In the years of his retirement, as younger leaders of the Republican party after the War of 1812 adopted a more nationalistic program than that of the old Jeffersonian Republican party, the ex-President became increasingly concerned about the constitutional relationships between the States and the national government. The Federal judiciary, in particular, became a subject of considerable concern. As the Supreme Court under Chief Justice John Marshall gave judicial sanction to the doctrine of implied powers—using the same arguments that Hamilton had used to defend the first national bank—and in a series of decisions went far to strengthen the national government at the expense of the States, Jefferson's correspondence became increasingly filled with expressions of alarm over judicial usurpation and Federal encroachment on State powers. One correspondent was Judge Spencer Roane of the Supreme Court of Appeals of Virginia (Documents VI and VII). Roane was likewise a strict constructionist who was an outspoken critic of what he too regarded as usurpation by the Supreme Court of the United States under Marshall.

Another Virginia defender of States' rights and strict construction, to whom Jefferson gave his endorsement, was John Taylor of Caroline. Taylor's book *Construction Construed and Constitutions Vindicated* (Richmond, 1820) received a rare public recommendation from the ex-President (Documents IX and X). About the same time, Jefferson took strong exception to portions of a book entitled *The Republican* (Pittsfield, Mass., 1820) written by William C. Jarvis, and in a letter to the Massachusetts author he discussed the role of the judiciary under republican government and emphasized that there was "no safe depository of the ultimate powers of the society but the people themselves" (Document VIII).

229

One of Jefferson's most extended discussions in regard to the Supreme Court is found in an 1823 letter to Justice William Johnson whom Jefferson as President had appointed to the Supreme Court (Document XI). It is clear that at the end of his life Jefferson was much concerned about the growing consolidation of national power and the usurpation of State authority. Six months before his death, he wrote to William B. Giles, a political comrade of many years past who was re-emerging as a leading champion of States' rights in Virginia: "I see, as you do, and with the deepest affliction, the rapid strides with which the federal branch of our government is advancing towards usurpation of all the rights reserved to the States, and the consolidation in itself of all powers, foreign and domestic . . ." (Document XII). Jefferson's final political legacy was thus a defense of States' rights; and, though the words of the aged Sage of Monticello were more passionate than at an earlier date, they were not inconsistent with the basic views on limited government which had always formed a part of his political creed. Nor is there any evidence to suggest that Jefferson had lost faith in "the holy cause of freedom" nor in the principles of self-government so eloquently expressed to his Albemarle neighbors more than three decades before when the Constitution was in its infancy.

The texts here reproduced are extracted from *The Writings of Thomas Jefferson*, edited by Paul Leicester Ford (10 volumes, New York, 1892-99).

☆ ☆ ☆ ☆ ☆ ☆ ☆ ☆ ☆ ☆ ☆ ☆ ☆

I

TO JAMES MADISON

Paris Dec. 20, 1787.

* * *

THE season admitting only of operations in the Cabinet, and these being in a great measure secret, I have little to fill a letter. I will therefore make up the deficiency by adding a few words on the Constitution proposed by our Convention. I like much the general idea of framing a government which should go on of itself peaceably, without needing continual recurrence to the State legislatures. I like the organization of the government into Legislative, Judiciary & Executive. I like the power given the Legislature to levy taxes, and for that reason solely approve of the greater house being chosen by the people directly. For tho' I think a house chosen by them will be very illy qualified to legislate for the Union, for foreign nations &c. yet this evil does not weigh against the good of preserving inviolate the fundamental principle that the people are not to be taxed but by representatives chosen immediately by themselves. I am captivated by the compromise of the opposite claims of the great & little States, of the latter to equal, and the former to proportional influence. I am much pleased too with the substitution of the method of voting by persons, instead of that of voting by States: and I like the negative given to the Executive with a third of either house, though I should have liked it better had the Judiciary been

231

associated for that purpose, or invested with a similar and separate power. There are other good things of less moment. I will now add what I do not like. First the omission of a bill of rights providing clearly & without the aid of sophisms for freedom of religion, freedom of the press, protection against standing armies, restriction against monopolies, the eternal & unremitting force of the habeas corpus laws, and trials by jury in all matters of fact triable by the laws of the land & not by the law of nations. To say, as Mr. Wilson does that a bill of rights was not necessary because all is reserved in the case of the general government which is not given, while in the particular ones all is given which is not reserved, might do for the audience to whom it was addressed, but is surely a gratis dictum, opposed by strong inferences from the body of the instrument, as well as from the omission of the clause of our present confederation which had declared that in express terms. It was a hard conclusion to say because there has been no uniformity among States as to the cases triable by jury, because some have been so incautious as to abandon this mode of trial, therefore the more prudent States shall be reduced to the same level of calamity. It would have been much more just & wise to have concluded the other way that as most of the States had judiciously preserved this palladium, those who had wandered should be brought back to it, and to have established general right instead of general wrong. Let me add that a bill of rights is what the people are entitled to against every government on earth, general or particular, & what no just government should refuse, or rest on inferences. The second feature I dislike, and greatly dislike, is the abandonment in every instance of the necessity of rotation in office, and most particularly in the case of the President. Experience concurs with reason in concluding that the first magistrate will always be re-elected if the Constitution permits it. He is then an officer for life. This once observed, it becomes of so much consequence to certain nations to have a friend or a foe at the head of our affairs that they will interfere with money & with arms. A Galloman or an Angloman will be supported by the nation he befriends. If once elected, and at a second or third election outvoted by one or two votes, he will pretend false votes, foul play, hold possession of the reins of government, be supported by the States voting for him, especially if they are the central ones lying in a compact body themselves & separating their opponents: and they will be aided by one nation of Europe, while the majority are aided by another. The election of a President of America some years hence will be much more interesting to certain nations of Europe than ever the election of a king of Poland was. Reflect on all the instances in history ancient & modern, of elective monarchies, and say if they do not give foundation for my fears. The Roman emperors, the popes, while they were of any importance, the German emperors till they became hereditary in practice, the kings of Poland, the Deys of the Ottoman dependances. It may be said that if elections are to be attended with these disorders, the seldomer they are renewed the better. But experience shews that the only way to prevent disorder is to render them uninteresting by frequent changes. An incapacity to be elected a second time would have been the only effectual preventative. The power of removing him every fourth year by the vote of the people is a power which will not be exercised. The king of Poland is removeable every day by the Diet, yet he is never removed.—Smaller objections are the Appeal in fact as well as law, and the binding all persons Legislative Executive & Judiciary by oath to maintain that constitution. I do not pretend to decide what would be the best method of procuring the establishment of the manifold good things in this constitution, and of getting rid of the bad.

Whether by adopting it in hopes of future amendment, or, after it has been duly weighed & canvassed by the people, after seeing the parts they generally dislike, & those they generally approve, to say to them 'We see now what you wish. Send together your deputies again, let them frame a constitution for you omitting what you have condemned, & establishing the powers you approve. Even these will be a great addition to the energy of your government.'—At all events I hope you will not be discouraged from other trials, if the present one should fail of its full effect.—I have thus told you freely what I like & dislike: merely as a matter of curiosity, for I know your own judgment has been formed on all these points after having heard everything which could be urged on them. I own I am not a friend to a very energetic government. It is always oppressive. The late rebellion in Massachusetts has given more alarm than I think it should have done. Calculate that one rebellion in 13 States in the course of 11 years, is but one for each State in a century & a half. No country should be so long without one. Nor will any degree of power in the hands of government prevent insurrections. France, with all its despotism, and two or three hundred thousand men always in arms has had three insurrections in the three years I have been here, in every one of which greater numbers were engaged than in Massachusetts & a great deal more blood was spilt. In Turkey, which Montesquieu supposes more despotic, insurrections are the events of every day. In England, where the hand of power is lighter than here, but heavier than with us, they happen every half dozen years. Compare again the ferocious depredations of their insurgents with the order, the moderation & the almost self extinguishment of ours.— After all, it is my principle that the will of the majority should always prevail. If they approve the proposed Convention in all its parts, I shall concur in it cheerfully, in hopes that they will amend it whenever they shall find it work wrong. I think our governments will remain virtuous for many centuries; as long as they are chiefly agricultural; and this will be as long as there shall be vacant lands in any part of America. When they get piled upon one another in large cities, as in Europe, they will become corrupt as in Europe. Above all things I hope the education of the common people will be attended to; convinced that on their good sense we may rely with the most security for the preservation of a due degree of liberty. I have tired you by this time with my disquisitions & will therefore only add assurances of the sincerity of those sentiments of esteem & attachment with which I am Dear Sir your affectionate friend & servant.

P.S. The instability of our laws is really an immense evil. I think it would be well to provide in our constitutions that there shall always be a twelve-month between the ingrossing a bill & passing it: that it should then be offered to its passage without changing a word: and that if circumstances should be thought to require a speedier passage, it should take two thirds of both houses instead of a bare majority.

II

OPINION ON THE CONSTITUTIONALITY OF A NATIONAL BANK

February 15, 1791.

The bill for establishing a National Bank undertakes among other things:—

1. To form the subscribers into a corporation.
2. To enable them in their corporate capacities to receive grants of land; and so far is against the laws of *Mortmain*.
3. To make alien subscribers capable of holding lands; and so far is against the laws of *Alienage*.
4. To transmit these lands, on the death of a proprietor, to a certain line of successors; and so far changes the course of *Descents*.
5. To put the lands out of the reach of forfeiture or escheat; and so far is against the laws of *Forfeiture and Escheat*.
6. To transmit personal chattels to successors in a certain line; and so far is against the laws of *Distribution*.
7. To give them the sole and exclusive right of banking under the national authority; and so far is against the laws of *Monopoly*.
8. To communicate to them a power to make laws paramount to the laws of the States: for so they must be construed, to protect the institution from the control of the State legislatures; and so, probably, they will be construed.

I consider the foundation of the Constitution as laid on this ground: That "all powers not delegated to the United States, by the Constitution, nor prohibited by it to the States, are reserved to the States [respectively] or to the people." To take a single step beyond the boundaries thus specially drawn around the powers of Congress, is to take possession of a boundless field of power, no longer susceptible of any definition.

The incorporation of a bank, and the powers assumed by this bill, have not, in my opinion, been delegated to the United States, by the Constitution.

I. They are not among the powers specially enumerated: for these are: 1st. A power to lay taxes for the purpose of paying the debts of the United States; but no debt is paid by this bill, nor any tax laid. Were it a bill to raise money, its origination in the Senate would condemn it by the Constitution.

2d. "To borrow money." But this bill neither borrows money nor ensures the borrowing it. The proprietors of the bank will be just as free as any other money holders, to lend or not to lend their money to the public. The operation proposed in the bill, first, to lend them two millions, and then to borrow them back again, cannot change the nature of the latter act, which will still be a payment, and not a loan, call it by what name you please.

3. To "regulate commerce with foreign nations, and among the States, and with the Indian tribes." To erect a bank, and to regulate commerce, are very different acts. He who erects a bank, creates a subject of commerce in its bills; so does he who makes a bushel of wheat, or digs a dollar out of the mines; yet neither of these persons regulates commerce thereby. To make a thing which may be bought and sold, is not to prescribe regulations for buying and selling. Besides, if this was an exercise of the power of regulating commerce, it would be void, as extending as much to the internal commerce of every State, as to its external. For the power given to Congress by the Constitution does not extend to the internal regulation of the commerce of a State, (that is to say of the commerce between citizen and citizen,) which remain exclusively with

its own legislature; but to its external commerce only, that is to say, its commerce with another State, or with foreign nations, or with the Indian tribes. Accordingly the bill does not propose the measure as a regulation of trade, but as "productive of considerable advantages to trade." Still less are these powers covered by any other of the special enumerations.

II. Nor are they within either of the general phrases, which are the two following:—

1. To lay taxes to provide for the general welfare of the United States, that is to say, "to lay taxes for *the purpose* of providing for the general welfare." For the laying of taxes is the *power*, and the general welfare the *purpose* for which the power is to be exercised. They are not to lay taxes *ad libitum for any purpose they please;* but only *to pay the debts or provide for the welfare of the Union.* In like manner, they are not *to do anything they please* to provide for the general welfare, but only to *lay taxes* for that purpose. To consider the latter phrase, not as describing the purpose of the first, but as giving a distinct and independent power to do any act they please, which might be for the good of the Union, would render all the preceding and subsequent enumerations of power completely useless.

It would reduce the whole instrument to a single phrase, that of instituting a Congress with power to do whatever would be for the good of the United States; and, as they would be the sole judges of the good or evil, it would be also a power to do whatever evil they please.

It is an established rule of construction where a phrase will bear either of two meanings, to give it that which will allow some meaning to the other parts of the instrument, and not that which would render all the others useless. Certainly no such universal power was meant to be given them. It was intended to lace them up straitly within the enumerated powers, and those without which, as means, these powers could not be carried into effect. It is known that the very power now proposed *as a means* was rejected as *an end* by the Convention which formed the Constitution. A proposition was made to them to authorize Congress to open canals, and an amendatory one to empower them to incorporate. But the whole was rejected, and one of the reasons for rejection urged in debate was, that then they would have a power to erect a bank, which would render the great cities, where there were prejudices and jealousies on the subject, adverse to the reception of the Constitution.

2. The second general phrase is, "to make all laws *necessary* and proper for carrying into execution the enumerated powers." But they can all be carried into execution without a bank. A bank therefore is not *necessary*, and consequently not authorized by this phrase.

It has been urged that a bank will give great facility or convenience in the collection of taxes. Suppose this were true: yet the Constitution allows only the means which are *"necessary,"* not those which are merely "convenient" for effecting the enumerated powers. If such a latitude of construction be allowed to this phrase as to give any non-enumerated power, it will go to every one, for there is not one which ingenuity may not torture into a *convenience* in some instance *or other*, to *some one* of so long a list of enumerated powers. It would swallow up all the delegated powers, and reduce the whole to one power, as before observed. Therefore it was that the Constitution restrained them to the *necessary* means, that is to say, to those means without which the grant of power would be nugatory.

But let us examine this convenience and see what it is. The report on this subject, page 3, states the only *general* convenience to be, the preventing the transportation and re-transportation of money between the States and the treasury, (for I pass over the increase of circulating medium, ascribed to it as a want, and which, according to my ideas of paper money, is clearly a demerit.) Every State will have to pay a sum of tax money into the treasury; and the treasury will have to pay, in every State, a part of the interest on the public debt, and salaries to the officers of government resident in that State. In most of the States there will still be a surplus of tax money to come up to the seat of government for the officers residing there. The payments of interest and salary in each State may be made by treasury orders on the State collector. This will take up the greater part of the money he has collected in his State, and consequently prevent the great mass of it from being drawn out of the State. If there be a balance of commerce in favor of that State against the one in which the government resides, the surplus of taxes will be remitted by the bills of exchange drawn for that commercial balance. And so it must be if there was a bank. But if there be no balance of commerce, either direct or circuitous, all the banks in the world could not bring up the surplus of taxes but in the form of money. Treasury orders then, and bills of exchange may prevent the displacement of the main mass of the money collected, without the aid of any bank; and where these fail, it cannot be prevented even with that aid.

Perhaps, indeed, bank bills may be a more *convenient* vehicle than treasury orders. But a little *difference* in the degree of *convenience*, cannot constitute the necessity which the Constitution makes the ground for assuming any non-enumerated power.

Besides; the existing banks will, without a doubt, enter into arrangements for lending their agency, and the more favorable, as there will be a competition among them for it; whereas the bill delivers us up bound to the national bank, who are free to refuse all arrangement, but on their own terms, and the public not free, on such refusal, to employ any other bank. That of Philadelphia, I believe, now does this business, by their post-notes, which, by an arrangement with the treasury, are paid by any State collector to whom they are presented. This expedient alone suffices to prevent the existence of that *necessity* which may justify the assumption of a non-enumerated power as a means for carrying into effect an enumerated one. The thing may be done, and has been done, and well done, without this assumption; therefore, it does not stand on that degree of *necessity* which can honestly justify it.

It may be said that a bank whose bills would have a currency all over the States, would be more convenient than one whose currency is limited to a single State. So it would be still more convenient that there should be a bank, whose bills should have a currency all over the world. But it does not follow from this superior conveniency, that there exists anywhere a power to establish such a bank; or that the world may not go on very well without it.

Can it be thought that the Constitution intended that for a shade or two of *convenience*, more or less, Congress should be authorised to break down the most ancient and fundamental laws of the several States; such as those against Mortmain, the laws of Alienage, the rules of descent, the acts of distribution, the laws of escheat and forfeiture, the laws of monopoly? Nothing but a necessity invincible by any other means, can justify such a prostitution of laws, which constitute the pillars of our whole system of jurisprudence. Will Congress be too strait-laced to carry the Constitution into honest effect, unless they may pass over the foundation-laws of the State government for the slightest convenience of theirs?

The negative of the President is the shield provided by the Constitution to protect against the invasions of the legislature:

1. The right of the Executive. 2. Of the Judiciary. 3. Of the States and State legislatures. The present is the case of a right remaining exclusively with the States, and consequently one of those intended by the Constitution to be placed under its protection.

It must be added, however, that unless the President's mind on a view of everything which is urged for and against this bill, is tolerably clear that it is unauthorised by the Constitution; if the pro and the con hang so even as to balance his judgment, a just respect for the wisdom of the legislature would naturally decide the balance in favor of their opinion. It is chiefly for cases where they are clearly misled by error, ambition, or interest, that the Constitution has placed a check in the negative of the President.

III

TO ELBRIDGE GERRY

Philadelphia, Jan 26, 1799.

* * *

I do then, with sincere zeal, wish an inviolable preservation of our present federal constitution, according to the true sense in which it was adopted by the States, that in which it was advocated by its friends, & not that which its enemies apprehended, who therefore became its enemies; and I am opposed to the monarchising its features by the forms of its administration, with a view to conciliate a first transition to a President & Senate for life, & from that to a hereditary tenure of these offices, & thus to worm out the elective principle. I am for preserving to the States the powers not yielded by them to the Union, & to the legislature of the Union its constitutional share in the division of powers; and I am not for transferring all the powers of the States to the general government, & all those of that government to the Executive branch. I am for a government rigorously frugal & simple, applying all the possible savings of the public revenue to the discharge of the national debt; and not for a multiplication of officers & salaries merely to make partisans, & for increasing, by every device, the public debt, on the principle of its being a public blessing. I am for relying, for internal defence, on our militia solely, till actual invasion, and for such a naval force only as may protect our coasts and harbors from such depredations as we have experienced; and not for a standing army in time of peace, which may overawe the public sentiment; nor for a navy, which, by its own expenses and the eternal wars in which it will implicate us, will grind us with public burthens, & sink us under them. I am for free commerce with all nations; political connection with none; & little or no diplomatic establishment. And I am not for linking ourselves by new treaties with the quarrels of Europe; entering that field of slaughter to preserve their balance, or joining in the confederacy of kings to war against the principles of liberty. I am for freedom of religion, & against all maneuvres to bring about a legal ascendancy of one sect over another: for freedom of the press, & against all violations of the Constitution to silence by force & not by reason the complaints or criticisms, just or unjust, of our citizens against the conduct of their agents. And I am for encouraging the progress of science in all its branches; and not for raising a hue and cry against the sacred name of philosophy; for awing the human mind by stories of raw-head & bloody bones to a distrust of its own vision, & to repose implicitly on that of others; to go backwards instead of forwards to look for improvement; to believe that government, religion, morality, & every other science were in the highest perfection in ages of the darkest ignorance, and that nothing can ever be devised more perfect than what was established by our forefathers. To these I will add, that I was a sincere well-wisher to the success of the French revolution, and still wish it may end in the establishment of a free & well-ordered republic; but I have not been insensible under the atrocious depredations they have committed on our commerce. The first object of my heart is my own country. In that is embarked my family, my fortune, & my own existence. I have not one farthing of interest, nor one fibre of attachment out of it, nor a single motive of preference of any one nation to another, but in proportion as they are more or less friendly to us. But though deeply feeling the injuries of France, I did not think war the surest means of redressing them. I did believe, that a mission sincerely disposed to preserve peace, would obtain for us a peaceable & honorable settlement & retribution; and I appeal to you to say, whether this might not have been obtained, if either of your colleagues had been of the same sentiment with yourself.

These, my friend, are my principles; they are unquestionably the principles of the great body of our fellow citizens, and I know there is not one of them which is not yours also. In truth, we never differed but on one ground, the funding system; and as, from the moment of its being adopted by the constituted authorities, I became religiously principled in the sacred discharge of it to the uttermost farthing, we are united now even on that single ground of difference.

* * *

IV

TO GIDEON GRANGER

[Monticello,] Aug 13, 1800.

DEAR SIR,—I received with great pleasure your favor of June 4, and am much comforted by the appearance of a change of opinion in your State; for tho' we may obtain, & I believe shall obtain, a majority in the legislature of the United States, attached to the preservation of the federal Constitution according to its obvious principles, & those on which it was known to be received; attached equally to the preservation to the States of those rights unquestionably remaining with them; friends to the freedom of religion, freedom of the press, trial by jury & to economical government; opposed to standing armies, paper systems, war, & all connection, other than commerce, with any foreign nation; in short, a majority firm in all those principles which we have espoused and the federalists have opposed uniformly; still, should the whole body of New England continue in opposition to these principles of government, either knowingly or through delusion, our government will be a very uneasy one. It can never be harmonious & solid, while so respectable a portion of its citizens support principles which go directly to a change of the federal Constitution, to sink the State governments, consolidate them into one, and to monarchize that. Our country is too large to have all its affairs directed by a single government. Public servants at such a distance, & from under the eye of their constituents, must, from the circumstance of distance, be unable to administer & overlook all the details necessary for the good government of the citizens, and the same circumstance, by rendering detection impossible to their constituents, will invite the public agents to corruption, plunder & waste. And I do verily believe, that if the principle were to prevail, of a common law being in force in the U. S., (which principle possesses the general government at once of all the powers of the State governments, and reduces us to a single consolidated government,) it would become the most corrupt government on the earth. You have seen the practises by which the public servants have been able to cover their conduct, or, where that could not be done, delusions by which they have varnished it for the eye of their constituents. What an augmentation of the field for jobbing, speculating, plundering, office-building & office-hunting would be produced by an assumption of all the State powers into the hands of the general government. The true theory of our Constitution is surely the wisest & best, that the States are independent as to everything within themselves, & united as to everything respecting foreign nations. Let the general government be reduced to foreign concerns only, and let our affairs be disentangled from those of all other nations, except as to commerce, which the merchants will manage the better, the more they are left free to manage for themselves, and our general government may be reduced to a very simple organization, & a very unexpensive one; a few plain duties to be performed by a few servants. But I repeat, that this simple & economical mode of government can never be secured, if the New England States continue to support the contrary system. I rejoice, therefore, in every appearance of their returning to those principles which I had always imagined to be almost innate in them. In this State, a few persons were deluded by the X. Y. Z. duperies. You saw the effect of it in our last Congressional representatives, chosen under their influence. This experiment on their credulity is now seen into, and our next representation will be as republican as it has heretofore been. On the whole, we hope, that by a part of the Union having held on to the principles of the Constitution, time has been given to the States to recover from the temporary frenzy into which they had been decoyed, to rally round the Constitution, & to rescue it from the destruction with which it had been threatened even at their own hands. I see copied from the American Magazine two numbers of a paper signed Don Quixotte, most excellently adapted to introduce the real truth to the minds even of the most prejudiced.

* * *

V

TO WILSON CARY NICHOLAS

Monticello, Sep. 7, 1803.

DEAR SIR,—Your favor of the 3d was delivered me at court; but we were much disappointed at not seeing you here, Mr. Madison & the Gov. being here at the time. I enclose you a letter from Monroe on the subject of the late treaty. You will observe a hint in it, to do without delay what we are bound to do. There is reason, in the opinion of our ministers, to believe, that if the thing were to do over again, it could not be obtained, & that if we give the least opening, they will declare the treaty void. A warning amounting to that has been given to them, & an unusual kind of letter written by their minister to our Secretary of State, direct. Whatever Congress shall think it necessary to do, should be done with as little debate as possible, & particularly so far as respects the constitutional difficulty. I am aware of the force of the observations you make on the power given by the Constn to Congress, to admit new States into the Union, without restraining the subject to the territory then constituting the U. S. But when I consider that the limits of the U. S. are precisely fixed by the treaty of 1783, that the Constitution expressly declares itself to be made for the U. S., I cannot help believing the intention was to permit Congress to admit into the Union new States, which should be formed out of the territory for which, & under whose authority alone, they were then acting. I do not believe it was meant that they might receive England, Ireland, Holland, &c. into it, which would be the case on your construction. When an instrument admits two constructions, the one safe, the other dangerous, the one precise, the other indefinite, I prefer that

249

which is safe & precise. I had rather ask an enlargement of power from the nation, where it is found necessary, than to assume it by a construction which would make our powers boundless. Our peculiar security is in possession of a written Constitution. Let us not make it a blank paper by construction. I say the same as to the opinion of those who consider the grant of the treaty making power as boundless. If it is, then we have no Constitution. If it has bounds, they can be no others than the definitions of the powers which that instrument gives. It specifies & delineates the operations permitted to the federal government, and gives all the powers necessary to carry these into execution. Whatever of these enumerated objects is proper for a law, Congress may make the law; whatever is proper to be executed by way of a treaty, the President & Senate may enter into the treaty; whatever is to be done by a judicial sentence, the judges may pass the sentence. Nothing is more likely than that their enumeration of powers is defective. This is the ordinary case of all human works. Let us go on then perfecting it, by adding, by way of amendment to the Constitution, those powers which time & trial show are still wanting. But it has been taken too much for granted, that by this rigorous construction the treaty power would be reduced to nothing. I had occasion once to examine its effect on the French treaty, made by the old Congress, & found that out of thirty odd articles which that contained, there were one, two, or three only which could not now be stipulated under our present Constitution. I confess, then, I think it important, in the present case, to set an example against broad construction, by appealing for new power to the people. If, however, our friends shall think differently, certainly I shall acquiesce with satisfaction; confiding, that the good sense of our country will correct the evil of construction when it shall produce ill effects.

No apologies for writing or speaking to me freely are necessary. On the contrary, nothing my friends can do is so dear to me, & proves to me their friendship so clearly, as the information they give me of their sentiments & those of others on interesting points where I am to act, and where information & warning is so essential to excite in me that due reflection which ought to precede action. I leave this about the 21st, and shall hope the District Court will give me an opportunity of seeing you.

Accept my affectionate salutations, & assurances of cordial esteem & respect.

VI

TO SPENCER ROANE

Monticello, October 12, 1815.

DEAR SIR,—I received in a letter from Colonel Monroe the enclosed paper communicated, as he said, with your permission, and even with a wish to know my sentiments on the important question it discusses. It is now more than forty years since I have ceased to be habitually conversant with legal questions; and my pursuits through that period have seldom required or permitted a renewal of my former familiarity with them. My ideas at present, therefore, on such questions, have no claim to respect but such as might be yielded to the common auditors of a law argument.

I well knew that in certain federal cases the laws of the United States had given to a foreign party, whether plaintiff or defendant, a right to carry his cause into the federal court; but I did not know that where he had himself elected the State judicature, he could, after an unfavorable decision there, remove his case to the federal court, and thus take the benefit of two chances where others have but one; nor that the right of entertaining the question in this case had been exercised or claimed by the federal judiciary after it had been postponed on the party's first election. His failure, too, to place on the record the particular ground which might give jurisdiction to the federal court, appears to me an additional objection of great weight. The question is of the first importance. The removal of it seems to be out of the analogies which guide the two governments on their separate tracts, and claims the solemn attention of both judicatures, and of the nation itself. I should fear to make up a final opinion on it, until I could see as able a development of the grounds of the federal claim as that which I have now read against it. I confess myself unable to foresee what those grounds would be. The paper enclosed must call them forth, and silence them too, unless they are beyond my ken. I am glad, therefore, that the claim is arrested, and made the subject of special and mature deliberation. I hope our courts will never countenance the sweeping pretensions which have been set up under the words "general defence and public welfare." These words only express the motives which induced the Convention to give to the ordinary legislature certain specified powers which they enumerate, and which they thought might be trusted to the ordinary legislature, and not to give them the unspecified also; or why any specification? They could not be so awkward in language as to mean, as we say, "all and some." And should this construction prevail, all limits to the federal government are done away. This opinion, formed on the first rise of the question, I have never seen reason to change, whether in or out of power; but, on the contrary, find it strengthened and confirmed by five and twenty years of additional reflection and experience: and any countenance given to it by any regular organ of the government, I should consider more ominous than anything which has yet occurred.

I am sensible how much these slight observations, on a question which you have so profoundly considered, need apology. They must find this in my zeal for the administration of our government according to its true spirit, federal as well as republican, and in my respect for any wish which you might be supposed to entertain for opinions of so little value. I salute you with sincere and high respect and esteem.

VII

TO SPENCER ROANE

Poplar Forest, September 6, 1819.

DEAR SIR,—I had read in the Enquirer, and with great approbation, the pieces signed Hampden, and have read them again with redoubled approbation, in the copies you have been so kind as to send me. I subscribe to every tittle of them. They contain the true principles of the revolution of 1800, for that was as real a revolution in the principles of our government as that of 1776 was in its form; not effected indeed by the sword, as that, but by the rational and peaceable instrument of reform, the suffrage of the people. The nation declared its will by dismissing functionaries of one principle, and electing those of another, in the two branches, executive and legislative, submitted to their election. Over the judiciary department, the Constitution had deprived them of their control. That, therefore, has continued the reprobated system, and although new matter has been occasionally incorporated into the old, yet the leaven of the old mass seems to assimilate to itself the new, and after twenty years' confirmation of the federal system by the voice of the nation, declared through the medium of elections, we find the judiciary on every occasion, still driving us into consolidation.

In denying the right they usurp of exclusively explaining the Constitution, I go further than you do, if I understand rightly your quotation from the Federalist, of an opinion that "the judiciary is the last resort in relation *to the other departments* of the government, but not in relation to the rights of the parties to the compact under which the judiciary is derived." If this opinion be sound, then indeed is our Constitution a complete *felo de se.* For intending to establish three departments, co-ordinate and independent, that they might check and balance one another, it has given, according to this opinion, to one of them alone, the right to prescribe rules for the government of the others, and to that one too, which is unelected by, and independent of the nation. For experience has already shown that the impeachment it has provided is not even a scare-crow; that such opinions as the one you combat, sent cautiously out, as you observe also, by detachment, not belonging to the case often, but sought for out of it, as if to rally the public opinion beforehand to their views, and to indicate the line they are to walk in, have been so quietly passed over as never to have excited animadversion, even in a speech of any one of the body entrusted with impeachment. The Constitution, on this hypothesis, is a mere thing of wax in the hands of the judiciary, which they may twist and shape into any form they please. It should be remembered, as an axiom of eternal truth in politics, that whatever power in any government is independent, is absolute also; in theory only, at first, while the spirit of the people is up, but in practice, as fast as that relaxes. Independence can be trusted nowhere but with the people in mass. They are inherently independent of all but moral law. My construction of the Constitution is very different from that you quote. It is that each department is truly independent of the others, and has an equal right to decide for itself what is the meaning of the Constitution in the cases submitted to its action; and especially, where it is to act ultimately and without appeal. I will explain myself by examples, which, having occurred while I was in office, are better known to me, and the principles which governed them.

A legislature had passed the sedition law. The federal courts had subjected certain individuals to its penalties of fine and imprisonment. On coming into office, I released these individuals by the power of pardon committed to executive discretion, which could never be more properly exercised than where citizens were suffering without the authority of law, or, which was equivalent, under a law unauthorized by the Constitution, and therefore null. In the case of Marbury and Madison, the federal judges declared that commissions, signed and sealed by the President, were valid, although not delivered. I deemed delivery essential to complete a deed, which, as long as it remains in the hands of the party, is as yet no deed, it is in *posse* only, but not in *esse*, and I withheld delivery of the commissions. They cannot issue a mandamus to the President or legislature, or to any of their officers. When the British treaty of —— arrived, without any provision against the impressment of our seamen, I determined not to ratify it. The Senate thought I should ask their advice. I thought that would be a mockery of them, when I was predetermined against following it, should they advise its ratification. The Constitution had made their advice necessary to confirm a treaty, but not to reject it. This has been blamed by some; but I have never doubted its soundness. In the cases of two persons, *antenati*, under exactly similar circumstances, the federal court had determined that one of them (Duane) was not a citizen; the House of Representatives nevertheless determined that the other (Smith, of South Carolina) was a citizen, and admitted him to his seat in their body. Duane was a republican, and Smith a federalist, and these decisions were made during the federal ascendancy.

These are examples of my position, that each of the three departments has equally the right to decide for itself what is its duty under the Constitution, without any regard to what the others may have decided for themselves under a similar question. But you intimate a wish that my opinion should be known on this subject. No, dear Sir, I withdraw from all contests of opinion, and resign everything cheerfully to the generation now in place. They are wiser than we were, and their successors will be wiser than they, from the progressive advance of science. Tranquillity is the *summum bonum* of age. I wish, therefore, to offend no man's opinion, nor to draw disquieting animadversions on my own. While duty required it, I met opposition with a firm and fearless step. But loving mankind in my individual relations with them, I pray to be permitted to depart in their peace; and like the superannuated soldier, "*quadragenis stipendiis emeritis,*" to hang my arms on the post. I have unwisely, I fear, embarked in an enterprise of great public concern, but not to be accomplished within my term, without their liberal and prompt support. A severe illness the last year, and another from which I am just emerged, admonish me that repetitions may be expected, against which a declining frame cannot long bear up. I am anxious, therefore, to get our University so far advanced as may encourage the public to persevere to its final accomplishment. That secured, I shall sing my *nunc dimittis*. I hope your labors will be long continued in the spirit in which they have always been exercised, in maintenance of those principles on which I verily believe the future happiness of our country essentially depends. I salute you with affectionate and great respect.

VIII

TO WILLIAM CHARLES JARVIS

Monticello, September 28, 1820.

I thank you, Sir, for the copy of your Republican which you have been so kind as to send me, and I should have acknowledged it sooner but that I am just returned home after a long absence. I have not yet had time to read it seriously, but in looking over it cursorily I see much in it to approve, and shall be glad if it shall lead our youth to the practice of thinking on such subjects and for themselves. That it will have this tendency may be expected, and for that reason I feel an urgency to note what I deem an error in it, the more requiring notice as your opinion is strengthened by that of many others. You seem, in pages 84 and 148, to consider the judges as the ultimate arbiters of all constitutional questions; a very dangerous doctrine indeed, and one which would place us under the despotism of an oligarchy. Our judges are as honest as other men, and not more so. They have, with others, the same passions for party, for power, and the privilege of their corps. Their maxim is *"boni judicis est ampliare jurisdictionem,"* and their power the more dangerous as they are in office for life, and not responsible, as the other functionaries are, to the elective control. The Constitution has erected no such single tribunal, knowing that to whatever hands confided, with the corruptions of time and party, its members would become despots. It has more wisely made all the departments co-equal and co-sovereign within themselves. If the legislature fails to pass laws for a census, for paying the judges and other officers of government, for establishing a militia, for naturalization as prescribed by the Constitution, or if they fail to meet in congress, the judges cannot issue their mandamus to them; if the President fails to supply the place of a judge, to appoint other civil or military officers, to issue requisite commissions, the judges cannot force him. They can issue their mandamus or distringas to no executive or legislative officer to enforce the fulfilment of their official duties, any more than the president or legislature may issue orders to the judges or their officers. Betrayed by English example, and unaware, as it should seem, of the control of our Constitution in this particular, they have at times overstepped their limit by undertaking to command executive officers in the discharge of their executive duties; but the Constitution, in keeping three departments distinct and independent, restrains the authority of the judges to judiciary organs, as it does the executive and legislative to executive and legislative organs. The judges certainly have more frequent occasion to act on constitutional questions, because the laws of *meum* and *tuum* and of criminal action, forming the great mass of the system of law, constitute their particular department. When the legislative or executive functionaries act unconstitutionally, they are responsible to the people in their elective capacity. The exemption of the judges from that is quite dangerous enough. I know no safe depository of the ultimate powers of the society but the people themselves; and if we think them not enlightened enough to exercise their control with a wholesome discretion, the remedy is not to take it from them, but to inform their discretion by education. This is the true corrective of abuses of constitutional power. Pardon me, Sir, for this difference of opinion. My personal interest in such questions is entirely extinct, but not my wishes for the longest possible continuance of our government on its pure principles; if the three powers maintain their mutual independence of each other it may last long, but not so if either can assume the authorities of the other....

IX

TO THOMAS RITCHIE

Monticello, December 25, 1820.

DEAR SIR,—On my return home after a long absence, I find here your favor of November the 23d, with Colonel Taylor's "Construction Construed," which you have been so kind as to send me, in the name of the author as well as yourself. Permit me, if you please, to use the same channel for conveying to him the thanks I render you also for this mark of attention. I shall read it, I know, with edification, as I did his Inquiry, to which I acknowledge myself indebted for many valuable ideas, and for the correction of some errors of early opinion, never seen in a correct light until presented to me in that work. That the present volume is equally orthodox, I know before reading it, because I know that Colonel Taylor and myself have rarely, if ever, differed in any political principle of importance. Every act of his life, and every word he ever wrote, satisfies me of this. So, also, as to the two Presidents, late and now in office, I know them both to be of principles as truly republican as any men living. If there be anything amiss, therefore, in the present state of our affairs, as the formidable deficit lately unfolded to us indicates, I ascribe it to the inattention of Congress to their duties, to their unwise dissipation and waste of the public contributions. They seemed, some little while ago, to be at a loss for objects whereon to throw away the supposed fathomless funds of the treasury. I had feared the result, because I saw among them some of my old fellow laborers, of tried and known principles, yet often in their minorities. I am aware that in one of their most ruinous vagaries, the people were themselves betrayed into the same phrenzy with their Representatives. The deficit produced, and a heavy tax to supply it, will, I trust, bring both to their sober senses.

But it is not from this branch of government we have most to fear. Taxes and short elections will keep them right. The judiciary of the United States is the subtle corps of sappers and miners constantly working under ground to undermine the foundations of our confederated fabric. They are construing our Constitution from a co-ordination of a general and special government to a general and supreme one alone. This will lay all things at their feet, and they are too well versed in English law to forget the maxim, *"boni judicis est ampliare jurisdictionem."* We shall see if they are bold enough to take the daring stride their five lawyers have lately taken. If they do, then, with the editor of our book, in his address to the public, I will say, that "against this every man should raise his voice," and more, should uplift his arm. Who wrote this admirable address? Sound, luminous, strong, not a word too much, nor one which can be changed but for the worse. That pen should go on, lay bare these wounds of our Constitution, expose the decisions *seriatim*, and arouse, as it is able, the attention of the nation to these bold speculators on its patience. Having found, from experience, that impeachment is an impracticable thing, a mere scare-crow, they consider themselves secure for life; they sculk from responsibility to public opinion, the only remaining hold on them, under a practice first introduced into England by Lord Mansfield. An opinion is huddled up in conclave, perhaps by a majority of one, delivered as if unanimous, and with the silent acquiescence of lazy or timid associates, by a crafty chief judge, who sophisticates the law to his mind, by the turn of his own reasoning. A judiciary law was once reported by the Attorney General to Congress, requiring each judge to deliver his opinion *seriatim* and openly, and then to give it in writing to the clerk to be entered in the record. A judiciary independent of a king or executive alone, is a good thing; but independence of the will of the nation is a solecism, at least in a republican government. But to return to your letter; you ask for my opinion of the work you send me, and to let it go out to the public. This I have ever made a point of declining, (one or two instances only excepted.) Complimentary thanks to writers who have sent me their works, have betrayed me sometimes before the public, without my consent having been asked. But I am far from presuming to direct the reading of my fellow citizens, who are good enough judges themselves of what is worth their reading. I am, also, too desirous of quiet to place myself in the way of contention. Against this I am admonished by bodily decay, which cannot be unaccompanied by corresponding wane of the mind. Of this I am as yet sensible, sufficiently to be unwilling to trust myself before the public, and when I cease to be so, I hope that my friends will be too careful of me to draw me forth and present me, like a Priam in armor, as a spectacle for public compassion. I hope our political bark will ride through all its dangers; but I can in future be but an inert passenger.

I salute you with sentiments of great friendship and respect.

X

TO SPENCER ROANE

Monticello, June 27, 1821

DEAR SIR,—I have received through the hands of the Governor, Colonel Taylor's letter to you. It is with extreme reluctance that I permit myself to usurp the office of an adviser of the public, what books they should read, and what not. I yield, however, on this occasion to your wish and that of Colonel Taylor, and do what (with a single exception only) I never did before, on the many similar applications made to me. On reviewing my letters to Colonel Taylor and to Mr. Thweat, neither appeared exactly proper. Each contained matter which might give offence to the judges, without adding strength to the opinion. I have, therefore, out of the two, cooked up what may be called "an extract of a letter from Th: J. to ——;" but without saying it is published *with my consent*. That would forever deprive me of the ground of declining the office of a Reviewer of books in future cases. I sincerely wish the attention of the public may be drawn to the doctrines of the book; and if this self-styled extract may contribute to it, I shall be gratified. I salute you with constant friendship and respect.

"EXTRACT OF A LETTER FROM TH: JEFFERSON TO ——.

"I have read Colonel Taylor's book of 'Constructions Construed,' with great satisfaction, and, I will say, with edification; for I acknowledge it corrected some errors of opinion into which I had slidden without sufficient examination. It is the most logical retraction of our governments to the original and true principles of the Constitution creating them, which has appeared since the adoption of that instrument. I may not perhaps concur in all its opinions, great and small; for no two men ever thought alike on so many points. But on all its important questions, it contains the true political faith, to which every catholic republican should steadfastly hold. It should be put into the hands of all our functionaries, authoritatively, as a standing instruction, and true exposition of our Constitution, as understood at the time we agreed to it. It is a fatal heresy to suppose that either our State governments are superior to the federal, or the federal to the States. The people, to whom all authority belongs, have divided the powers of government into two distinct departments, the leading characters of which are *foreign* and domestic; and they have appointed for each a distinct set of functionaries. These they have made co-ordinate, checking and balancing each other, like the three cardinal departments in the individual States: each equally supreme as to the powers delegated to itself, and neither authorized ultimately to decide what belongs to itself, or to its coparcenor in government. As independent, in fact, as different nations, a spirit of forbearance and compromise, therefore, and not of encroachment and usurpation, is the healing balm of such a constitution; and each party should prudently shrink from all approach to the line of demarcation, instead of rashly overleaping it, or throwing grapples ahead to haul to hereafter. But, finally, the peculiar happiness of our blessed system is, that in differences of opinion between these different sets of servants, the appeal is to neither, but to their employers peaceably assembled by their representatives in Convention. This is more rational than the *jus fortioris*, or the cannon's mouth, the *ultima et sola ratio regum*."

XI

TO WILLIAM JOHNSON

Monticello, June 12, 1823

* * *

I have stated above, that the original objects of the federalists were, 1st, to warp our government more to the form and principles of monarchy, and, 2d, to weaken the barriers of the State governments as coördinate powers. In the first they have been so completely foiled by the universal spirit of the nation, that they have abandoned the enterprise, shrunk from the odium of their old appellation, taken to themselves a participation of ours, and under the pseudo-republican mask, are now aiming at their second object, and strengthened by unsuspecting or apostate recruits from our ranks, are advancing fast towards an ascendancy. I have been blamed for saying, that a prevalence of the doctrines of consolidation would one day call for reformation or *revolution*. I answer by asking if a single State of the Union would have agreed to the Constitution, had it given all powers to the General Government? If the whole opposition to it did not proceed from the jealousy and fear of every State, of being subjected to the other States in matters merely its own? And if there is any reason to believe the States more disposed now than then, to acquiesce in this general surrender of all their rights and powers to a consolidated government, one and undivided?

You request me confidentially, to examine the question, whether the Supreme Court has advanced beyond its constitutional limits, and trespassed on those of the State authorities? I do not undertake it, my dear Sir, because I am unable. Age and the wane of mind consequent on it, have disqualified me from investigations so severe, and researches so laborious. And it is the less necessary in this case, as having been already done by others with a logic and learning to which I could add nothing. On the decision of the case of Cohens *vs.* The State of Virginia, in the Supreme Court of the United States, in March, 1821, Judge Roane, under the signature of Algernon Sidney, wrote for the Enquirer a series of papers on the law of that case. I considered these papers maturely as they came out, and confess that they appeared to me to pulverize every word which had been delivered by Judge Marshall, of the extra-judicial part of his opinion; and all was extra-judicial, except the decision that the act of Congress had not purported to give to the corporation of Washington the authority claimed by their lottery law, of controlling the laws of the States within the States themselves. But unable to claim that case, he could not let it go entirely, but went on gratuitously to prove, that notwithstanding the eleventh amendment of the Constitution, a State *could* be brought as a defendant, to the bar of his court; and again, that Congress might authorize a corporation of its territory to exercise legislation within a State, and paramount to the laws of that State. I cite the sum and result only of his doctrines, according to the impression made on my mind at the time, and still remaining. If not strictly accurate in circumstance, it is so in substance. This doctrine was so completely refuted by Roane, that if he can be answered, I surrender human reason as a vain and useless faculty, given to bewilder, and not to guide us. And I mention this particular case as one only of several, because it gave occasion to that thorough examination of the constitutional limits between the General and State jurisdictions, which you have asked for. There were two other writers in the same paper, under the signatures of Fletcher of Saltoun, and Somers, who, in a few essays, presented some very luminous and striking views of the question. And there was a particular paper which recapitulated all the cases in which it was thought the federal court had usurped on the State jurisdictions. These essays will be found in the Enquirers of 1821, from May the 10th to July the 13th. It is not in my present power to send them to you, but if Ritchie can furnish them, I will procure and forward them. If they had been read in the other States, as they were here, I think they would have left, there as here, no dissentients from their doctrine. The subject was taken up by our legislature of 1821-'22, and two draughts of remonstrances were prepared and discussed. As well as I remember, there was no difference of opinion as to the matter of right; but there was as to the expediency of a remonstrance at that time, the general mind of the States being then under extraordinary excitement by the Missouri question; and it was dropped on that consideration. But this case is not dead, it only sleepeth. The Indian Chief said he did not go to war for every petty injury by itself, but put it into his pouch, and when that was full, he then made war. Thank Heaven, we have provided a more peaceable and rational mode of redress.

This practice of Judge Marshall, of travelling out of his case to prescribe what the law would be in a moot case not before the court, is very irregular and very censurable. I recollect another instance, and the more particularly, perhaps, because it in some measure bore on myself. Among the midnight appointments of Mr. Adams, were commissions to some federal justices of the peace for Alexandria. These were signed and sealed by him, but not delivered. I found them on the table of the department of State, on my entrance into office, and I forbade their delivery. Marbury, named in one of them, applied to the Supreme Court for a mandamus to the Secretary of State (Mr. Madison) to deliver the commission intended for him. The court determined at once, that being an original process, they had no cognizance of it; and therefore the question before them was ended. But the Chief Justice went on to lay down what the law would be, had they jurisdiction of the case, to wit: that they should command the delivery. The object was clearly to instruct any other court having the jurisdiction, what they should do if Marbury should apply to them. Besides the impropriety of this gratuitous interference, could anything exceed the perversion of law? For if there is any principle of law never yet contradicted, it is that delivery is one of the essentials to the validity of the deed. Although signed and sealed, yet as long as it remains in the hands of the party himself, it is in *fieri* only, it is not a deed, and can be made so only by its delivery. In the hands of a third person it may be made an escrow. But whatever is in the executive offices is certainly deemed to be in the hands of the President; and in this case, was actually in my hands, because, when I countermanded them, there was as yet no Secretary of State. Yet this case of Marbury and Madison is continually cited by bench and bar, as if it were settled law, without any animadversion on its being merely an *obiter* dissertation of the Chief Justice.

It may be impracticable to lay down any general formula of words which shall decide at once, and with precision, in every case, this limit of jurisdiction. But there are two canons which will guide us safely in most of the cases. 1st. The capital and leading object of the Constitution was to leave with the States all authorities which respected their own citizens only, and to transfer to the United States those which respected citizens of foreign or other States: to make us several as to ourselves, but one as to all others. In the latter case, then, constructions should lean to the general jurisdiction, if the words will bear it; and in favor of the States in the former, if possible to be so construed. And indeed, between citizens and citizens of the same State, and under their own laws, I know but a single case in which a jurisdiction is given to the General Government. That is, where anything but gold or silver is made a lawful tender, or the obligation of contracts is any other wise impaired. The separate legislatures had so often abused that power, that the citizens themselves chose to trust it to the general, rather than to their own special authorities. 2d. On every question of construction, carry ourselves back to the time when the Constitution was adopted, recollect the spirit manifested in the debates, and instead of trying what meaning may be squeezed out of the text, or invented against it, conform to the probable one in which it was passed. Let us try Cohen's case by these canons only, referring always, however, for full argument, to the essays before cited.

1. It was between a citizen and his own State, and under a law of his State. It was a domestic case, therefore, and not a foreign one.

2. Can it be believed, that under the jealousies prevailing against the General Government, at the adoption of the Constitution, the States meant to surrender the authority of preserving order, of enforcing moral duties and restraining vice, within their own territory? And this is the present case, that of Cohen being under the ancient and general law of gaming. Can any good be effected by taking from the States the moral rule of their citizens, and subordinating it to the general authority, or to one of their corporations, which may justify forcing the meaning of words, hunting after possible constructions, and hanging inference on inference, from heaven to earth, like Jacob's ladder? Such an intention was impossible, and such a licentiousness of construction and inference, if exercised by both governments, as may be done with equal right, would equally authorize both to claim all power, general and particular, and break up the foundations of the Union. Laws

are made for men of ordinary understanding, and should, therefore, be construed by the ordinary rules of common sense. Their meaning is not to be sought for in metaphysical subtleties, which may make anything mean everything or nothing, at pleasure. It should be left to the sophisms of advocates, whose trade it is, to prove that a defendant is a plaintiff, though dragged into court, *torto collo*, like Bonaparte's volunteers, into the field in chains, or that a power has been given, because it ought to have been given, *et alia talia*. The States supposed that by their tenth amendment, they had secured themselves against constructive powers. They were not lessoned yet by Cohen's case, nor aware of the slipperiness of the eels of the law. I ask for no straining of words against the General Government, nor yet against the States. I believe the States can best govern our home concerns, and the General Government our foreign ones. I wish, therefore, to see maintained that wholesome distribution of powers established by the Constitution for the limitation of both; and never to see all offices transferred to Washington, where, further withdrawn from the eyes of the people, they may more secretly be bought and sold as at market.

But the Chief Justice says, "there must be an ultimate arbiter somewhere." True, there must; but does that prove it is either party? The ultimate arbiter is the people of the Union, assembled by their deputies in convention, at the call of Congress, or of two-thirds of the States. Let them decide to which they mean to give an authority claimed by two of their organs. And it has been the peculiar wisdom and felicity of our Constitution, to have provided this peaceable appeal, where that of other nations is at once to force.

I rejoice in the example you set of *seriatim* opinions. I have heard it often noticed, and always with high approbation. Some of your brethren will be encouraged to follow it occasionally, and in time, it may be felt by all as a duty, and the sound practice of the primitive court be again restored. Why should not every judge be asked his opinion, and give it from the bench, if only by yea or nay? Besides ascertaining the fact of his opinion, which the public have a right to know, in order to judge whether it is impeachable or not, it would show whether the opinions were unanimous or not, and thus settle more exactly the weight of their authority.

The close of my second sheet warns me that it is time now to relieve you from this letter of unmerciful length. Indeed, I wonder how I have accomplished it, with two crippled wrists, the one scarcely able to move my pen, the other to hold my paper. But I am hurried sometimes beyond the sense of pain, when unbosoming myself to friends who harmonize with me in principle. You and I may differ occasionally in details of minor consequence, as no two minds, more than two faces, are the same in every feature. But our general objects are the same, to preserve the republican form and principles of our Constitution and cleave to the salutary distribution of powers which that has established. These are the two sheet anchors of our Union. If driven from either, we shall be in danger of foundering. To my prayers for its safety and perpetuity, I add those for the continuation of your health, happiness, and usefulness to your country.

XII

TO WILLIAM BRANCH GILES

Monticello, December 26, 1825.

DEAR SIR,—I wrote you a letter yesterday, of which you will be free to make what use you please. This will contain matters not intended for the public eye. I see, as you do, and with the deepest affliction, the rapid strides with which the federal branch of our government is advancing towards the usurpation of all the rights reserved to the States, and the consolidation in itself of all powers, foreign and domestic; and that, too, by constructions which, if legitimate, leave no limits to their power. Take together the decisions of the federal court, the doctrines of the President, and the misconstructions of the constitutional compact acted on by the legislature of the federal branch, and it is but too evident, that the three ruling branches of that department are in combination to strip their colleagues, the State authorities, of the powers reserved by them, and to exercise themselves all functions foreign and domestic. Under the power to regulate commerce, they assume indefinitely that also over agriculture and manufactures, and call it regulation to take the earnings of one of these branches of industry, and that too the most depressed, and put them into the pockets of the other, the most flourishing of all. Under the authority to establish post roads, they claim that of cutting down mountains for the construction of roads, of digging canals, and aided by a little sophistry on the words "general welfare," a right to do, not only the acts to effect that which are specifically enumerated and permitted, but whatsoever they shall think, or pretend will be for the general welfare. And what is our resource for the preservation of the Constitution? Reason and argument? You might as well reason

272

and argue with the marble columns encircling them. The representatives chosen by ourselves? They are joined in the combination, some from incorrect views of government, some from corrupt ones, sufficient voting together to out-number the sound parts; and with majorities only of one, two, or three, bold enough to go forward in defiance. Are we then *to stand to our arms*, with the hot-headed Georgian? No. That must be the last resource, not to be thought of until much longer and greater sufferings. If every infraction of a compact of so many parties is to be resisted at once, as a dissolution of it, none can ever be formed which would last one year. We must have patience and longer endurance then with our brethren while under delusion; give them time for reflection and experience of consequences; keep ourselves in a situation to profit by the chapter of accidents; and separate from our companions only when the sole alternatives left, are the dissolution of our Union with them, or submission to a government without limitation of powers. Between these two evils, when we must make a choice, there can be no hesitation. But in the meanwhile, the States should be watchful to note every material usurpation on their rights; to denounce them as they occur in the most peremptory terms; to protest against them as wrongs to which our present submission shall be considered, not as acknowledgments or precedents of right, but as a temporary yielding to the lesser evil, until their accumulation shall overweigh that of separation. I would go still further, and give to the federal member, by a regular amendment of the Constitution, a right to make roads and canals of intercommunication between the States, providing sufficiently against corrupt practices in Congress, (log-rolling, &c.,) by declaring that the federal proportion of each State of the moneys so employed, shall be in works within the State, or elsewhere with its consent, and with a due *salvo* of jurisdiction. This is the course which I think safest and best as yet.

* * *

THE FORT HILL ADDRESS
OF
JOHN C. CALHOUN

☆ ☆ ☆ ☆ ☆ ☆ ☆ ☆ ☆ ☆ ☆ ☆ ☆

THE FORT HILL ADDRESS
OF JOHN C. CALHOUN

On the Relation which the States and General
Government Bear to Each Other

HE question of the relation which the States and General Government bear to each other is not one of recent origin. From the commencement of our system, it had divided public sentiment. Even in the convention, while the Constitution was struggling into existence, there were two parties as to what this relation should be, whose different sentiments constituted no small impediment in forming that instrument. After the General Government went into operation, experience soon proved that the question had not terminated with the labors of the Convention. The great struggle that preceded the political revolution of 1801, which brought Mr. Jefferson into power, turned essentially on it, and the doctrines and arguments on both sides were embodied and ably sustained;—on the one, in the Virginia and Kentucky Resolutions, and the Report to the Virginia Legislature;—and on the other, in the replies of the Legislature of Massachusetts and some of the other States.

These Resolutions and this Report, with the decision of the Supreme Court of Pennsylvania about the same time (particularly in the case of Cobbett, delivered by Chief Justice M'Kean, and concurred in by the whole bench), contain what I believe to be the true doctrine on this important subject. I refer to them in order to avoid the necessity of presenting my views, with the reasons in support of them, in detail.

As my object is simply to state my opinions, I might pause with this reference to documents that so fully and ably state all the points immediately connected with this deeply-important subject; but as there are many who may not have the opportunity or leisure to refer to them, and as it is possible, however clear they may be, that different persons may place different interpretations on their meaning, I will, in order that my sentiments may be fully known, and to avoid all ambiguity, proceed to state, summarily, the doctrines which I conceive they embrace.

The great and leading principle is, that the General Government emanated from the people of the several States, forming distinct political communities, and acting in their separate and sovereign capacity, and not from all of the people forming one aggregate political community; that the Constitution of the United States is, in fact, a compact, to which each State is a party, in the character already described; and that the several States, or parties, have a right to judge of its infractions; and in case of a deliberate, palpable, and dangerous exercise of power not delegated, they have the right, in the last resort, to use the language of the Virginia Resolutions, *"to interpose for arresting the progress of the evil, and for maintaining, within their respective limits, the authorities, rights, and liberties appertaining to them."* This right of interposition, thus solemnly asserted by the State of Virginia, be it called what it may,—State-right, veto, nullification, or by any other name,—I conceive to be the fundamental principle of our system, resting on facts historically as certain as our revolution itself, and deductions as simple and demonstrative as that of any political or moral truth whatever; and I firmly believe that on its recognition depend the stability and safety of our political institutions.

I am not ignorant that those opposed to the doctrine have always, now and formerly, regarded it in a very different light, as anarchical and revolutionary. Could I believe such, in fact, to be its tendency, to me it would be no recommendation. I yield to none, I trust, in a deep and sincere attachment to our political institutions and the union of these States. I never breathed an opposite sentiment; but, on the contrary, I have ever considered them the great instruments of preserving our liberty, and promoting the happiness of our selves and our posterity; and next to these I have ever held them most dear. Nearly half my life has been passed in the service of the Union, and whatever public reputation I have acquired is indissolubly identified with it. To be too national has, indeed, been considered by many, even of my friends, my greatest political fault.

With these strong feelings of attachment, I have examined, with the utmost care, the bearing of the doctrine in question; and, so far from anarchical or revolutionary, I solemnly believe it to be the only solid foundation of our system, and of the Union itself; and that the opposite doctrine, which denies to the States the right of protecting their reserved powers, and which would vest in the General Government (it matters not through what department) the right of determining, exclusively and finally, the powers delegated to it, is incompatible with the sovereignty of the States, and of the Constitution itself, considered as the basis of a Federal Union. As strong as this language is, it is not stronger than that used by the illustrious Jefferson, who said, to give to the General Government the final and exclusive right to judge of its powers, is to make "*its discretion,* and *not the Constitution, the measure of its powers;*" and that, "*in all cases of compact between parties having no common judge, each party has an equal right to judge for itself, as well of the infraction as of the mode and measure of redress.*" Language cannot be more explicit, nor can higher authority be adduced.

That different opinions are entertained on this subject, I consider but as an additional evidence of the great diversity of the human intellect. Had not able, experienced, and patriotic individuals, for whom I have the highest respect, taken different views, I would have thought the right too clear to admit of doubt; but I am taught by this, as well as by many similar instances, to treat with deference opinions differing from my own. The error may, possibly, be with me; but if so, I can only say that, after the most mature and conscientious examination, I have not been able to detect it. But, with all proper deference, I must think that theirs is the error who deny what seems to be an essential attribute of the conceded sovereignty of the States, and who attribute to the General Government a right utterly incompatible with what all acknowledge to be its limited and restricted character: an error originating principally, as I must think, in not duly reflecting on the nature of our institutions, and on what constitutes the only rational object of all political constitutions.

It has been well said by one of the most sagacious men of antiquity, that the object of a constitution is, to *restrain the government, as that of laws* is to restrain *individuals.* The remark is correct; nor is it less true where the government is vested in a majority, than where it is in a single or a few individuals—in a republic, than a monarchy or aristocracy. No one can have a higher respect for the maxim that the majority ought to govern than I have, taken in its proper sense, subject to the restrictions imposed by the Constitution, and confined to objects in which every portion of the community have similar interests; but it is a great error to suppose, as many do, that the right of a majority to govern is a natural and not a conventional right, and therefore absolute and unlimited. By nature, every individual has the right to govern himself; and governments, whether founded on majorities or minorities, must derive their right from the assent, expressed or implied, of the governed, and be subject to such limitations as they may impose. Where the interests are the same, that is, where the laws that may benefit one will benefit all, or the reverse, it is just and proper to place them under the control of the majority; but where they are dissimilar, so that the law that may benefit one portion may be ruinous to another, it would be, on the contrary, unjust and absurd to subject them to its will; and such I conceive to be the theory on which our Constitution rests.

That such dissimilarity of interests may exist, it is impossible to doubt. They are to be found in every community, in a greater or less degree, however small or homogeneous; and they constitute every where the great difficulty of forming and preserving free institutions. To guard against the unequal action of the laws, when applied to dissimilar and opposing interests, is, in fact, what mainly renders a constitution indispensable; to overlook which, in reasoning on our Constitution, would be to omit the principal element by which to determine its character. Were there no contrariety of interests, nothing would be more simple and easy than to form and preserve free institutions. The right of suffrage alone would be a sufficient guarantee. It is the conflict of opposing interests which renders it the most difficult work of man.

Where the diversity of interests exists in separate and distinct classes of the community, as is the case in England, and was formerly the case in Sparta, Rome, and most of the free States of antiquity, the rational constitutional provision is, that each should be represented in the government, as a separate estate, with a distinct voice, and a negative on the acts of its co-estates, in order to check their encroachments. In England, the Constitution has assumed expressly this form, while in the governments of Sparta and Rome, the same thing was effected under different, but not much less efficacious forms. The perfection of their organization, in this particular, was that which gave to the constitutions of these renowned States all their celebrity, which secured their liberty for so many centuries, and raised them to so great a height of power and prosperity. Indeed, a constitutional provision giving to the great and separate interests of the community the right of self-protection, must appear, to those who will duly reflect on the subject, not less essential to the preservation of liberty than the right of suffrage itself. They, in fact, have a common object, to effect which the one is as necessary as the other to secure *responsibility;* that is, *that those who make and execute the laws should be accountable to those on whom the laws in reality operate—the only solid and durable foundation of liberty.* If, without the right of suffrage, our rulers would oppress us, so, without the right of self-protection, the major would equally oppress the minor interests of the community. The absence of the former would make the governed the slaves of the rulers; and of the latter, the feebler interests, the victim of the stronger.

Happily for us, we have no artificial and separate classes of society. We have wisely exploded all such distinctions; but we are not, on that account, exempt from all contrariety of interests, as the present distracted and dangerous condition of our country, unfortunately, but too clearly proves. With us they are almost exclusively geographical, resulting mainly from difference of climate, soil, situation, industry, and production; but are not, therefore, less necessary to be protected by an adequate constitutional provision, than where the distinct interests exist in separate classes. The necessity is, in truth, greater, as such separate and dissimilar geographical interests are more liable to come into conflict, and more dangerous, when in that state, than those of any other description: so much so, that *ours is the first instance on record where they have not formed, in an extensive territory, separate and independent* communities, *or subjected the whole to despotic sway*. That such may not be our unhappy fate also, must be the sincere prayer of every lover of his country.

So numerous and diversified are the interests of our country, that they could not be fairly represented in a single government, organized so as to give to each great and leading interest a separate and distinct voice, as in governments to which I have referred. A plan was adopted better suited to our situation, but perfectly novel in its character. The powers of government were divided, not, as heretofore, in reference to classes, but geographically. One General Government was formed for the whole, to which were delegated all the powers supposed to be necessary to regulate the interests common to all the States, leaving others subject to the separate control of the States, being, from their local and peculiar character, such that they could not be subject to the will of a majority of the whole Union, without the certain hazard of injustice and oppression. It was thus that the interests of the whole were subjected, as they ought to be, to the will of the whole, while the peculiar and local interests were left under the control of the States separately, to whose custody only they could be safely confided. This distribution of power, settled solemnly by a constitutional compact, to which all the States are parties, constitutes the peculiar character and excellence of our political system. It is truly and emphatically *American, without example or parallel.*

To realize its perfection, we must view the General Government and those of the States as a whole, each in its proper sphere independent; each perfectly adapted to its respective objects; the States acting separately, representing and protecting the local and peculiar interests; and acting jointly through one General Government, with the weight respectively assigned to each by the Constitution, representing and protecting the interest of the whole; and thus perfecting, by an admirable but simple arrangement, the great principle of representation and responsibility, without which no government can be free or just. To preserve this sacred distribution as originally settled, by coercing each to move in its prescribed orbit, is the great and difficult problem, on the solution of which the duration of our Constitution, of our Union, and, in all probability, our liberty depends. How is this to be effected?

The question is new, when applied to our peculiar political organization, where the separate and conflicting interests of society are represented by distinct but connected governments; but it is, in reality, an old question under a new form, long since perfectly solved. Whenever separate and dissimilar interests have been separately represented in any government; whenever the sovereign power has been divided in its exercise, the experience and wisdom of ages have devised but one mode by which such political organization can be preserved,—the mode adopted in England, and by all governments, ancient and modern, blessed with constitutions deserving to be called free,—to give to each co-estate the right to judge of its powers, with a negative or veto on the acts of the others, in order to protect against encroachments the interests it particularly represents: a principle which all of our constitutions recognize in the distribution of power among their respective departments, as essential to maintain the independence of each; but which, to all who will duly reflect on the subject, must appear far more essential, for the same object, in that great and fundamental distribution of powers between the General and State Governments.

So essential is the principle, that, to withhold the right from either, where the sovereign power is divided, is, in fact, *to annul the division* itself, and to *consolidate*, in the one left in the exclusive possession of the right, *all* powers of government; for it is not possible to distinguish, practically, between a government having all power, and one having the right to take what powers it pleases. Nor does it in the least vary the principle, whether the distribution of power be between co-estates, as in England, or between distinctly organized but connected governments, as with us. The reason is the same in both cases, while the necessity is greater in our case, as the danger of conflict is greater where the interests of a society are divided geographically than in any other, as has already been shown.

These truths do seem to me to be incontrovertible; and I am at a loss to understand how any one, who has maturely reflected on the nature of our institutions, or who has read history or studied the principles of free government to any purpose, can call them in question. The explanation must, it appears to me, be sought in the fact that, in every free State there are those who look more to the necessity of maintaining power than guarding against its abuses. I do not intend reproach, but simply to state a fact apparently necessary to explain the contrariety of opinions among the intelligent, where the abstract consideration of the subject would seem scarcely to admit of doubt.

If such be the true cause, I must think the fear of weakening the government too much, in this case, to be in a great measure unfounded, or, at least, that the danger is much less from that than the opposite side. I do not deny that a power of so high a nature may be abused by a State; but when I reflect that the States unanimously called the General Government into existence with all its powers, which they freely delegated on their part, under the conviction that their common peace, safety, and prosperity required it; that they are bound together by a common origin, and the recollection of common suffering and common triumph in the great and splendid achievement of their independence; and that the strongest feelings of our nature, and among them the love of national power and distinction, are on the side of the Union, it does seem to me that the fear which would strip the States of their sovereignty, and degrade them, in fact, to mere dependent corporations, lest they should abuse a right indispensable to the peaceable protection of those interests which they reserved under their own peculiar guardianship when they created the General Government, is unnatural and unreasonable. If those who voluntarily created the system cannot be trusted to preserve it, who can?

So far from extreme danger, I hold that there never was a free State in which this great conservative principle, indispensable to all, was ever so safely lodged. In others, when the co-estates representing the dissimilar and conflicting interests of the community came into contact, the only alternative was compromise, submission, or force. Not so in ours. Should the General Government and a State come into conflict, we have a higher remedy: the power which called the General Government into existence, which gave it all its authority, and can enlarge, contract, or abolish its powers at its pleasure, may be invoked. The States themselves may be appealed to,—three fourths of which, in fact, form a power, whose decrees are the Constitution itself, and whose voice can silence all discontent.

The utmost extent, then, of the power is, that a State, acting in its sovereign capacity as one of the parties to the constitutional compact, may compel the Government, created by that compact, to submit a question touching its infraction, to the parties who created it; to avoid the supposed dangers of which, it is proposed to resort to the novel, the hazardous, and, I must add, fatal project of giving to the General Government the sole and final right of interpreting the Constitution;—thereby reversing the whole system, making that instrument the creature of its will, instead of a rule of action impressed on it at its creation, and annihilating, in fact, the authority which imposed it, and from which the Government itself derives its existence.

That such would be the result, were the right in question vested in the Legislative or Executive branch of the Government, is conceded by all. No one has been so hardy as to assert that Congress or the President ought to have the right, or deny that, if vested finally and exclusively in either, the consequences which I have stated would necessarily follow; but its advocates have been reconciled to the doctrine, on the supposition that there is one department of the General Government which, from its peculiar organization, affords an independent tribunal, through which the Government may exercise the high authority which is the subject of consideration, with perfect safety to all.

I yield, I trust, to few in my attachment to the Judiciary Department. I am fully sensible of its importance, and would maintain it, to the fullest extent, in its constitutional powers and independence; but it is impossible for me to believe it was ever intended by the Constitution that it should exercise the power in question, or that it is competent to do so; and, if it were, that it would be a safe depository of the power. Its powers are judicial, and not political; and are expressly confined by the Constitution "to all *cases* in law and equity arising under this Constitution, the laws of the United States, and the treaties made, or which shall be made, under its authority;" and which I have high authority in asserting excludes political questions, and comprehends those only where there are parties amenable to the process of the court.* Nor is its incompetency less clear than its want of constitutional authority. There may be many, and the most dangerous infractions on the part of Congress, of which, it is conceded by all, the court, as a judicial tribunal, cannot, from its nature, take cognizance. The Tariff itself is a strong case in point; and the reason applies equally *to all others where Congress perverts a power from an object intended, to one not intended, the most insidious and dangerous of all infractions; and which may be extended to all of its powers, more especially to the taxing and appropriating.* But, supposing it competent to take cognizance of all infractions of every description, the insuperable objection still remains, that it would not be a safe tribunal to exercise the power in question.

It is a universal and fundamental political principle, that the power to protect can safely be confided only to those interested in protecting, or their responsible agents,—a maxim not less true in private than in public affairs. The danger in our system is, that the General Government, which represents the interests of the whole, may encroach on the States,

---

* I refer to the authority of Chief Justice Marshall, in the case of Jonathan Robbins. I have not been able to refer to the speech, and speak from memory.*

* The following are the remarks referred to by Mr. Calhoun:—

"By extending the judicial power to all cases in law and equity, the Constitution *had never been understood* to confer on that department any *political power whatever*. To come within this description, a question must assume a *legal* form, for forensic litigation and judicial decision. There must

which represent the peculiar and local interests, or that the latter may encroach on the former.

In examining this point, we ought not to forget that the Government, through all its departments, judicial as well as others, is administered by delegated and responsible agents; and that the *power which really controls, ultimately, all the movements, is not in the agents, but those who elect or appoint them.* To understand, then, its real character, and what would be the action of the system in any supposable case, we must raise our view from the mere agents to this high controlling power, which finally impels every movement of the machine. By doing so, we shall find all under the control of the will of a majority, compounded of the majority of the States, taken as political bodies, and the majority of the people of the States, estimated in federal numbers. These, united, constitute the real and final power which impels and directs the movements of the General Government. The majority of the States elect the majority of the Senate; of the people of the States, that of the House of Representatives; the two united, the President; and the President and a majority of the Senate appoint the judges: a majority of whom, and a majority of the Senate and House, with the President, really exercise all the powers of the Government, with the exception of the cases where the Constitution requires a greater number than a majority.

---

be parties to come into court, who can be reached by its process, and bound by its power; whose rights admit of ultimate decision by a tribunal, to which they are bound to submit. A 'case in Law and Equity,' proper for judicial decision, may arise under a treaty, where the *rights of invididuals,* acquired or secured by a treaty, are to be asserted or defended in court;— as under the fourth and sixth articles of the treaty of peace with Great Britain; or under those articles of our late treaties with France, Prussia, and other nations, which secure to *the subjects* of these nations *their property* within the United States; but the *judicial power cannot extend to political compacts.*" Speech in the House of Representatives, in the case of Thomas Nash, *alias* Jonathan Robbins, Sept. 1797.—*Editor.*

The judges are, in fact, as truly the judicial representatives of this united majority, as the majority of Congress itself, or the President, is its legislative or executive representative; and to confide the power to the Judiciary to determine finally and conclusively what powers are delegated and what reserved, would be, in reality, to confide it to the majority, whose agents they are, and by whom they can be controlled in various ways; and, of course, to subject (against the fundamental principle of our system and all sound political reasoning) the reserved powers of the States, with all the local and peculiar interests they were intended to protect, to the will of the very majority against which the protection was intended. Nor will the tenure by which the judges hold their office, however valuable the provision in many other respects, materially vary the case. Its highest possible effect would be to *retard*, and not *finally* to *resist*, the will of a dominant majority.

But it is useless to multiply arguments. Were it possible that reason could settle a question where the passions and interests of men are concerned, this point would have been long since settled for ever by the State of Virginia. The report of her Legislature, to which I have already referred, has really, in my opinion, placed it beyond controversy. Speaking in reference to this subject, it says: "It has been objected" (to the right of a State to interpose for the protection of her reserved rights) "that the judicial authority is to be regarded as the sole expositor of the Constitution. On this objection it might be observed, first, that there may be instances of usurped powers which the forms of the Constitution could never draw within the control of the Judicial Department; secondly, that, if the decision of the judiciary be raised above the sovereign parties to the Constitution, the decisions of the other departments, not carried by the forms of the Constitution before the Judiciary, must be equally authoritative and final with the decision of that department. But the proper answer to the objection is, that the resolution of the General Assembly relates to those great and extraordinary cases, in which all the forms of the Constitution may prove ineffectual against infractions dangerous to the essential rights of the parties to it. The resolution supposes that dangerous powers, not delegated, may not only be usurped and executed by the other departments, but that the Judicial Department may also exercise or sanction dangerous powers, beyond the grant of the Constitution, and, consequently, that the ultimate right of the parties to the Constitution to judge whether the compact has been dangerously violated, must extend to violations by one delegated authority, as well as by another,—by the judiciary, as well as by the executive or legislative."

Against these conclusive arguments, as they seem to me, it is objected that, if one of the parties has the right to judge of infractions of the Constitution, so has the other; and that, consequently, in cases of contested powers between a State and the General Government, each would have a right to maintain its opinion, as is the case when sovereign powers differ in the construction of treaties or compacts; and that, of course, it would come to be a mere question of force.

The error is in the assumption that the General Government is a party to the constitutional compact. The States, as has been shown, formed the compact, acting as sovereign and independent communities. The General Government is but its creature; and though, in reality, a government, with all the rights and authority which belong to any other government, within the orbit of its powers, it is, nevertheless, a government emanating from a compact between sovereigns, and partaking, in its nature and object, of the character of a joint commission, appointed to superintend and administer the interests in which all are jointly concerned; but having, beyond its proper sphere, no more power than if it did not exist.

To deny this would be to deny the most incontestable facts and the clearest conclusions; while to acknowledge its truth is to destroy utterly the objection that the appeal would be to force, in the case supposed. For, if each party has a right to judge, then, under our system of government, the final cognizance of a question of contested power would be in the States, and not in the General Government. It would be the duty of the latter, as in all similar cases of a contest between one or more of the principals and a joint commission or agency, to refer the contest to the principals themselves. Such are the plain dictates of both reason and analogy. On no sound principle can the agents have a right to final cognizance, as against the principals, much less to use force against them to maintain their construction of their powers. Such a right would be monstrous, and has never, heretofore, been claimed in similar cases.

That the doctrine is applicable to the case of a contested power between the States and the General Government, we have the authority, not only of reason and analogy, but of the distinguished statesman already referred to. Mr. Jefferson, at a late period of his life, after long experience and mature reflection, says, "With respect to our State and Federal Governments, I do not think their relations are correctly understood by foreigners. They suppose the former are subordinate to the latter. This is not the case. They are co-ordinate departments of one simple and integral whole. But you may ask, If the two departments should claim each the same subject of power, where is the umpire to decide between them? In cases of little urgency or importance, the prudence of both parties will keep them aloof from the questionable ground; but, if it can neither be avoided nor compromised, a convention of the States must be called to ascribe the doubtful power to that department which they may think best."

It is thus that our Constitution, by authorizing amendments, and by prescribing the authority and mode of making them, has, by a simple contrivance, with its characteristic wisdom, provided a power which, in the last resort, supersedes effectually the necessity, and even the pretext for force: a power to which none can fairly object; with which the interests of all are safe; which can definitively close all controversies in the only effectual mode, by freeing the compact of every defect and uncertainty, by an amendment of the instrument itself. It is impossible for human wisdom, in a system like ours, to devise another mode which shall be safe and effectual, and, at the same time, consistent with what are the relations and acknowledged powers of the two great departments of our Government. It gives a beauty and security peculiar to our system, which, if duly appreciated, will transmit its blessings to the remotest generations; but, if not, our splendid anticipations of the future will prove but an empty dream.

Stripped of all its covering, the naked question is, whether ours is a federal or a consolidated government; a constitutional or absolute one; a government resting ultimately on the solid basis of the sovereignty of the States or on the unrestrained will of a majority; a form of government, as in all other unlimited ones, in which injustice, and violence, and force must finally prevail. *Let it never be forgotten that, where the majority rules without restriction, the minority is the subject;* and that, if we should absurdly attribute to the former the exclusive right of construing the Constitution, there would be, in fact, between the sovereign and subject, under such a government, no Constitution, or, at least, nothing deserving the name, or serving the legitimate object of so sacred an instrument.

How the States are to exercise this high power of interposition, which constitutes so essential a portion of their reserved rights that it *cannot be delegated without an entire surrender of their sovereignty*, and converting our system from a *federal* into a *consolidated* Government, is a question that the States only are competent to determine. The arguments which prove that they possess the power, equally prove that they are, in the language of Jefferson, *"the rightful judges of the mode and measure of redress."* But the spirit of forbearance, as well as the nature of the right itself, forbids a recourse to it, except in cases of dangerous infractions of the Constitution; and then only in the last resort, when all reasonable hope of relief from the ordinary action of the Government has failed; when, if the right to interpose did not exist, the alternative would be submission and oppression on one side, or resistance by force on the other. That our system should afford, in such extreme cases, an intermediate point between these dire alternatives, by which the Government may be brought to a pause, and thereby an interval obtained to compromise differences, or, if impracticable, be compelled to submit the question to a constitutional adjustment, through an appeal to the States themselves, is an evidence of its high wisdom: an element not, as is supposed by some, of weakness, but of strength; not of anarchy or revolution, but of peace and safety. *Its general recognition would of itself, in a great measure, if not altogether, supersede the necessity of its exercise, by impressing on the movements of the Government that moderation and justice so essential to harmony and peace, in a country of such vast extent and diversity of interests as ours;* and would, if controversy should come, turn the resentment of the aggrieved from the system to those who had abused its powers (a point all-important), and cause them to seek redress, *not in revolution or overthrow, but in reformation.* It is, in fact, properly understood, *a substitute,—where the alternative would be force,—tending to prevent, and, if that fails, to correct peace-*

ably the aberrations to which all systems are liable, and which, if permitted to accumulate without correction, must finally end in a general catastrophe.

NOTE: [*At this point, in a portion of his address here omitted, Mr. Calhoun expounded his views upon the tariff questions that so bitterly divided the Republic at that time. He felt strongly that a tariff imposed for purposes of protection, and not for purposes of revenue only, was unconstitutional; he urged a reduction on those rates having a punitive effect upon the South; and he pleaded eloquently that "in a country of such great extent and diversity as ours," extreme caution and moderation should be observed in imposing upon one region the economic theories of another.*]

In thus placing my opinions before the public, I have not been actuated by the expectation of changing the public sentiment. Such a motive, on a question so long agitated, and so beset with feelings of prejudice and interest, would argue, on my part, an insufferable vanity, and a profound ignorance of the human heart. To avoid, as far as possible, the imputation of either, I have confined my statement, on the many and important points on which I have been compelled to touch, to a simple declaration of my opinion, without advancing any other reasons to sustain them than what appeared to me to be indispensable to the full understanding of my views; and if they should, on any point, be thought to be not clearly and explicitly developed, it will, I trust, be attributed to my solicitude to avoid the imputations to which I have alluded, and not from any desire to disguise my sentiments, nor the want of arguments and illustrations to maintain positions, which so abound in both, that it would require a volume to do them any thing like justice. I can only hope the truths which, I feel assured, are essentially connected with all that we ought to hold most dear, may not be weakened in the public estimation by the imperfect manner in which I have been, by the object in view, compelled to present them.

With every caution on my part, I dare not hope, in taking the step I have, to escape the imputation of improper motives; though I have, without reserve, freely expressed my opinions, not regarding whether they might or might not be popular. I have no reason to believe that they are such as will conciliate public favor, but the opposite, which I greatly regret, as I have ever placed a high estimate on the good opinion of my fellow-citizens. But, be that as it may, I shall, at least, be sustained by feelings of conscious rectitude. I have formed my opinions after the most careful and deliberate examination, with all the aids which my reason and experience could furnish; I have expressed them honestly and fearlessly, regardless of their effects personally, which, however interesting to me individually, are of too little importance to be taken into the estimate, where the liberty and happiness of our country are so vitally involved.

JOHN C. CALHOUN.

FORT HILL, *July 26th*, 1831.

A QUESTION OF INTENT

THE STATES, THEIR SCHOOLS
AND THE FOURTEENTH AMENDMENT

A QUESTION OF INTENT

A Statement Before the
Subcommittee on Constitutional Amendments,
United States Senate

DAVID J. MAYS

R. Chairman and members of the Committee, I am David J. Mays of Richmond, Virginia, and appear in my capacity as Chairman of the Virginia Commission on Constitutional Government, whose purpose is to bring to the attention of our people basic concepts relating to the Constitution of the United States.

I am grateful for the opportunity of appearing before you in connection with Senate Joint Resolution 32.

Since many arguments have been and will be made concerning this Resolution, I believe that I can be of most use to you in confining myself to the historical background of the Fourteenth Amendment, and more particularly to the interpretations placed thereon by the Congress and by the States at the time of its ratification. The source of this information is the legal brief prepared by my law office and the counsel with whom we were associated in the School Cases decided by the Supreme Court of the United States in 1954. This résumé clearly demonstrates that the court did not follow the interpretations placed upon the Fourteenth Amendment by the Congress and the States at the time of its adoption, and that action is needed to restore the meaning of the Amendment as it was understood for nearly a century.

The Effect of the Fourteenth Amendment Upon Racial Segregation in the Public Schools, as Interpreted by the Congress

The starting point in any such discussion is the Civil Rights Act of 1866, since it was designed to cover the same field as the Amendment. The bill provided:

> That there shall be no discrimination in the civil rights or immunities among the inhabitants of any State or Territory of the United States on account of race, color, or previous condition of slavery; but the inhabitants of every race and color ... shall have the same rights to make and enforce contracts, to sue, be parties, and give evidence, to inherit, purchase, lease, sell, hold and convey real and personal property, and to full and equal benefit of all laws and proceedings for the security of person and property, and shall be subject to like punishment, pains, and penalties, and to none others, any law, statutes, ordinance, regulation, or custom to the contrary notwithstanding.[1]

When the bill came before the Senate, there was some concern on the part of Senator Cowan, Pennsylvania Republican,

that it would end segregation in the schools;[2] but he was
assured by Senator Trumbull, of Illinois, the bill's patron, that
it affected only civil rights.[3] When the bill reached the House,
the floor leader, Mr. Wilson of Iowa, Chairman of the Judiciary Committee to which the bill had been committed, stated
in opening the debate:

> What do these terms mean? Do they mean that in
> all things civil, social, political, all citizens, without
> distinction of race or color, shall be equal? By no
> means can they be so construed. . . . Nor do they
> mean that . . . their children shall attend the same
> schools. These are no civil rights or immunities.[4]

And he repeated that assurance later in the course of debate.[5]

The Civil Rights act is important in this discussion since it
referred to the "full and equal benefit of all laws," which
could mean nothing less than full protection.

The resolution proposing the Fourteenth Amendment had
been introduced before the Civil Rights Act and both were
before the Congress at the same time. There is nothing in
the proceedings of the House Committee that considered it
to indicate that school segregation was discussed, and there
is nothing to that effect in the majority and minority reports
that came from the Committee. Mr. Thaddeus Stevens, one of
the strongest advocates of the Amendment, did not indicate
that it went beyond the Civil Rights Act. His position was
that the Amendment was necessary since "the first time the
South with their copperhead allies obtained control of Congress the Civil Rights Act would be repealed."[6] He was
anxious to put the Civil Rights Act beyond the reach of
transient congressional majorities.

In the midst of the debate on the Amendment in the House
the Senate passed "an Act donating certain Lots in the City

of Washington for schools for colored children in the District of Columbia."[7] And another statute was enacted to provide for equitable apportionment of school funds to Negro schools.[8]

The Congress would hardly have taken such a course in the midst of the debates over the Civil Rights Act and the Fourteenth Amendment had it been thought that they barred segregation in the public schools. Moreover, when the Congress codified the laws relating to the District of Columbia in 1874, it specifically preserved the mandatory segregation requirements enacted in 1866.[9] These statutes remained in effect until declared unconstitutional in *Bolling* v. *Sharpe*, 347 U.S. 497.

THE EFFECT OF THE FOURTEENTH AMENDMENT UPON RACIAL SEGREGATION IN THE PUBLIC SCHOOLS AS INTERPRETED BY THE STATES

ALABAMA rejected the Fourteenth Amendment in 1866.[10] After its government was reorganized under Federal military rule, the Amendment was ratified without debate (1868).[11] A new constitution was adopted in the same year without reference to segregated schools although there is evidence that it was recognized that segregation would be practiced.[12] The Legislature, less than a month after its ratification of the Amendment, adopted a general school law requiring segregation.[13] Obviously, the Legislature saw no conflict between the Amendment and the school statute. The next constitution (1875) made segregation mandatory.[14]

ARKANSAS at first rejected the Amendment.[15] Committee reports in both houses of the Assembly stated objections in detail, but there is no indication that the Amendment was thought to affect segregation.[16] The same Assembly specifically required it.[17] The Amendment was ratified in 1868 by a military Legislature, which then directed the State Board of Education to set up segregated schools.[18]

CALIFORNIA never ratified the Amendment, but its Assembly must have concluded that it did not ban segregation in the public schools, since the statutes requiring segregation in 1863 and 1864 were repeated in 1866 and 1870.[19]

CONNECTICUT abolished school segregation in 1868,[20] but there is nothing to indicate that the Amendment was in any way related to the statute. Of course, this was not a grave issue in that State since it had only 9,668 Negroes according to the 1870 census.

DELAWARE did not ratify the Fourteenth Amendment until 1901. At that time its constitution, adopted in 1897, required segregation.[21] Certainly, Delaware did not consider the Amendment in contravention of its constitution.

FLORIDA ratified the Amendment in 1868,[22] and in the same year adopted a new constitution under pressure of the Reconstruction Act.[23] Nothing was said about school segregation, although there was quite a cross section represented in the Assembly: 23 Democrats, 13 carpetbaggers, 21 scalawags and 19 Negroes.[24] It is true that Florida prohibited segregation by statute in 1873;[25] but, according to the Florida Attorney General, the statute was not enforced, and in the constitution which became effective in 1887 segregation was required.[26] There is no affirmative evidence that the Amendment was considered to have outlawed school segregation.

GEORGIA ratified the Amendment in 1870.[27] The same Assembly passed the first statute establishing a public school system and it expressly required segregation.[28] The Governor was a Republican and a majority in both houses were Republicans, but they defeated an amendment to eliminate the segregation provision.[29]

ILLINOIS ratified the Amendment in 1867.[80] There is nothing in the official publications or in current newspaper accounts to indicate any intention to affect public schools. The Superintendent of Public Instruction reported (1865-1866) that no schools were provided for Negroes since the law did not contemplate their mixing with the whites.[81] In his next report he stated:

> The question of co-attendance, or of separate schools, is an entirely separate and distinct one, and may safely be left to be determined by the respective districts and communities, to suit themselves. In many places there will be but one school for all; in many others there will be separate schools. This is a matter of but little importance, and one which need not and cannot be regulated by legislation.[82]

The Illinois Constitution of 1870 required compulsory education, but made no reference to segregation.[83] The Governor, in his message to the Assembly, urged statutes to implement the Constitution, and said:

> The question whether children of different complexions shall be admitted to and instructed in the same school is one of mere local and temporary interest, and may be safely left to those who vote and pay the taxes.[84]

The constituted authorities of Illinois obviously thought that the Fourteenth Amendment did not wipe out segregation in the schools. Nor did Illinois bar segregation in its schools until 1874.[85]

INDIANA adopted the Amendment in 1867.[86] None of those advocating adoption suggested that segregation in the schools would be affected. Under the School Law of 1865, there was no provision for Negro pupils.[37] In 1869, however, the statute was amended and separate schools were provided for Negroes.[88] The debate was extensive, but there was no suggestion that the Fourteenth Amendment was violated.[89] Segregated schools were made permissive by statute in 1877.[40] In 1874, the Supreme Court of Indiana rejected the argument that the Fourteenth Amendment was violated by school segregation statutes, citing the action of Congress in maintaining segregation in the schools of the District of Columbia.[41] It did so again in 1926.[42]

IOWA's constitution barred school segregation before the adoption of the Amendment, according to its Supreme Court.[43] After the adoption of the Amendment, an effort was made to segregate the schools, but the Iowa Supreme Court held this violative of Iowa statutes. The Fourteenth Amendment was not mentioned.[44]

KANSAS ratified the Amendment in 1867.[45] The same Legislature in the same year authorized segregated schools in the cities of the second class;[46] and, in 1868, authorized such schools in cities of the first class.[47] Except for one adverse vote in the house, action on the latter was unanimous.[48] Except for the period 1876-1879, segregated schools were maintained until the *Brown* decision.[49]

KENTUCKY rejected the Amendment in 1867[50] and never again considered it. There is nothing to indicate that the Amendment affected that decision. The Legislature obviously thought the Amendment was not related to school segregation since it established separate schools for Negroes that same year.[51] And the Constitution of 1891 required segregated schools.[52]

LOUISIANA rejected the Amendment unanimously in 1867.[53] Reconstruction caused the 1868 Legislature to be composed mostly of Negroes who adopted the Amendment by a wide margin.[54] That same year a constitution was adopted barring school segregation.[55] Several members gave reasons for their votes, but none mentioned the Fourteenth Amendment.[56] Riots followed, and no effective schools were established while the 1868 Constitution was in effect.[57] In 1879 a new Constitution was adopted requiring school segregation.[58] There is no affirmative evidence that the people of Louisiana thought that the Amendment affected segregated schools.

MAINE never had segregation, and its Negro population in 1870 was only 1,606, about one-quarter of one percent of its population.

MARYLAND never ratified the Amendment.[59] In his message of submission, the Governor did not mention the Amendment;[60] nor did the lengthy report of the Joint Committee on Federal Relations to which the Amendment was referred.[61] Maryland adopted a new constitution in 1867 and it did not require segregation in the schools. But the debates in convention make it clear that the delegates did not think the subject required discussion, much less prohibition.[62] When a comprehensive school system was set up by statute in 1868, it provided for separate schools for the races.[63] All of this was contemporaneous with the early history of the Fourteenth Amendment and clearly shows that Maryland thought it had no application.

MASSACHUSETTS prohibited segregated schools by statute in 1855,[64] and its adoption of the Fourteenth Amendment throws no light. The Governor reviewed the Amendment in detail but made no reference to its application to schools.[65]

MICHIGAN passed a statute in 1867 providing that "all residents of any district shall have an equal right to attend any school therein."[66] The Supreme Court of Michigan construed this as permitting Negroes to attend white schools. The opinion made no reference to the Fourteenth Amendment.[67]

MINNESOTA abolished segregated schools in 1864,[68] and throws no light on our problem. Minnesota had only 759 Negroes in the 1870 census.

MISSISSIPPI at first rejected the Amendment out of hand.[69] Reconstruction followed and the provisional Governor, a Major General of the U. S. Army, compelled ratification.[70] Segregation was not mentioned in the Constitution of 1868,[71] nor in the 1870 statute setting up a school system.[72] However, the Republican Lieutenant Governor recognized that the statute accomplished segregation in effect, since in a speech to the Senate he said: "If the people desire to provide separate schools for white and black, or for good and bad children, or large or small, or male or female children, there is nothing in this law that prohibits it."[73] The schools established under this statute were nearly always segregated,[74] and segregation was expressly required by statute in 1878.[75] The Mississippi Legislature that ratified the Fourteenth Amendment, dominated as it was by Republicans and former slaves, did not consider that ratification made school segregation unlawful.

MISSOURI ratified the Amendment in 1867,[76] but no reference to schools is found in the proceedings. It has been consistent in maintaining segregated schools: The Constitution of 1865,[77] and statutes enacted in 1865, 1868, 1869 and 1874.[78] Segregation was again required by the Constitution of 1875 without debate,[79] and subsequent statutes laid down the same requirements in 1879, 1887, and 1889.[80]

NEBRASKA was admitted to the Union in 1867 and immediately ratified the Amendment.[81] While the first school statute, enacted in 1867, made no reference to segregation,[82] the Legislature specifically declared against segregation at the University of Nebraska when it was established two years later.[83] There is nothing in the record to indicate that school segregation was thought to be required by the Amendment. Nebraska had only 789 Negroes in the 1870 census, and the matter of racial mixing gave no concern.

NEVADA ratified the Amendment in 1867.[84] The same Legislature provided for segregated schools.[85] There was a minority report by the committee that recommended this legislation, but there is nothing to indicate that the division of opinion was caused by the Amendment.[86] In 1872, the Nevada Supreme Court held that a particular statute providing separate schools for Negroes was invalid under the Constitution of Nevada though not under the Fourteenth Amendment.[87] The dissenting opinion stated:

> The case of relator was sought to be maintained on the ground that the statute was in violation of the

Fourteenth Amendment to the Constitution of the United States. I fully agree with my associates that proposal of counsel is utterly untenable.

So there was unanimity only to extent of agreeing that the Amendment had no application to segregation.

NEW JERSEY ratified the Amendment in 1866.[88] Although when the Democrats got control of the Assembly in 1868 they rescinded that action over the veto of the Governor, and stated numerous objections to the Amendment, none of them related to its effect upon the school system.[89] New Jersey never had mandatory school segregation by law, but in 1868 the State Superintendent of Schools interpreted the statute to permit segregation,[90] and there was no amendment of the statute until 1881, when segregation in the schools was abolished.[91]

NEW YORK ratified in 1867.[92] It had long permitted separate schools for the races. In 1864, as part of the general revision of the school laws, local authorities were empowered to establish separate schools for Negroes,[93] and this act was continued in effect in subsequent codifications.[94] Authorities in some localities took advantage of the act and maintained separate schools.[95] Although the New York Constitutional Convention of 1867 adopted a strong resolution on civil rights, there was nothing said about abolishing school segregation.[96] Efforts were made over a period of more than thirty years to have school segregation statutes declared unconstitutional in the New York courts, but in each case the court refused.[97]

NORTH CAROLINA ratified in 1868.[98] A new constitution,

adopted that same year, did not expressly require segregation, but the Convention adopted a resolution asserting that the interest and happiness of the races would be promoted by separate schools.[99] This convention, it will be observed, was dominated by the radical Republicans who recognized the validity of segregation statutes.[100] Within two weeks after ratification of the Fourteenth Amendment, the Assembly adopted a joint resolution asserting that it was the duty of the Assembly to adopt a system of free public schools, but that the races should be separated.[101] Accordingly, legislation was adopted to carry out that purpose,[102] and segregated schools were thereafter maintained under law until North Carolina was recently required to integrate by force of Federal court order.

Оню ratified in 1867.[103] No mention was made in those proceedings of school segregation. The following year, a resolution was passed by both Houses rescinding its previous action.[104] Again, no mention of school segregation. Ohio had a long record of segregated schools. A statute providing schools for Negroes was enacted as early as 1831.[105] Others were enacted in 1847 and 1848.[106] In 1860 separate schools were required where there were more than thirty children in a school district.[107] In 1874 separate schools were authorized in the discretion of local authorities,[108] and this provision was codified in 1880.[109] Segregation was not barred by statute until 1887.[110]

OREGON ratified in 1866[111] and rescinded in 1868.[112] There is no mention of school segregation in either record. Nor was any segregation statute passed. Oregon had only 346 Negroes in 1870 and there was no problem.

PENNSYLVANIA ratified in 1867.[113] The debates are preserved, and there are some references to segregation, but it is not clear that the Legislature believed that school segregation was involved. Subsequently, however, the Legislature did make it clear that the Fourteenth Amendment did not affect school segregation, since it required separate schools in Pittsburgh in 1869,[114] and did not abolish school segregation until 1881.[115] Meantime, the constitutionality of segregation had been upheld in the courts.[116]

RHODE ISLAND ratified in 1867,[117] but school segregation had been abolished by statute in January, 1866.[118] The Fourteenth Amendment, therefore, was never involved.

SOUTH CAROLINA in 1866 unanimously rejected the Amendment for one vote in the House.[119] Then came Reconstruction, followed by the adoption of a constitution (1868) which abolished segregation in the public schools.[120] Three months after the convention adjourned the Fourteenth Amendment was ratified.[121] There is nothing to indicate that the Amendment was a factor either in the Convention or the Legislature. Even though the radical element was then in control in South Carolina and had abolished segregation by law, its Governor, a Brigadier General, United States Army, advocated that in practice the races be separated in the schools, and that the ultimate solution of the problem be left to time.[122] The Legislature followed his advice and never set up the system of schools contemplated by the framers of the Constitution, but something "very different."[123] In 1870, a Massachusetts Negro was named the first Superintendent of Public Education. He submitted a report to the Legislature which contained recommendations from local school authorities, twelve of the thirteen reporting advocating segregation.[124] In practice, there

311

was little integration. When the Superintendent ordered integration for the School of the Deaf, Dumb and Blind, it closed down, and remained closed until it was reopened three years later on a segregated basis. Efforts to integrate the State University also failed.[125]

TENNESSEE ratified the Amendment in 1866 after some members were put under arrest to make a quorum. Efforts were made by the opponents to except various State rights from its operation, but no one seemed to consider it necessary to make exceptions to cover segregation in the public schools.[126] The same Legislature which ratified the Amendment amended the school law (March 5, 1867) to require segregated education in Tennessee,[127] a statute which the Republican Governor referred to in his second inaugural address as "wise and desirable." In 1870, school segregation was written into the constitution,[128] and reenacted in a further amendment to the school laws in 1873.[129] They have remained segregated until our day.

TEXAS at first rejected the Amendment.[130] Both House and Senate committees on Federal Relations filed long reports opposing ratification, pointing out that the Amendment might give the Negroes the vote, the right to serve on juries, to bear arms, etc.; but no one seemed to think it necessary to mention segregation in the schools, which was not enumerated among the objections.[131] Then came Reconstruction and ratification of the Amendment in 1870.[132] Again, there is no record of any reference to schools. The 1869 Constitution required establishment of a free school system, but segregation was not mentioned.[133] The same Legislature that ratified the Amendment enacted a statute which left it to the localities, "when in their opinion, the harmony and success of the schools require it, to make any separation of the students or schools necessary to insure success..."[134] The report of the committee that recommended adoption made it plain enough that it was intended to establish segregation on the local level.[135] Segregated schools were required by the 1876 Constitution,[136] and that requirement has been continued.

VERMONT ratified in 1866.[137] Throughout the proceeding no mention was made of the school problem. But Vermont seems never to have had segregated schools, and it had no problem since it had only 924 Negroes in 1870.

VIRGINIA refused to ratify in 1867. There were no favorable votes in the Senate and only one in the House.[138] There was no mention of public schools in the proceedings. Ratification followed Reconstruction in the 1869-70 session of the Legislature.[139] In 1869, a constitution was adopted which made no reference to segregated schools, but in 1870 the same Legislature which ratified the Fourteenth Amendment provided for segregated schools and resisted every effort to strike this provision from the school statute.[140] On Virginia's statute books this has been the law ever since.

WEST VIRGINIA ratified in 1867,[141] and the same Legislature only six weeks later adopted a statute providing that "white and colored persons shall not be taught in the same schools..."[142] In 1872 a new constitution was adopted. It required segregation in the schools,[143] and West Virginia has continued that provision ever since.

WISCONSIN ratified in 1867.[144] There was no reference in the proceedings to segregated schools, but it was immaterial anyway since Wisconsin never had segregation in its schools, and in 1870 had only 2,113 Negroes to segregate.

CONCLUSION

The foregoing summary seems conclusive that the Congress which initiated the Fourteenth Amendment did not believe that it barred segregation in the public schools, and that in not one of the thirty-seven States that considered the Amendment is there substantial evidence to indicate that the Amendment was deemed such a prohibition.

The Supreme Court of the United States on March 20 of this year decided a case involving an interpretation of the Amendment by a careful examination of the constitutions of the several States at the time of the Amendment's adoption, and felt bound thereby.[145] It, therefore, approves that method of interpretation. However, all of the material above cited and more, was supplied to the Court in the School Cases, but was held by it to be "inconclusive."[146] Surely we have the right respectfully to differ when the evidence is so overwhelming and irrefutable.

There are only two possible ways of restoring the original meaning of the Fourteenth Amendment: by the reversal of its position by the Supreme Court itself or by action of the Congress and orderly amendment. The first seems out of the question since the Court has adopted the policy of committing new justices to the rule laid down in the School Cases as they take their places on the bench.[147] The remedy, therefore, is in the hands of Congress alone.

Again, I wish to thank you gentlemen for the opportunity of appearing before you.

NOTES

1. Cong. Globe, 39th Cong., 1st Sess. (1866) 211.
2. *Ibid.*, p. 500.
3. *Ibid.*, p. 600.
4. *Ibid.*, p. 1117.
5. *Ibid.*, p. 1294.
6. *Ibid.*, p. 2459.
7. *Ibid.*, p. 2719.
8. 14 Stat. 216 (1866).
9. Revised Statutes of the District of Columbia, 18 Stat. part 2 (1874).
10. Ala. Sen. J. (1866-7) 155; Ala. House J. (1866-7) 84.
11. Ala. Sen. J. (1868) 10; Ala. House J. (1868) 10.
12. Bond, *Negro Education in Alabama, A Study in Cotton and Steel* (1939).
13. Ala. Acts (1868) 148.
14. Ala. Const. (1875) Art. 13, 51.
15. Ark. S. J. (1866) 262; Ark. H. J. (1866-7) 291.
16. Ark. S. J. (1866) 258; Ark. H. J. (1866-7) 288.
17. Ark. Stat. (1866-7) 100.
18. Ark. Stat. (1868) No. LII, S 107.
19. Cal. Stat. (1863) Ch. CLIX, S68; (1864), Ch. CCIX, S13 (1866), Ch. CCCXLII, Ss 57-9; (1870), Ch. DLVI, Ss 56-7.
20. Conn. Public Acts (1868) Ch. CVIII.
21. Del. Const. (1897) Art. 10, S2.
22. Fla. S. J. (1868) 9; Fla. H. J. (1868) 9.
23. Fla. Const. (1868) Art. VIII, S1.
24. Davis, *Civil War and Reconstruction in Florida* (1913), 259.
25. Fla. Laws (1873) Ch. 1947.
26. Art. XII, S12.
27. Ga. S. J. (1870) v. I. 74; Ga. H. J. (1870) 74.
28. Ga. Public Laws (1870) 49.
29. Ga. H. J. (1870) 449.
30. Ill. S. J. (1867); Ill. H. J. (1867) 134.
31. Report of Superintendent of Public Instruction of Illinois (1865-6) 28; Ill. Laws (1865) 105.
32. Report of Superintendent of Public Instruction of Ill. (1867-8) 21.
33. Ill. Const. (1870) Art. VIII, S1. A proposal to require segregated schools was defeated, Journal of Const. Conv. of Ill. (1869) 234, but the majority did not bar segregation.
34. Message to Legislature by Governor of Ill. (1871) 26.
35. Ill. Rev. Stat. (1874) Ch. 122, S 100.
36. Brevier Legislative Reports (1867) 58, 90.
37. Ind. Laws (1865) 3.
38. Brevier Legislative Reports (1867) 267-268, 353, 444. *cf. id.* pp. 356, 444.
39. *Idem* (1869) 34, 341-2, 419-96, 506-12, 533.
40. Ind. Laws (1877) 124.
41. *Cory v. Carter*, 48 Ind. 327 (1874).
42. *Greathouse v. Board of School Commissioners*, 194 Ind. 95, 151 N. E. 411.
43. *District v. City of Dubuque*, 7 Iowa 262 (1858).
44. *Clark v. Board of Directors*, 24 Iowa 266 (1868).

45. Kan. S. J. (1867) 76, 128; Kan. H. J. (1867) 79.

46. Kan. Laws (1867) Ch. 49, S7.

47. Kan. Gen. Stat. (1868) Ch. 18, Art. V, S75. cont. 4 and 5 p. 9.

48. Kan. H. J. (1868) 637; Kan. S. J. (1868) 389, 391, 399.

49. Kan. Laws (1876) Ch. 122; Kan. Laws (1879); Kan. Gen. Stat. (1949) Ss 72-1724.

50. Ky. S. J. (1867) 64; Ky. H. J. (1867) 63.

51. Ky. Acts (1867) 94.

52. S 187.

53. La. S. J. (1867) 20; La. H. J. (1867) 23.

54. La. S. J. (1868) 21; La. H. J. (1868) 8.

55. La. Const. (1868) Art. 135.

56. Journal of La. Const. Conv. J 1868, pp. 200-01.

57. Annual Rept. of La. State Supt. of Public Education (1874) LII-LXXVI; idem (1875) 40-73; Idem (1877) IV.

58. Art. 224; cf. Art. 231.

59. Actually, Maryland ratified the Amendment after this statement was prepared. The Governor approved the resolution of the General Assembly on April 28, 1959.

60. Message of the Governor of Md. to the Legislature of 1867, p. 22.

61. Documents of the General Assembly of Md., Regular Session, 1867.

62. Debates of the Md. Const. Conv. of 1867, pp. 199-203, 243-48, 251-57.

63. Md. Laws (1868) Ch. 407; idem, p. 766.

64. Mass. Acts and Resolves (1855) Ch. 256.

65. Message of the Governor of Mass. to the General Court, Jan. 4, 1867, pp. 67 et seq.

66. Mich. Laws (1867) 43.

67. People ex. rel. Workman v. Board of Education of Detroit 18 Mich. 400 (1869).

68. Minn. Laws (1864) 25-6.

69. Miss. H. J. (1867) 201-2, App. p. 77; Miss. S. J. (1867) 195-6.

70. Miss. H. J. (1870) 13, 26; Miss. S. J. (1870) 19.

71. See Art. VIII relating to Education.

72. Miss. Laws (1870) Ch. 1.

73. Miss. S. J. (1870) 440.

74. Message of the Governor of Miss. (1871) 6; Annual Rept. of Supt. of Public Instruction of Miss. (1871) 66, 124-7, showing only two mixed schools in the entire State.

75. Miss. Laws (1878) Ch. XIV, § 35.

76. Mo. S. J. (1867) 30; Mo. H. J. (1867) 50.

77. Mo. Const. (1865) Art. IX, S2.

78. Mo. Laws (1865) 177; (1868) 170; (1869) 86; (1874) 163-4.

79. Mo. Const. (1875) Art. XI S 3.

80. Mo. Rev. Stat. (1879) S 7052; Mo. Laws (1887) 264; Mo. Laws (1889) 226.

81. Neb. H. J. (1867) 15; Neb. S. J. (1867) 174.

82. Neb. Laws (1867) 101.

83. Neb. Laws (1869) 172, 177.

84. Nev. S. J. (1867) 47; Nev. Assembly J. (1867) 25.

85. Nev. Stat. (1867) 95.

86. Nev. Assembly J. (1867) 208, 211.

87. State v. Duffy, 7 Nev. 342, 8 Am. Rep. 713 (1872).

88. N. J. S. J. (Extra Session, 1866) 14; Minutes of the Assembly (1866) 8, 17.

89. N. J. Acts (1868) 1225.

90. Annual Report of State Supt. of Schools (1868), 41-2.

91. N. J. Laws (1881) Ch. CXLIX, p. 186.

92. N. Y. S. J. (1867) 34; N. Y. H. J. (1867) 77.

93. N. Y. Laws (1864) Ch. 555, Title X, S 1.

94. N. Y. Laws (1894) Ch. 556, Title XV, Art. 11; N. Y. Laws (1909), Ch. 21, Art. 10.

95. Report of N. Y. Supt. of Public Education (1867) 75-6, 206, 208-9; (1868) 19, 219-20, 247-9; (1869) 78-9, 202-3, 227; (1870) 97-8, 230.

96. N. Y. Const. (1868) Art. IX; Documents of the Convention of the State of New York (1868) No. 15.

97. *Dallas* v. *Fosdick*, 40 How. Prac. 249 (1869); *People* ex. rel. *Dietz* v. *Easton*, 13 Abb. Prac. (N. S.) 159 (1872); *People* ex. rel. *King* v. *Gallagher* 93 New York 438 (1883); *People* ex. rel. *Cisco* v. *School Board of Queens*, 161 N. Y. 598, 56 N. E. 81.

98. N. C. Laws (1868) 89.

99. Constitution of the State of North Carolina, Together with Ordinances and Resolutions of the Constitutional Convention Assembled in the City of Raleigh, January 14, 1868 (1868) 122.

100. Noble, *A History of Public Schools in North Carolina* (1930) 299.

101. N. C. H. J. (1868) 54; N. C. S. J. (1868) 237.

102. N. C. Laws (1868-9) Ch. 184.

103. Ohio S. J. (1867) 7; Ohio H. J. (1867) 12; Ohio Laws (1867) 320.

104. Ohio H. J. (1868) 33; Ohio S. J. (1868) 39; Ohio Laws (First Session, 1867) 280.

105. Ohio Laws (1831) 414.

106. Ohio Laws (1847) 81; (1848) 17.

107. 2 Ohio Rev. Stat. (1860) 1357.

108. Ohio Laws (1874) 513.

109. Ohio Rev. Stat. (1880) S 4008.

110. Ohio Laws (1887) 34.

111. Ore. S. J. (1866) 35; Ore. H. J. (1866) 74.

112. Ore. S. J. (1868) 32, 131; Ore. H. J. (1868) 271.

113. Penna. S. J. (1867) No. 125; Penna. H. J. (1867) 278.

114. Penna. Laws (1869) No. 133, S 15.

115. Act of June 8, 1881, P. L. 76.

116. *Commonwealth* v. *Williamson*, 30 Legal. Int. 406 (1873).

117. 25 Journal of the R. I. Sen. (1865-8) Feb. 5, 1867; 41 Journal of the R. I. House (1866-9) Feb. 7, 1867.

118. R. I. Acts and Resolves (1866) Ch. 609.

119. Charleston Daily Courier, Dec. 20, 22, 1866.

120. Art. X, S 10.

121. Charleston Daily Courier, July 8, 9, 1868.

122. *Ibid.*, July 10, 1868.

123. *Holler* v. *Rock Hill School District*, 60 S. C. 41, 38 S. E. 220, 221 (1901).

124. Reports and Resolutions of the S. C. General Assembly (1870) 403-87.

125. Simpkins and Woody, *South Carolina Reconstruction* (1932) 439-42.

126. Tenn. S. J. (Called Session, 1866), 4, 23, 24, 41; Tenn. H. J. (Called Session, 1866) 25, 36.

127. Tenn. Stat. (1866-7) Ch. XXVII, S 17.

128. Art. XI, S 12.

129. Tenn. Stat. (1873) Ch. XXV, S 30.

130. Texas H. J. (1866) 584; Texas S. J. (1866) 471.

131. Texas H. J. (1866) 578; Texas S. J. (1866) 421.

132. Daily State Journal, v. I, No. 19 (Feb. 19, 1870).

133. Texas Const. (1869) Art. IX, S IV.

134. Texas Gen. Laws (1870) 113.

135. Texas S. J. (1870) 482.

136. Art. VII, S 7.

137. Vt. S. J. (1866) 75; Vt. H. J. (1866) 140.

138. Va. H. J. (1866-7) 108; Va. S. J. (1866-7) 103; Va. Acts (1866-7) Ch. 46.

139. Va. H. J. (1869-70) 36, Va. S. J. (1869-70) 27.

140. Va. Acts (1869-70) Ch. 259, S 47; Va. S. J. (1869-70) 485, 489, 507; Va. H. J. (1869-70) 606-7, 615.

141. W. Va. S. J. (1867) 24; W. Va. H. J. (1867) 10.

142. W. Va. Acts (1867) Ch. 98.

143. W. Va. Const. (1872) Art. XII, S 8.

144. Wis. S. J. (1867) 119; Wis. H. J. (1867) 223.

145. *Bartkus* v. *People of the State of Illinois*, 27 L. W. 4233.

146. *Brown* v. *Board of Education of Topeka*, 347 U. S. 483, 489.

147. *Cooper* v. *Aaron*, 3 L ed. 5, 18.

THE MEANING OF THE FOURTEENTH AMENDMENT

IN TERMS OF A STATE'S POWER TO OPERATE
RACIALLY SEPARATE PUBLIC SCHOOLS,
AS DEFINED BY THE COURTS

DID THE COURT
INTERPRET OR *AMEND?*

The Meaning of the Fourteenth Amendment, in
Terms of a State's power to operate Racially
Separate Public Schools, as defined by the Courts.

GREAT danger to constitutional government lies in popular misunderstanding of its precise methods and purposes. In many ways the small minority who would treat the United States Constitution as an archaic hindrance to their centralist purposes, and willingly would discard or subvert it, pose less threat than that far greater number who vocally support the Constitution, but who unwittingly approve or participate in actions that tend to destroy its protective features.

One striking instance of this is to be found in the so-called school segregation cases. There are other instances, of course, but none perhaps as conspicuously in the public view nor so clear in dangerous implications. It is not the purpose of the Virginia Commission on Constitutional Government to argue the merits and demerits of racial segregation in any form; the problem is as old and as complex as man himself. It is our purpose, however, to show that the Supreme Court, in order to accomplish what it presumably thought was a worthwhile end, committed a breach of basic constitutional limitations.

321

John C. Calhoun said that just as laws are written to restrain men, so constitutions are written to restrain governments. The framers of the United States Constitution had this goal in mind when they drafted the basic compact by which the States are bound in Union. They had fired the crucible of the Revolution with a great political ideal, that governments derive their just powers only from the consent of the governed; and newly freed from the tyrannies of the British crown, they did not propose to embrace a system that would permit fresh tyranny of domestic origin. Thus, out of the reservoir of the States' inherent political powers, certain specific powers were to be delegated to the central government, but all powers not so delegated were to be retained, to the end that the people themselves, acting in their respective States, might control their own destinies.

It was recognized, of course, that in time their compact, i.e., the Constitution, might require amendment, but it was recognized also that it was as necessary to protect the Constitution from being amended by the very government it was designed to control as it was to establish controls on that government initially. Consistent with this grand plan for a federated union, Article V was drafted carefully to preserve ultimate control of the Constitution in the States themselves. The agreement was that no change would be made in this most basic of all law without the consent of a full three-fourths of the States. Amendments could not even be proposed without the approval of two-thirds of each House of Congress, or as an alternative, without the approval of two-thirds of the States.

The purpose of this deliberately restrictive procedure was plain: it was to protect a minority of the people, in a minority of the States, from the tyranny of simple majority rule. The framers realized, with magnificent vision, that similarities among the States would take care of themselves; the framers' concern was that the *differences* among the States be respected. And when it came to their fundamental law—to the Constitution itself—they wanted to be positive that changes in the compact were not made easily or impulsively.

An understanding of the design and purpose of Article V is essential to an understanding of the position advanced in this paper. A Constitution does not consist of empty words. A Constitution has meaning only as its words have meaning, and the plain meaning of Article V was, and is, that the States alone have the power to amend their compact.

But words, it is said, often have different meanings, and it may be necessary to have them construed or interpreted by resort to the judicial function. Where, then, does "interpretation" of the Constitution end, and where does "amendment" begin? Granted that courts have power to interpret; how is one to know when the necessary power to interpret has been corrupted into a usurped power to amend?

The question answers itself if we return to the point of beginning: Words have meanings. And the words of a contractual instrument, as applied to particular events or conditions in the minds of the parties at the time the instrument is agreed to, have a permanent meaning. Such a meaning is necessarily fixed. It becomes, in fact, the instrument itself; to alter it would be to alter the instrument itself. This is true even if some disagreement among the parties themselves led or forced them to have the Courts interpret the instrument and judicially establish this meaning for them. If that original meaning, however determined, is to be abandoned, then it must be by consent of the parties and the instrument must be formally amended.

Coming then to the point at hand we find that some of the words and phrases of the Fourteenth Amendment are, on the surface, rather nebulous. When men speak of a State's "abridging a citizen's privileges or immunities," or of a State's denying any person "due process of law," or of a State's denying to any person within its jurisdiction the "equal protection of the laws," it is fair enough to inquire what these apparently ambiguous phrases mean.

To answer these questions, one must go to the primary source. What did these words and phrases mean, as applied to particular situations, *to the framers who drafted the Amendment and to the States that ratified it?* If the meaning and intent can be established on this basis, the search is done. That meaning, so fixed, actually becomes and is the Constitution; and no effort to change that meaning can be legal unless it comes through the amendatory process provided in Article V. To contend otherwise would be to nullify the very purpose of the Constitution—the control of government.

This is not an argument of disgruntled Southerners; it is an established maxim of law echoed in every accepted legal treatise on the subject. It is succinctly stated in Judge Cooley's great work on Constitutional Limitations:

A cardinal rule in dealing with written instruments is that they are to receive an unvarying interpretation, and that their practical construction is to be uniform. *A Constitution is not to be made to mean one thing at one time, and another at some subsequent time when the circumstances may have so changed as perhaps to make a different rule in the case seem desirable. A principal share of the benefit expected from written constitutions would be lost if the rules they established were so flexible as to bend to circumstances or be modified by public opinion.* It is with special reference to the varying moods of public opinion, and with a view to putting the fundamentals of government beyond their control, that these instruments are framed; and there can be no such steady and imperceptible change in their rule as inheres in the principles of the common law.

. . .

A court or legislature which should allow a change in public sentiment to influence it in giving construction to a written constitution not warranted by the intention of its founders, would be justly chargable with reckless disregard of official oath and public duty; *and if its course could become a precedent, these instruments would be of little avail.* The violence of public passion is quite as likely to be in the direction of oppression as in any other; and the necessity for Bills of Rights in our fundamental laws lies mainly in the danger that the legislature will be influenced by temporary excitements and passions among the people to adopt oppressive enactments. What a court is to do, therefore, is to declare the law as written, leaving it to the people themselves to make such changes as new circumstances may require. *The meaning of the Constitution is fixed when it is adopted, and it is not different at any subsequent time when a Court has occasion to pass upon it.* [Emphasis supplied]

What "meaning of the Constitution" are we searching for here? We are undertaking to find the meaning of the Fourteenth Amendment to the framers who drafted it and to the States that ratified it, in terms of (1) the *power* of a State to maintain racially separate public schools, and (2) the *right* of an individual to attend a school not segregated by law.

This is a survey, it will be seen, to determine a boundary line—the line that separates the powers of government, or of society, from the rights of the individual citizen. If the metaphor may be pursued for a moment, it will be seen that some striking analogies can be found with the law of real property. Just as the precise bounds of wilderness tracts may remain uncertain for a time, until it is necessary to fix them exactly, so the delineation of constitutional rights and powers may remain for a while obscure. It is only when some specific question is raised that the surveyors are brought in with chain and transit, that titles are examined with care, and that suit is filed to determine precise metes and bounds. Thus A is told that his authority extends to this point, and no farther; and B is told that his rights extend to this point, and no farther, and by obedience to this lawful process, order is established among contending parties. The line becomes fixed. It cannot be changed thereafter except by consent of the parties.

Precisely this lawful process was followed long ago in settling the boundary here under study. Prior to adoption of the Fourteenth Amendment, the States individually possessed a vast domain of political power; it was as if they held all land stretching to some unmapped mountain range. The Amendment reduced this holding drastically. Now the States were prohibited from doing certain things they had had power to do before. The effect of this constriction, obviously, was to expand the area of liberty possessed by the individual in his relationship to the State.

At once a specific question arose. Plainly, the States prior to 1868 had possessed the power, and had exercised the power, to operate racially separate public schools. With the execution of this constitutional deed, had the power now been taken from them? Just as plainly, the Negro prior to 1868 had possessed no right to attend school on a non-segregated basis. In this metaphorical transfer of political property, had he now acquired that right?

So the surveyors were called in, and the title examiners were called in, and the questions were answered and the lines were fixed in the only orderly way these boundaries can be fixed, and that is by judicial determination.

Within fifteen years after adoption of the Fourteenth Amendment, while the understandings and intentions and circumstances of the instrument were fresh in everyone's mind, seven cases were decided on this specific question of right and power. Five of these decisions were written by the highest courts of Ohio, Indiana, Nevada, California and New York. Two of them were written by Federal courts, one in Ohio, the other in Louisiana. These cases so clearly established the mean-

ing of the Fourteenth Amendment in regard to racially separate public schools that the Supreme Court of the United
States later could dismiss the question as settled beyond further argument.

In OHIO:

The first of these cases was *Garnes* v. *McCann*, 21 Ohio
198, decided in December, 1871. Ohio's school laws at this
time required that each township or district have one or more
common schools for its children. However, these laws also
classified and separated pupils by race and permitted adjoining
townships or districts, if they had only a few Negro children,
to form a *joint* school district and operate one school for the
colored children in both original districts. Plaintiff's children,
Negroes, were refused instruction in the established white
school in the district in which they resided, and they refused
to attend the school established in the joint district for colored
children. Garnes sought a writ of mandamus to compel admission of his children to the white school. Basing his case
squarely on the Fourteenth Amendment, his attorney presented these arguments:

[The] school law discriminates against colored children.
The statute providing for the classification of school children
according to color, or at least that part of it which would, as in
this instance, compel colored children to go outside of the limits
of the subdistrict in which they reside, to attend school, and, in
certain contingencies, debar them from the privileges of common
schools altogether, cannot be enforced without abridging the
privileges of citizens within the meaning of the amendment to the
Constitution. Again, the enforcement of this law would be a violation of this amendment, because it would compel a certain class
of citizens to submit the management and control of their school
fund to a board not chosen by themselves, while it secures to
another class the privilege of having their proportion of the school

327

fund appropriated and managed by the electors elected by the voters of the subdistrict. In this particular the statute secures to one class a privilege it denies to another.

In *Van Camp* v. *Board of Education of Logan*, (9 Ohio St. 406), our school law was held to be one of classification and not of exclusion. Class legislation was then permitted—color could then be made a basis of classification, as well as age or sex, without violating the Constitution of the United States, but not so since the amendment.

The relator claims the right to send his children to the public school which is kept in the district in which he resides. It is the only school within the district. Our school law would drive his children forth to some other district where there is maintained a separate school for colored children. To refuse this writ would be to enforce a law which denies to him the privileges that belong to other citizens living in the same district. They possess the advantages and conveniences of having their children instructed in a school located within the limits of their subdistrict, and under the control of officers elected by themselves. To deny to the relator these advantages and conveniences, is to abridge his privileges, since the denial is placed solely on the ground that he is colored.

The citizen is bound to give obedience, and the government must furnish protection. The relator "cannot be a citizen to obey, and an alien to demand protection."

Mr. Justice Day, speaking for a unanimous court, reviewed the facts and then said this:

. . . During all the time the plaintiff insisted on having his children instructed in subdistrict number nine, in the school established for white children, an equally good school was open for them in the joint district established for colored children, as provided by law, where they could enjoy the full advantages and privileges of a public common school.

The defendants, in refusing to recognize the children of the plaintiff as pupils in the school of subdistrict number nine, acted in good faith, and without any design of depriving them of a common school education; but they claim that they may properly insist that the children of the plaintiff shall be educated in the

328

school established for colored children in the joint district, and that they rightfully refuse them instruction in the school for white children in subdistrict number nine.

It is quite apparent from this state of the case, that the proceeding is brought, not because the children of the plaintiff are excluded from the public schools, but to test the right of those having charge of them to make a classification of scholars on the basis of color. This is the principal question in the case, and we propose to consider it without reference to the question made as to the proper parties to the proceeding, for, in the view we take of the case, this becomes unnecessary.

The system of public education in Ohio is the creature of the constitution and statutory laws of the State. The constitution provides that "it shall be the duty of the General Assembly to pass suitable laws * * * * to encourage schools and the means of instruction." (Art. 1, sec. 7.) Again, it provides that "The General Assembly shall make such provision, by taxation or otherwise, as, with the income arising from the school trust fund, will secure a thorough and efficient system of common schools throughout the State." (Art. 6, sec. 2.)

It is left to the discretion of the General Assembly, in the exercise of the general legislative power conferred upon it, to determine what laws are "suitable" to secure the organization and management of the contemplated system of common schools, without express restriction, except that "no religious or other sect or sects shall ever have any exclusive right to, or control of, any part of the school funds of the State." (Art. 6, sec. 2.)

Under these powers and requirements of the constitution, the General Assembly has attempted to organize, by "suitable laws," an "efficient system of common schools," for the purpose (as expressed in the 63d section of the act of 1853) "of affording the advantages of a free education to all the youth of this State."

. . .

As to the validity of the provisions of this section we express no opinion further than is necessary to the determination of this case, in which it clearly appears that the clauses applicable to it did not operate to exclude the colored children of that locality from a common school education equal to that of the other youth.

329

Were this not the fact, more doubt would arise. But where both classes of children, as in the case before us, enjoy substantially equal advantages in different schools, and the separate school for colored children is clearly authorized by the statute, the only doubt that arises is as to the constitutional validity of the law which authorizes such separation on the basis of color: and that is the real question in this case.

The constitution confers the legislative power of the State upon the General Assembly, and "that includes all legislative power which the object and purposes of the State government may require; and we must look to other provisions of the constitution to see how far, and to what extent, legislative discretion is qualified or restricted." (Per Gholson, J. in *Baker* v. *The City of Cincinnati*, 11 Ohio St. 542.) The constitution contains no restrictions upon the "legislative discretion," in regard to the classification of the youth of the State for school purposes. Those, then, enjoying equal privileges with all, cannot complain of a want of power to regulate the manner in which such privileges shall be enjoyed, for in this, as in all cases, the legislature has the power to regulate, for the general good, the mode in which parties shall enjoy their rights, without coming in conflict with any of those constitutional principles which are established for the protection of private rights.

But the question of legislative power to authorize the classification of the youth of the State for school purposes on the basis of color, has been determined by the Supreme Court of this State, both under the present constitution and that of 1802. The 25th section of the bill of rights in the latter contains express provisions guaranteeing "equal participation" to all in the schools endowed, in whole or in part, from the revenue arising from donations made by the United States for the support of schools. But it was held in *The State ex rel. &c.* v. *The City of Cincinnati*, (19 Ohio 178), that, inasmuch as "the whole subject of organizing and regulating schools is very properly left to the General Assembly, in the exercise of its legislative powers," an act to authorize the establishment of separate schools for the education of colored children was constitutional; and it was said by Hitchcock, C. J., in that case, that, "as a matter of policy, it is unquestionably better that the white and colored youth should be placed in separate schools, and that the school fund should be divided to them in proportion to their numbers." After this expression of opinion by that eminent judge, we might at least hesitate to conclude, that the classification of the youth of the State for school purposes, on the basis of color, was an unauthorized or unreasonable exercise of the legislative discretion in the regulation of the public schools of the State.

But in *Van Camp* v. *The Board of Education of Logan*, (9 Ohio St. 406), the question under consideration was expressly determined by this court, upon the original statute, which, so far as material to the question, was the same as that under which the classification was made in this case. In that case the legislative power of classification on the basis of color was sanctioned, and it was held, that, inasmuch as the statute "is a law of *classification* and not of *exclusion*," colored children "are not, *as of right*, entitled to admission into the common schools set apart under said act for the instruction of white youths." The application, however, made in that case, of the principle settled by it, we are not required to approve or disapprove in this, for in that case there had not been, as there was in this, a separate school established for colored children.

It would seem, then, that under the constitution and laws of this State, the right to classify the youth of the State for school purposes, on the basis of color, and to assign them to separate schools for education, both upon well recognized legal principles and the repeated adjudications of this court, is too firmly established to be now judicially disturbed.

But it is claimed that the law authorizing the classification in question contravenes the provisions of the 14th Amendment of the Constitution of the United States, and is, therefore, abrogated thereby.

The section of the amendment relied upon is as follows:

"SECTION 1. All persons born or naturalized in the United States, and subject to the jurisdiction thereof, are citizens of the United States and of the State wherein they reside. No State shall make or enforce any law which shall abridge the privileges or immunities of citizens of the United States; nor shall any State deprive any person of life, liberty or property without due process of law,

331

nor deny to any person within its jurisdiction the equal protection of the laws."

Unquestionably all doubts, wheresoever they existed, as to the citizenship of colored persons, and their right to the "equal protection of the laws," are settled by this amendment. But neither of these was denied to them in this State before the adoption of the amendment. At all events, the statutes classifying the youth of the State for school purposes on the basis of color, and the decisions of this court in relation thereto, were not at all based on a denial that colored persons were citizens, or that they are entitled to the equal protection of the laws. It would seem, then, that these provisions of the amendment contain nothing conflicting with the statute authorizing the classification in question, nor the decisions heretofore made touching the point in controversy in this case. Nor do we understand that the contrary is claimed by counsel in the case. But the clause relied on, in behalf of the plaintiff, is that which forbids any State to "make or enforce any law which shall abridge the privileges or immunities of citizens of the United States."

This involves the enquiry as to what privileges or immunities are embraced in the inhibition of this clause. We are not aware that this has been as yet judicially settled. The language of the clause, however, taken in connection with other provisions of the amendment, and of the Constitution of which it forms a part, affords strong reasons for believing that it includes only such privileges or immunities as are derived from, or recognized by, the Constitution of the United States. A broader interpretation opens into a field of conjecture limitless as the range of speculative theories, and might work such limitations of the power of the States to manage and regulate their local institutions and affairs as were never contemplated by the amendment.

If this construction be correct, the clause has no application to this case, for all the privileges of the school system of this State are derived solely from the constitution and laws of the State. If the General Assembly should pass a law repealing all laws creating and regulating the system, it cannot be claimed that the 14th Amendment could be interposed to prevent so grievous an abridgement of the privileges of the citizens of the State, for they would thereby be deprived of privileges derived from the State, and not of privileges derived from the United States.

But we need not now further discuss this point, as the true meaning and exact limits of the clause in question are not necessarily involved in this case. For, conceding that the 14th Amendment not only provides equal securities for all, but guarantees equality of rights to the citizens of a State, as one of the privileges of citizens of the United States, it remains to be seen whether this privilege has been abridged in the case before us. The law in question surely does not attempt to deprive colored persons of any rights. On the contrary it recognizes their right, under the constitution of the State, to equal common school advantages, and secures to them their equal proportion of the school fund. It only regulates the mode and manner in which this right shall be enjoyed by all classes of persons. The regulation of this right arises from the necessity of the case. Undoubtedly it should be done in a manner to promote the best interests of all. But this task must, of necessity, be left to the wisdom, and discretion of some proper authority. The people have committed it to the General Assembly, and the presumption is that it has discharged its duty in accordance with the best interests of all. At all events, the legislative action is conclusive, unless it clearly infringes the provisions of the Constitution.

At most, the 14th Amendment only affords to colored citizens an additional guaranty of equality of rights to that already secured by the constitution of the State.

The question, therefore, under consideration is the same that has, as we have seen, been heretofore determined in this State, that a classification of the youth of the State for school purposes, upon any basis which does not exclude either class from equal school advantages, is no infringement of the equal rights of citizens secured by the constitution of the State.

We have seen that the law, in the case before us, works no substantial inequality of school privileges between the children of both classes in the locality of the parties. Under the lawful regulation of equal educational privileges, the children of each class are required to attend the school provided for them, and to which they are assigned by those having the lawful official control of all. The plaintiff, then, cannot claim that his privileges are abridged on the ground of inequality of school advantages for his children. Nor can he dictate where his children shall be instructed, or what teacher shall perform that office, without obtaining privileges not enjoyed by white citizens. *Equality of rights does not involve the necessity of educating white and colored persons in the same school, any more than it does that of educating children of both sexes in the same school, or that different grades of scholars must be kept in the same school. Any classification which preserves substantially equal school advantages is not prohibited by either the State or Federal Constitution, nor would it contravene the provisions of either.* There is, then, no ground upon which the plaintiff can claim that his rights under the Fourteenth Amendment have been infringed. [Emphasis supplied]

The action of the defendants was warranted by the authority conferred by the General Assembly in the exercise of its constitutional powers. "Where the power which is exercised is legislative in its character, the courts can enforce only those limitations which the Constitution imposes, and not those implied restrictions, which, resting on theory only, the people have been satisfied to leave to the judgment, patriotism, and sense of justice of their representatives." Cooley's Con. Lim. [*129].

In NEVADA:

In 1872, the Supreme Court of Nevada had before it the question of whether racial classification in public schools contravened the provisions of the Fourteenth Amendment. (*State ex rel Stoutmeyer* v. *Duffy,* 7 Nevada 342) The colored plaintiff raised some arguments identical to those advanced by Negro petitioners in 1953 and 1954, viz:

. . .

V. The separation of the children in the public schools, on account of race or color, is in the nature of caste, and is a violation of equality. It is clear that the trustees may classify scholars according to age and sex, for these distinctions are inoffensive and recognized as legal; or according to their moral and intellectual qualifications, because such a power is necessary to the government of schools. But the legislature cannot assume, without individual examination, that an entire race possess certain moral or intellectual qualities, which renders it proper to place them all in

334

a school by themselves. Nor is it any good answer to say that separate schools may be established for their instruction, because such separate schools are not the public schools designed by the constitution.

VI. The attempt to discriminate against and to abridge and impair the rights of colored citizens, comes with bad taste from the State of Nevada. It will be remembered that this State was organized in the midst of a great war, fought for the enfranchisement of the slaves and for the establishment of the great doctrine that all men are free and equal, and that, in that contest, this State enthusiastically supported that doctrine. It will be further remembered, that this State, with the utmost alacrity, ratified the Thirteenth, Fourteenth and Fifteenth amendments to the United States Constitution, the object and intent of which were to declare and fix the absolute equality of all men before the law.

The case was decided on other points, but the Nevada court's broad answer to the foregoing argument is clear:

... While on the one hand they may not deny to any resident person of proper age an equal participation in the benefits of the common schools; and while in the present case upon the facts presented, the defendants should have admitted the relator into the public school in question; yet, on the other hand, it is perfectly within their power to send all blacks to one school, and all whites to another; or, without multiplying words, to make such a classification, whether based on age, sex, race, or any other existent condition, as may seem to them best. *Van Camp* v. *Board of Education of Logan*, 9 O. S. 406; *Roberts* v. *Boston*, 5 Cush. 108.

Whether it be well or ill to classify or divide, on either or all of the conditions suggested, or upon any other, is entirely within the discretion of the trustees, acting intelligently within their powers.

In CALIFORNIA:

Apparently unwilling to accept these precedents, a California resident two years later challenged the legality of school segregation under the Fourteenth Amendment. *Ward* v. *Flood*,

48 California 36 (1874). He, too, presaged events to come by reference to sociological and international implications, as follows:

This is a case which can hardly be argued, any further than its statement alone is an argument. It is admitted now, by the highest masters of thought, even among theologians, that the existence of God himself cannot be proved, nor the duty of children to love and cherish their parents, nor that of general benevolence. But we know that God exists, and that these duties are of imperative obligation. We know that persons of African descent have been degraded by an odious hatred of caste, and that the Constitution of the United States has provided that this social repugnance shall no longer be crystallized into a political disability. This was the object of the Fourteenth Amendment, and its terms are above being the subject of criticism. We know, too, that a State must always have laws equal to its obligations. This was always true as a proposition of municipal law. The world is still ringing with the echoes of its announcement as a proposition of the public law of nations, by the highest tribunal that ever existed in the world, which has just closed its session at Geneva.

The Supreme Court of California, speaking through Chief Justice Wallace, met the issue head on:

Nor is it perceived that the State law in question, in obedience to which the respondent proceeded, is obnoxious to those provisions of the Fourteenth Amendment to the Federal Constitution securing the privileges and immunities of citizens of the United States, and protecting all persons against the deprivation of life, liberty or property, without due process of law. That Amendment, so far as claimed to be material to the question, is as follows: "No State shall make or enforce any law which shall abridge the privileges and immunities of citizens of the United States. Nor shall any State deprive any person of life, liberty or property, without due process of law, nor deny to any person within its jurisdiction the equal protection of the laws."

. . .

The last clause of so much of the Amendment as has been

recited, however, forbids the State to "deny to any person within its jurisdiction the equal protection of the laws," and it remains to inquire if the statute of the State, providing for a system of common schools, in so far as it directs that schools shall be maintained for the education of colored children separate from those provided for the education of white children, be obnoxious to this portion of the Federal Constitution.

The opportunity of instruction at public schools is afforded the youth of the State by the statute of the State, enacted in obedience to the special command of the Constitution of the State, directing that the Legislature shall provide for a system of common schools, by which a school shall be kept up and supported in each district, at least three months in every year, etc. (Art. 19, Sec. 3.) The advantage or benefit thereby vouchsafed to each child, of attending a public school is, therefore, one derived and secured to it under the highest sanction of positive law. It is, therefore, a right—a legal right—as distinctively so as the vested right in property owned is a legal right, and as such it is protected, and entitled to be protected by all the guarantees by which other legal rights are protected and secured to the possessor.

The clause of the Fourteenth Amendment referred to did not create any new or substantive legal right, or add to or enlarge the general classification of rights of persons or things existing in any State under the laws thereof. It, however, operated upon them as it found them already established, and it declared in substance that, such as they were in each State, they should be held and enjoyed alike by all persons within its jurisdiction. The protection of law is indeed inseparable from the assumed existence of a recognized legal right, through the vindication of which the protection is to operate. To declare, then, that each person within the jurisdiction of the State shall enjoy the equal protection of its laws, is necessarily to declare that the measure of legal rights within the State shall be equal and uniform, and the same for all persons found therein—according to the respective condition of each—each child as all other children—each adult person as all other adult persons.

· · ·

But we do not find in the Act of April, 1870, providing for a system of common schools, which is substantially repeated in the

337

Political Code now in force, any legislative attempt [to exclude Negroes]; nor do we discover that the statute is, in any of its provisions, obnoxious to objections of a constitutional character. It provides in substance that schools shall be kept open for the admission of white children, and that the education of children of African descent must be provided for in separate schools.

In short, the policy of separation of the races for educational purposes is adopted by the legislative department, and it is in this mere policy that the counsel for the petitioner professes to discern "an odious distinction of caste, founded on a deep-rooted prejudice in public opinion." But it is hardly necessary to remind counsel that we cannot deal here with such matters, and that our duties lie wholly within the much narrower range of determining whether this statute, in whatever motive it originated, denies to the petitioner, in a constitutional sense, the equal protection of the laws; and in the circumstances that the races are separated in the public schools, there is certainly to be found no violation of the constitutional rights of the one race more than of the other, and we see none of either, for each, though separated from the other, is to be educated upon equal terms with that other, and both at the common public expense.

A question similar to this came before the Supreme Judicial Court of the State of Massachusetts in 1849 (*Roberts* v. *The City of Boston*, 5 Cushing R. 198), and was determined by the Court in accordance with the views just expressed by us. That was an action on the case brought by a colored child against the city to recover damages claimed by reason of her exclusion from a public school as a pupil. It appeared that primary schools to the number of about one hundred and sixty were maintained for the instruction of children of both sexes between five and seven years of age, and that of these schools two were appropriated to the exclusive instruction of colored children, and the residue to the exclusive instruction of white children. It also appeared that the plaintiff had been excluded from the primary school nearest her father's residence, which was a school devoted exclusively to the instruction of white children, and that the school appropriated to the education of colored children nearest her father's residence was about a fifth of a mile more distant therefrom than was the school from which she had been excluded. The Constitution of the State of Massachusetts contained the following clauses, which were relied upon by the counsel for the plaintiff to show that the separation of colored from white children for educational purposes was not justified by law. (Part 1, Art. 1:) "All men are born free and equal, and have certain natural, essential and inalienable rights; among which may be reckoned the right of enjoying and defending their lives and liberties, that of acquiring, possessing and protecting property; in fine, that of seeking and obtaining their safety and happiness. Art. 6: No man nor corporation or association of men, have any other title to obtain advantages or particular and exclusive privileges distinct from those of the community, than what arise from consideration of services rendered to the public." * * *

It will be seen that the language of the Massachusetts Constitution prohibiting "particular and exclusive privileges," was fully as significant, to say the least, in its bearing on the general question in hand as is that of the Fourteenth Amendment of the Federal Constitution, securing "the equal protection of the laws."

The argument of the counsel for the plaintiff in the Massachusetts case, much like that of the counsel for the petitioner here, was that the separation of the races for educational purposes, "is the occasion of inconveniences to colored children, to which they would not be exposed if they had access to the nearest public schools; it inflicts upon them the stigma of caste; and although the matters taught in the two schools may be precisely the same, a school exclusively devoted to one class must differ essentially, in its spirit and character, from that public school known to the law, where all classes meet together in equality."

The opinion of the Court, delivered by Mr. Chief Justice Shaw, maintained the rightful authority of the school committee, to separate the colored children from the white children in the public schools of the city of Boston, and in the course of the opinion, the learned Chief Justice remarked as follows:

"It will be considered that this is a question of power, or of the legal authority of the committee intrusted by the city with this department of public instruction; because if they have the legal authority, the expediency of exercising it in any particular way is exclusively with them. The great principle advanced by the learned and eloquent advocate of the plaintiff, is that by the Constitution and laws of Massachusetts, all persons, without distinction of age or sex, birth or color, origin or condition, are equal before the law. This, as a broad general principle, such as ought to appear in a declaration of rights, is perfectly sound; it is not only expressed in terms, but pervades and animates the whole spirit of our Constitution of free government. But when this great principle comes to be applied to the actual and various conditions of persons in society, it will not warrant the assertion that men and women are legally clothed with the same civil and political powers, and that children and adults are legally to have the same functions and be subject to the same treatment; but only that the rights of all, as they are settled and regulated by law, are equally entitled to the paternal consideration and protection of the law, for their maintenance and security. What those rights are, to which individuals in the infinite variety of circumstances by which they are surrounded in society, are entitled, must depend on laws adapted to their respective relations and conditions. . . .

"The committee, apparently upon great deliberation, have come to the conclusion that the good of both classes of schools will be best promoted by maintaining the separate primary schools for colored and for white children, and we can perceive no ground to doubt that this is the honest result of their experience and judgment. It is urged that this maintenance of separate schools tends to deepen and perpetuate the odious distinction of caste, founded on a deep-rooted prejudice in public opinion. This prejudice, if it exists, is not created by law, and probably cannot be changed by law. Whether this distinction and prejudice, existing in the opinion and feelings of the community, would not be as effectually fostered by compelling colored and white children to associate together in the same schools, may well be doubted; at all events, it is a fair and proper question for the committee to consider and decide upon, having in view the best interests of both classes of children placed under their superintendence; and we cannot say that their decision upon it is not founded on just grounds of reason and experience, and in the results of a discriminating and honest judgment."

We concur in these views, and they are decisive of the present controversy. In order to prevent possible misapprehension, however, we think proper to add that in our opinion, and as the result of the views here announced, the exclusion of colored children from schools where white children attend as pupils, cannot be supported, except under the conditions appearing in the present case; that is, except where separate schools are actually maintained for the education of colored children; and that, unless such separate schools be in fact maintained, all children of the school district, whether white or colored, have an equal right to become pupils at any common school organized under the laws of the State, and have a right to registration and admission as pupils in the order of their registration, pursuant to the provisions of subdivision fourteen of section 1,617 of the Political Code.

In INDIANA:

That same year the Supreme Court of Indiana was called upon to decide the issue. (*Cory et al.* v. *Carter*, 48 Ind. 327, 1874). The court's opinion by Mr. Justice Buskirk represented extensive research into the field of State and Federal relations, and the court's conclusions and citations of authority merit respectful attention today.

Having decided that the Constitution of the State of Indiana did not prohibit racial segregation in the public schools, the Court said:

. . . the next step is to find out the extent of its qualification or change by the Constitution of the United States.

Section 2 of article 4 of the Constitution of the United States declares, that "the citizens of each State shall be entitled to all privileges and immunities of citizens in the several States."

This section, at an early date, received a construction in the case of *Corfield* v. *Coryell,* which has ever since been recognized and approved. It relates only to "those privileges and immunities which are fundamental," and which may all be comprehended under the following heads: "Protection by the government, with the right to acquire and possess property of every kind, and to pursue and obtain happiness and safety, subject, nevertheless, to such restraints as the government may prescribe for the general good of the whole."

In the *Slaughter-House Cases*, the Supreme Court of the United States said: "Its sole purpose was to declare to the several States, that whatever those rights, as you grant or establish them to your own citizens, or as you limit or qualify, or impose restrictions on their exercise, the same, neither more nor less, shall be the measure of the rights of citizens of other States within your jurisdiction." It did not compel the State, into which the citizen of another State removed, to allow him the exercise of the same rights which he enjoyed in the State from which he removed. *Corfield v. Coryell*, 4 Wash. C. C. 371; *Slaughter-House Cases*, 16 Wal. 76, 77; *Bradwell v. The State*, 16 Wal. 130; *Ward v. Maryland*, 12 Wal. 430; *Conner v. Elliott*, 18 How. 591; *Brown v. State of Md.*, 12 Wheat. 448, 449; *People v. Brady*, 40 Cal. 198; Story Const., secs. 1805, 1806; Cooley Const. Lim. 15, 16, 397; Potter's Dwarris on Stat. 525, 526; *Sears v. The Board, etc.*, 36 Ind. 267; *The Jeffersonville, etc., R. R. Co. v. Hendricks*, 41 Ind. 48.

It is well settled by repeated decisions of the Federal and State courts, that with the exception of the limitations imposed upon the powers of the States by section 10 of article 1 of the Constitution of the United States, the several States were left as before the Federal Union was formed, with full power to declare the rights of their citizens, without interference from the Federal Government.

It is a familiar rule of construction of the Constitution of the Union, that the sovereign powers vested in the State governments by their respective constitutions, remain unaltered and unimpaired, except so far as they were granted to the government of the United States. In one of the States of the Union, colored children were entitled to admission into schools for white children, and to be taught with white children, and yet, if a person residing in such State should remove into some other State, where such right is denied, the right so exercised in the State from which the person removed would be lost, because it was not one of those fundamental rights which accompany the person, but a domestic regulation exclusively within the constitutional and legislative power of each State, and to be regarded in the nature of a domestic regulation necessary for the good of the whole people, or which the good of the people of one State, in their sovereign judgment, required to be different from the regulation in another, as best securing "the general comfort and prosperity of the State." Story Const., secs. 1353, 1409; Cooley Const. Lim. 573, 574; 2 Kent Com. 71; 2 Op. Att'y Gen'l, 426; *Commonwealth* v. *Alger*, 7 Cush. 84; *The City of New York* v. *Miln*, 11 Pet. 139; *Slaughter-House Cases*, 16 Wal. 62; *Bradwell* v. *The State*, 16 Wal. 130; *Thayer* v. *Hedges*, 22 Ind. 282; Potter's Dwarris on Stat. 352, 452, 455, 461.

It is very plain that the Tenth Amendment of the Constitution of the United States cannot receive such construction as will aid the claim of the appellee. It declares, that "the powers not delegated to the United States by the Constitution, nor prohibited by it to the States, are reserved to the States respectively, or to the people;" and the power to fix the qualifications of the citizen of the State, and to establish his rights in the State, is one of the powers expressly reserved to the State by this amendment; for there is no express limitation of the power of the States in the Federal Constitution in this respect, as it then stood, and such limitation could not exist without express mention. Rawle Const. 84, 87; Story Const., sec. 1904; Works of Webster, vol. 3, p. 322; Cooley Const. Lim. 19; Federalist, 140; *Slaughter-House Cases*, 16 Wal. 70, 71, 72, 73; *Barron* v. *Mayor, etc.*, 7 Pet. 243; *Smith* v. *State of Md.*, 18 How. 71; *Pervear* v. *The Commonwealth*, 5 Wal. 475; *Barker* v. *The People*, 3 Cow. 686; *James* v. *The Commonwealth*, 12 S. & R. 220; *Jane* v. *Commonwealth*, 3 Met. Ky. 18; *Lincoln* v. *Smith*, 27 Vt. 336; *Warren* v. *Paul*, 22 Ind. 276; *The State, ex rel. Lakey*, v. *Garton*, 32 Ind. 1.

That the views hereinbefore expressed correctly represent the relative powers of the Federal and State governments at the close of the great civil war, and until after the ratification of the amendments to the Constitution of the United States, which followed the termination of that contest, cannot, we think, be successfully controverted.

We next proceed to determine whether such amendments, or either of them, have worked a change, and, if they have, to what extent.

The Thirteenth Amendment was proposed by Congress on the 1st day of February, 1865, and declared by the Secretary of State to have been ratified December 18th, 1865. It declares that "neither slavery nor involuntary servitude, except as a punishment for crime whereof the party shall have been duly convicted, shall exist within the United States, or any place subject to their jurisdiction;" and "Congress shall have power to enforce this article by appropriate legislation."

This amendment was to prevent any question in the future as to the effect of the war and the President's proclamation of emancipation upon slavery; and its obvious purpose was to forbid all shades and conditions of African slavery. *Slaughter-House Cases*, 16 Wal. 68, 69.

It had no other office, and its real effect was more for the future than the present. As to the matter of social and political rights, the African was left just where section 37, article 1, of our State constitution left him, and subject to all the inconveniences and burdens incident to his color and race, except his former one of servitude. He was a person whose place and office, in the body politic, was yet to be designated and established. He possessed no political rights, in the usual and proper sense of that term, through, or had none conferred by, this enactment. . . .

The Fourteenth Amendment to the Federal Constitution was proposed by Congress July 16th, 1866, and declared by the Secretary of State to have been ratified July 28th, 1868. It consists of several sections, but section 1 is the only one necessary to this examination. It declares, that "all persons born or naturalized in the United States, and subject to the jurisdiction thereof, are citizens of the United States and of the State wherein they reside. No State shall make or enforce any law which shall abridge the privileges or immunities of citizens of the United States; nor shall any State deprive any person of life, liberty, or property, without due process of law, nor deny to any person within its jurisdiction the equal protection of the laws."

This section can better be understood or construed, by dividing and considering it in four paragraphs or clauses, the last, however, being a mere re-statement of what precedes it:

First. "All persons born or naturalized in the United States, and subject to the jurisdiction thereof, are citizens of the United States and of the State wherein they reside."

In the *Slaughter-House Cases*, the Supreme Court of the United States says this is a declaration "that persons may be citizens of the United States without regard to their citizenship of a particular State, and it overturns the Dred Scott decision by making all persons born within the United States and subject to its jurisdiction citizens of the United States. That its main purpose was to establish the citizenship of the Negro can admit of no doubt. The phrase, 'subject to its jurisdiction,' was intended to exclude from its operation children of ministers, consuls, and citizens or subjects of foreign states born within the United States." It recognizes and establishes a "distinction between citizenship of the United States and citizenship of a State." "Not only may a man be a citizen of the United States without being a citizen of a State, but an important element is necessary to convert the former into the latter. He must reside within the State to make him a citizen of it, but it is only necessary that he should be born or naturalized in the United States to be a citizen of the Union. It is quite clear, then, that there is a citizenship of the United States, and a citizenship of a State, which are distinct from each other, and which depend upon different characteristics or circumstances in the individual." Hence, a Negro may be a citizen of the United States and reside without its territorial limits, or within some one of the territories; but he cannot be a citizen of a State until he becomes a *bona fide* resident of the State.

Second. "No State shall make or enforce any law which shall abridge the privileges or immunities of citizens of the United States."

This clause does not refer to citizens of the States. It embraces only citizens of the United States. It leaves out the words "citizen of the State," which is so carefully used, and used in contradistinction to citizens of the United States, in the preceding sentence. It places the privileges and immunities of citizens of the United States under the protection of the Federal Constitution, and leaves the privileges and immunities of citizens of a State under the protection of the State constitution. This is fully shown by the recent decision of the Supreme Court of the United States in the *Slaughter-House Cases*, 16 Wal. 36.

Mr. Justice Miller, in delivering the opinion of the court and in speaking in reference to the clause under examination, says:

"It is a little remarkable, if this clause was intended as a protection to the citizen of a State against the legislative power of his own State, that the word citizen of the State should be left out when it is so carefully used, and used in contradistinction to citizens of the United States, in the very sentence which precedes it. It is too clear for argument that the change in phraseology was adopted understandingly and with a purpose.

"Of the privileges and immunities of the citizen of the United States, and of the privileges and immunities of the citizen of the State, and what they respectively are, we will presently consider; but we wish to state here that it is only the former which are placed by this clause under the protection of the Federal Constitution, and that the latter, whatever they may be, are not intended to have any additional protection by this paragraph of the amendment.

"If, then, there is a difference between the privileges and immunities belonging to a citizen of the United States as such, and those belonging to the citizen of the State as such, the latter must rest for their security and protection where they have heretofore rested; for they are not embraced by this paragraph of the amendment."

The same learned judge, in the further examination of the second clause, says:

"It would be the vainest show of learning to attempt to prove by citations of authority, that up to the adoption of the recent amendments, no claim or pretence was set up that those rights depended on the Federal Government for their existence or protection, beyond the very few express limitations which the Federal Constitution imposed upon the States—such, for instance, as the prohibition against *ex post facto* laws, bills of attainder, and laws impairing the obligation of contracts. But with the exception of these and a few other restrictions, the entire domain of the privileges and immunities of citizens of the States, as above defined, lay within the constitutional and legislative power of the States, and without that of the Federal Government. Was it the purpose of the Fourteenth Amendment, by the simple declaration that no State should make or enforce any law which shall abridge the privileges and immunities of citizens of the United States, to transfer the security and protection of all the civil rights which we have mentioned, from the States to the Federal Government?

And where it is declared that Congress shall have the power to enforce that article, was it intended to bring within the power of Congress the entire domain of civil rights heretofore belonging exclusively to the States?

"All this and more must follow, if the proposition of the plaintiffs in error be sound. For not only are these rights subject to the control of Congress whenever in its discretion any of them are supposed to be abridged by State legislation, but that body may also pass laws in advance, limiting and restricting the legislative power of the States, in their most ordinary and usual functions, as in its judgment it may think proper on all such subjects. And still further, such a construction followed by the reversal of the judgments of the Supreme Court of Louisiana in these cases" (these judgments sustained the validity of the grant, by the legislature of Louisiana, of an exclusive right, guarded by certain limitations as to price, etc., to a corporation created by it, for twenty-five years, to build and maintain slaughter-houses, etc., and prohibited the right to all others, within a certain locality), "would constitute this court a perpetual censor upon all legislation of the States, on the civil rights of their own citizens, with authority to nullify such as it did not approve as consistent with those rights, as they existed at the time of the adoption of this amendment.

"The argument we admit is not always the most conclusive which is drawn from the consequences urged against the adoption of a particular construction of an instrument. But when, as in the case before us, these consequences are so serious, so far-reaching and pervading, so great a departure from the structure and spirit of our institutions; when the effect is to fetter and degrade the State governments by subjecting them to the control of Congress, in the exercise of powers heretofore universally conceded to them of the most ordinary and fundamental character; when in fact it radically changes the whole theory of the relations of the State and Federal Governments to each other and of both these governments to the people; the argument has a force that is irresistible, in the absence of language which expresses such a purpose too clearly to admit of doubt. *We are convinced that no such results were intended by the Congress which proposed these amendments, nor by the legislatures of the States which ratified them.*" [Emphasis supplied]

Third. "Nor shall any State deprive any person of life, liberty, or property, without due process of law."

This clause is the same contained in the Fifth Amendment to the Constitution of the United States, but there applied to the action of the Federal Government, and here placed as a check upon the States. But the constitution of our State contains, and perhaps those of all the States contain just such a provision, so that it expresses no new principle, but is the old rule in force since the foundation of the State governments. It prohibits the States from depriving any person of life, liberty, or property, except "in due course of legal proceedings, according to those rules and forms which have been established" by the State, "for the protection of private rights." Cooley Const. Lim. 356, 357; *Westervelt* v. *Gregg*, 12 N. Y. 209.

Fourth. "Nor deny to any person within its jurisdiction the equal protection of the laws."

In regard to this clause, the Supreme Court of this State, in *The State* v. *Gibson*, 36 Ind. 389, says it "seems to have been added in the abundance of caution, for it provides in express terms what was the fair, logical, and just implication from what had preceded it, and that was, that the persons made citizens by the amendment should be protected by the laws in the same manner, and to the same extent, that white citizens were protected."

In the case of *The State* v. *Gibson*, *supra*, this court was called upon to place a construction upon the Fourteenth Amendment to the Constitution of the United States. It was claimed in that case, that such amendment had abolished the laws of this State prohibiting the intermarriage of Negroes and whites. We held that marriage was a purely domestic institution, and subject to the exclusive control of the State; that such amendment had not conferred on the Federal Government any power to interfere with the institution of marriage, and that such amendment had not enlarged the powers of the Federal Government nor diminished those of the States. We then said:

"The Fourteenth Amendment contains no new grant of power from the people, who are the inherent possessors of all power, to the Federal Government. It did not enlarge the powers of the Federal Government, nor diminish those of the States. The inhibitions against the States doing certain things have no force or effect. They do not prohibit the States from doing any act that they could have done without them. * * * The only effect of the amendment under consideration was to extend the protection and blessings of the Constitution and laws to a new class of persons. When they were made citizens they were as much entitled to the protection of the Constitution and the laws as were the white citizens, and the States could no more deprive them of privileges and immunities than they could citizens of the white race. Citizenship entitled them to the protection of life, liberty, and property, and the full and equal protection of the laws. Nor has the ratification of this amendment in any manner or to any extent impaired, weakened, or taken away any of the reserved rights of the States, as they had existed and been fully recognized by every department of the national government from its creation."

What was then intended to be expressed was, that the Fourteenth Amendment had not delegated to the Federal Government the power to regulate and control the domestic institutions of a State. As will be hereinafter shown, it imposes some limitations upon the powers of the States as to slavery and the equal protection of the rights of citizens of the United States and of the States.

We were then unaided by any judicial construction of the Fourteenth Amendment; and we are gratified to know that the views then expressed have been, in all substantial respects, sustained by the highest judicial tribunal in this country, and the one especially charged with the construction and interpretation of the Federal Constitution. By the solemn decision of that high court, the privileges and immunities belonging to the citizens of the States, as such, rest for their security and protection where they have heretofore rested, with the States themselves.

. . .

How far, then, have the amendments operated to change the constitution of Indiana or imposed limitations or restrictions upon the sovereign power of the State? We answer, in the following particulars:

1. The State cannot in the future, while a member of the Federal Union, change her constitution so as to create or establish slavery or involuntary servitude, except as a punishment for

crimes whereof the party shall have been convicted; thus protecting the new class of citizens, *i. e.*, Negroes and mulattoes, from being again reduced to slavery.

2. The State cannot deny to, or deprive a citizen of the United States, *i. e.*, any Negro or mulatto, of, those national rights, privileges, or immunities which belong to him as such citizen.

3. The State must recognize as its citizen any citizen of the United States, *i. e.*, any Negro or mulatto, who is or becomes a *bona fide* resident therein.

4. The State must give to such, *i. e.*, to such Negro or mulatto, who is or who becomes a *bona fide* resident therein, the same rights, privileges, and immunities, secured by her constitution and laws to her other, *i. e.*, to her white citizens.

In our opinion, such amendments have not in any other respect imposed restrictions or limitations upon the sovereign power of the State. From this it results, that there is no limitation upon the power of the State, within the limits of her own constitution, to fix, secure, and protect the rights, privileges, and immunities of her citizens, as such, of whatever race or color they may be, so as to secure her own internal peace, prosperity, and happiness.

This will preserve in their purity and vigor the structure and spirit of our complex system of government, as it came from the hands of the great and illustrious men who achieved our independence and formed our matchless form of government. Anterior to the adoption of the Federal Constitution, the States existed as independent sovereignties, possessing supreme and absolute power over all questions of local and internal government. To the States the whole charge of interior regulation is left by the Federal Constitution; to them and to the people thereof all powers not expressly, or by necessary implication, delegated to the national government, and not prohibited to the States, are reserved to the States.

. . .

The Federal Constitution does not provide for any general system of education, to be conducted and controlled by the national government, nor does it vest in Congress any power to exercise a general or special supervision over the States on the subject of education. . . .

This system of common schools must consist of many schools in different localities or geographical divisions; and these schools may be of different grades. In some of these localities or divisions there may be school-houses, and in others none. In some the school-house or houses may not be sufficient to accommodate all, and the revenue may not be sufficient to provide for them.

In this system, there ought to be and must be a classification of the children. This classification ought to and will be with reference to some properties or characteristics common to or possessed by a certain number out of the whole; and these classes may be put into and taught in different parts of the same school, or different rooms in the same school-house, or different school-houses, as convenience and good policy may require.

This is too reasonable to admit of question; for it concerns the general good, and does not affect the quality of the privilege, but regulates the manner of its enjoyment.

This being settled, what is there to prevent the classification of children, equally entitled to the privileges of the system of common schools, with reference to difference of race or color, if the judgment of the legislature should hold such a classification to be most promotive of, or conducive to, the good order and discipline of the schools in the system, and the interest of the public?

It being settled that the legislature must provide for the education of the colored children as well as for the white children, we are required to determine whether the legislature may classify such children, by color and race, and provide for their education in separate schools, or whether they must attend the same school without reference to race or color. In our opinion, the classification of scholars, on the basis of race or color, and their education in separate schools, involve questions of domestic policy which are within the legislative discretion and control, and do not amount to an exclusion of either class. In other words, the placing of the white children of the State in one class and the Negro children of the State in another class, and requiring these classes to be taught separately, provision being made for their education in the same branches, according to age, capacity, or advancement, with capable teachers, and to the extent of their *pro rata* share in the school revenue, does not amount to a denial of equal privileges to either, or conflict with the open character of the system required by the constitution. The system would be equally open to all. The tuition would be free. The privileges of the schools would be denied to none. The white children go to one school, or to certain of the schools in the system of common schools. The colored children go to another school, or to certain others of the schools in the system of the common schools. Or, if there are not a sufficient number of colored children within attending distance, the several districts may be consolidated and form one district. But if there are not a sufficient number within reasonable distance to be thus consolidated, the trustee or trustees shall provide such other means of education for said children as shall use their proportion, according to number, of school revenue to the best advantage. If there be cause of complaint, the white class has as much, if not greater cause than the colored class, for the latter class receive their full share of the school revenue, although none of it may have been contributed by such class; and when districts can not be consolidated so as to form a school, such class is entitled to receive their full share of the school revenue, according to number, which shall be expended for their benefit to the best advantage, a privilege which is not granted to the white class.

In our opinion, there would be as much lawful reason for complaint, by one scholar in the same school, that he could not occupy the seat of another scholar therein at the same time the latter occupied it, or by scholars in the different classes in the same school, that they were not all put in the same class, or by the scholars in different schools, that they were not all placed in one school, as there is that white and black children are placed in distinct classes and taught separately, or in separate schools.

The action of Congress, at the same session at which the Fourteenth Amendment was proposed to the States, and at a session subsequent to the date of its ratification, is worthy of consideration as evincing the concurrent and after-matured conviction of that body that there was nothing whatever in the amendment which prevented Congress from separating the white and colored races, and placing them, as classes, in different schools, and that such separation was highly proper and conducive to the well-being of the races, and calculated to secure the peace, harmony, and welfare of the public; and if no obligation was expected to be or was imposed upon Congress by the amendment, to place the

352

two races and colors in the same school, with what show of reason can it be pretended that it has such a compelling power upon the sovereign and independent States forming the Federal Union?

We refer to the legislation of Congress relative to schools in the District of Columbia, at the first session of the Thirty-Ninth Congress, and the third session of the Forty-Second Congress.

On the 23d day of July, 1866, the act of Congress, entitled "an act relating to public schools in the District of Columbia," took effect. It requires the cities of Washington and Georgetown to pay over to the trustees of colored schools of said cities such a proportionate part of all moneys received or expended for school or educational purposes in said cities, including the cost of sites, buildings, improvements, furniture, and books, and all other expenditures on account of schools, as the colored children between the ages of six and seventeen years, in the respective cities, bear to the whole number of children, white and colored, between the same ages. Acts sess. 1, 39th Cong. 222.

This was followed at the same session of Congress by an act, entitled "an act donating certain lots in the city of Washington for schools for colored children in the District of Columbia," approved July 28th, 1866, which authorized and required the Commissioner of Public Buildings to convey certain described lots, in the city of Washington, which belonged to the United States, to the trustees for colored schools for the cities of Washington and Georgetown in said District, for the sole use of schools for colored children in that District; the said lots having been designated and set apart by the Secretary of the Interior to be used for colored schools; and the said lots whenever converted to any other use to revert to the United States. Act sess. 1, 39th Cong. 354.

At its 42d session an act was passed, entitled "an act to amend an act entitled 'An act governing the colored schools of the District of Columbia,' " approved March 3d, 1873, which fixes the number of the board of trustees of schools for colored children in the District of Columbia, their mode of appointment, their duties, etc., and authorizes the Governor of the District to appoint a superintendent of schools for colored children, who is to receive a salary of twenty-five hundred dollars annually, for his services, etc., and directs the proportion of school money then due, or afterward to become due, to the board of trustees of colored schools from the cities of Washington and Georgetown, to be paid to the treasurer of said board, and not to the trustees, as provided in the act of July 23d, 1866. Acts sess. 3, 42d Cong. 260.

This legislation of Congress continues in force, at the present time, as a legislative construction of the Fourteenth Amendment, and as a legislative declaration of what was thought to be lawful, proper, and expedient under such amendment, by the same body that proposed such amendment to the States for their approval and ratification.

We are very clearly of the opinion that the act of May 13th, 1869, is constitutional, and that while it remains in force colored children are not entitled to admission into the common schools which are provided for the education of the white children.

In LOUISIANA:

And what did Federal Circuit Judge Woods, a former Union General, have to say on the question? Referring to his opinion in the case of *Bertonneau* v. *The Directors of City Schools,* 3 Woods 177 (Federal) La. (1878), we read in part as follows:

The grievance, and the sole grievance, set out in the bill is that complainant's children, being of African descent, are not allowed to attend the same public schools as those in which children of white parents are educated.

Is this a deprivation of a right granted by the Constitution of the United States? The complainant says that the action of the defendants deprives him and his children of the equal protection of the laws, and therefore impairs a right granted to him and them by the Fourteenth Amendment to the Constitution of the United States, and the act of Congress passed to secure the same.

Is there any denial of equal rights in the resolution of the board of directors of the city schools, or in the action of the subordinate officers of the schools, as set out in the bill? Both races are treated precisely alike. White children and colored children are compelled to attend different schools. That is all. The State, while conceding equal privileges and advantages to both races, has the right to manage its schools in the manner which, in its judgment, will best promote the interest of all.

The State may be of opinion that it is better to educate the sexes separately, and therefore establishes schools in which the children of different sexes are educated apart. By such a policy can it be said that the equal rights of either sex are invaded? Equality of right does not involve the necessity of educating children of both sexes, or children without regard to their attainments or age in the same school. Any classification which preserves substantially equal school advantages does not impair any rights, and is not prohibited by the Constitution of the United States. *Equality of rights does not necessarily imply identity of rights.* [Emphasis supplied]

In OHIO:

Federal Circuit Judge Baxter, of Ohio, adopted the same position in giving his charge to the jury in *United States* v. *Buntin*, 10 Fed. 730 (1882). He said:

The Supreme Court of the State has held that such a classification of the two races is within the constitutional discretion of the legislature, and that the separate education of the whites and blacks in accordance with the terms of the law is no wrong to either. I concur in and adopt this decision as a correct exposition of the Constitution, and instruct you that if there was such a school in the district for the education of colored children, affording substantially the same educational advantages as were afforded by the school from which the prosecuting witness was excluded, and reasonably accessible, it was his duty to have gone there, and the defendant did him no wrong in the exclusion complained of.

In NEW YORK:

The State of New York for some years has prohibited racial segregation in its public schools. This, to be sure, is New York's legislative prerogative. But it is useful to keep in mind that New York maintained racially separate schools long after

355

ratification of the Fourteenth Amendment, and abandoned this dual system by its own voluntary action and not under compulsion of any court decree.

Among the most significant cases to arise in the period immediately following the amendment's approval was *People ex rel King* v. *Gallagher*, 93 N. Y. 438 (1883). In pertinent part, New York's highest court said this:

The argument of the appellant's counsel is to the effect that the Fourteenth Amendment, under the laws of this State, giving equal privileges in its common schools to every citizen, confers upon the relator not only the right of equal educational facilities with white children, but that such education shall be furnished at the same time and place with that afforded to any other child, otherwise it is claimed that she is abridged of some "privilege or immunity" which of right belongs to her, or that she is denied the equal protection of the law.

The history of this amendment is familiar to all, and for all of the purposes of this argument may be briefly summarized. At the time of its adoption the colored race had been recently emancipated from a condition of servitude and made citizens of the States. It was apprehended that in some, if not all, of the States of the Union, feelings of antipathy between the races would cause the dominant race, by unfriendly legislation, to abridge the rights of the other, and deny to them equal privileges and the protection of the laws. To guard the previously subject race from the effect of such discrimination, these provisions were made a part of the fundamental law of the land, and their rights were placed under the protection of the Federal Government. Their object has been defined by Mr. Justice Strong in *Ex parte Virginia* (100 U. S. 344), where it is said that "one great purpose of these amendments was to raise the colored race from that condition of inferiority and servitude, in which most of them had previously stood, into perfect equality of *civil rights* with all other persons within the jurisdiction of the States." The same learned judge in *Strauder* v. *West Virginia* (100 U. S. 306), also says: "It was designed to assure to the colored race the enjoyment of all of the *civil rights* that, under the law, are enjoyed by white persons, and to give that race the protection of the general government, in that enjoyment, when it should be denied by the States."

It will be observed that the language of the amendment is peculiar in respect to the rights which the State is forbidden to abridge. Although the same section makes all persons born or naturalized in the United States, and subject to the jurisdiction thereof, citizens of the United States and of the State wherein they reside, yet, in speaking of the class of privileges and immunities which the State is forbidden to deny the citizen, they are referred to as the privileges and immunities which belong to them as citizens of the United States. It has been argued from this language that such rights and privileges as are granted to its citizens, and depend solely upon the laws of the State for their origin and support, are not within the constitutional inhibition and may lawfully be denied to any class or race by the States at their will and discretion. This construction is distinctly and plainly held in *The Slaughter-House Cases* (16 Wall. 36), by the Supreme Court of the United States. The doctrine of that case has not, to our knowledge, been retracted or questioned by any of its subsequent decisions. . . .

But we are of the opinion that our decision can also be sustained upon another ground, and one which will be equally satisfactory as affording a practical solution of the questions involved. It is believed that this provision will be given its full scope and effect when it is so construed as to secure to all citizens, wherever domiciled, equal protection under the laws and the enjoyment of those privileges which belong, as of right, to each individual citizen. This right, as affected by the questions in this case in its fullest sense, is the privilege of obtaining an education under the same advantages and with equal facilities for its acquisition with those enjoyed by any other individual. It is not believed that these provisions were intended to regulate or interfere with the social standing or privileges of the citizen, or to have any other effect than to give to all, without respect to color, age or sex, the same legal rights and the uniform protection of the same laws.

In the nature of things there must be many social distinctions and privileges remaining unregulated by law and left within the control of the individual citizens, as being beyond the reach of the legislative functions of government to organize or control.

The attempt to enforce social intimacy and intercourse between the races, by legal enactments, would probably tend only to embitter the prejudices, if any such there are, which exist between them, and produce an evil instead of a good result. (*Roberts* v. *City of Boston*, 5 Cush. 198.)

As to whether such intercourse shall ever occur must eventually depend upon the operation of natural laws and the merits of individuals, and can exist and be enjoyed only by the voluntary consent of the persons between whom such relations may arise, but this end can neither be accomplished nor promoted by laws which conflict with the general sentiment of the community upon whom they are designed to operate. When the government, therefore, has secured to each of its citizens equal rights before the law and equal opportunities for improvement and progress, it has accomplished the end for which it is organized and performed all of the functions respecting social advantages with which it is endowed. . . .

If the [complainant's] argument should be followed out to its legitimate conclusion, it would also forbid all classification of the pupils in public schools founded upon distinctions of sex, nationality or race, and which, it must be conceded, are essential to the most advantageous administration of educational facilities in such schools. Seeing the force of these contentions the appellant concedes that discrimination may be exercised by the school authorities with respect to age, sex, intellectual acquirements and territorial location, but he claims that this cannot, under the Constitution, be extended to distinctions founded upon difference in color or race. We think the concession fatal to his argument.

The language of the amendment is broad, and prohibits every discrimination between citizens as to those rights which are placed under its protection. If the right, therefore, of school authorities to discriminate, in the exercise of their discretion, as to the methods of education to be pursued with different classes of pupils be conceded, how can it be argued that they have not the power, in the best interests of education, to cause different races and nationalities, whose requirements are manifestly different, to be educated in separate places? We cannot see why the establishment of separate institutions for the education and benefit of different races should be held any more to imply the inferiority of one race than that of the other, and no ground for such an implication exists in the act of discrimination itself. . . .

A natural distinction exists between these races which was not created neither can it be abrogated by law, and legislation which recognizes this distinction and provides for the peculiar wants or conditions of the particular race can in no just sense be called a discrimination against such race or an abridgment of its civil rights. The implication that the Congress of 1864, and the State legislature of the same year, sitting during the very throes of our civil war, who were respectively the authors of legislation providing for the separate education of the two races, were thereby guilty of unfriendly discrimination against the colored race, will be received with surprise by most people and with conviction by none. Recent movements on the part of the colored people of the South, through their most intelligent leaders, to secure Federal sanction to the separation of the two races, so far as the same is compatible with their joint occupation of the same geographical territory, afford strong evidence of the wishes and opinions of that people as to the methods which in their judgments will conduce most beneficially to their welfare and improvement. . . .

If regard be had to that established rule for the construction of statutes and constitutional enactments which require courts, in giving them effect, to regard the intent of the law-making power, it is difficult to see why the considerations suggested are not controlling upon the question under discussion.

The question here presented has also been the subject of much discussion and consideration in the courts of the various States of the Union, and it is believed has been, when directly adjudicated upon, uniformly determined in favor of the proposition that the separate education of the white and colored races is no abridgment of the rights of either.

Admittedly State courts of last resort are final judicial authority only as to the meaning of their respective State Constitutions; in all cases involving the United States Constitution, their decisions are subject to review by the Supreme Court of the United States. But, unless and until reversed, decisions of State appellate courts regarding the Federal Constitution are final, and as none of the foregoing cases was reviewed by the Supreme Court the decisions normally would be considered controlling authority. However, reliance on State court interpretations, even though unreversed, is unnecessary here because the Supreme Court of the United States long ago fixed this boundary line itself—that is, the Court determined, by specific pronouncement, the meaning, intent and effect of the Fourteenth Amendment as regards operation of racially segregated public schools by the States.

In the case of *Plessy* v. *Ferguson*, 163 U. S. 537, 16 S. Ct. 1138 (1896) the Court was called upon to decide a question concerning segregation in public transportation under the Fourteenth Amendment, but in the process of passing on that question the Court, through Mr. Justice Brown, said:

The object of the amendment was undoubtedly to enforce the absolute equality of the two races before the law, but, in the nature of things, it could not have been intended to abolish distinctions based upon color, or to enforce social, as distinguished from political equality, or a commingling of the two races upon terms unsatisfactory to either. Laws permitting, and even requiring, their separation, in places where they are liable to be brought into contact do not necessarily imply the inferiority of either race to the other, and have been generally, if not universally, recognized as within the competency of the State legislatures in the exercise of their police power. *The most common instance of this is connected with the establishment of separate schools for white and colored children, which have been held to be a valid exercise of the legislative power even by courts of States where the political rights of the colored race have been longest and most earnestly enforced.* [Emphasis supplied]

Then in 1899, the Supreme Court decided a case directly involving segregated schools (*Cumming* v. *Richmond County Board of Education*, 175 U. S. 528, 20 S. Ct. 197). Not only were the schools in Richmond County segregated, but a considerable difference existed in the financial support which the Board of Education extended toward the high school education of the two races. However, taking note of the fact that by reason of colored high schools in an adjacent community, Negroes had substantially equal opportunities with whites for such an education, the Court declined to interfere with the situation in Richmond County.

Mr. Justice Harlan, who, incidentally, had dissented strongly from the majority view in the *Plessy* case regarding segregation in transportation, wrote the unanimous opinion of the Court in this case. Directing his remarks to the power of States in regard to *education*, he had this to say:

. . . the education of the people in schools maintained by State taxation is a matter belonging to the respective States, and any interference on the part of Federal authority with the management of such schools cannot be justified except in the case of a clear and unmistakable disregard of rights secured by the supreme law of the land.

Any conceivable doubt on this point was settled beyond dispute in the case of *Gong Lum* v. *Rice*, 275 U. S. 78, 48 S. Ct. 91 (1927). The problem and the Supreme Court's answer to it is summed up in the following brief quotation from the majority opinion by Mr. Justice Taft.

The question here is whether a Chinese citizen of the United States is denied equal protection of the laws when he is classed among the colored races and furnished facilities for education equal to that offered to all. . . . Were this a new question, it would call for very full argument and consideration, but we think it is the same question which has been many times decided to be within the constitutional power of the State Legislature to settle without intervention of the Federal courts under the Federal Constitution.
. . . The decision [to separate races] is within the discretion of the

State in regulating its public schools, *and does not conflict with the Fourteenth Amendment.*"

The judiciary thus performed its *interpretive* function. In the field of public education, the Constitution stood clearly defined and, so far as education is concerned, the people have changed it not one iota.

Did the Supreme Court then have the right to issue the opinion it did in *Brown?* The answer is found by adverting again to the argument advanced in the beginning of this exposition, the truth of which the members of the Supreme Court apparently recognize, albeit only when it suits them.

The Court, referring to the *Brown* case, made this statement which must of necessity be equally applicable to all other Supreme Court decisions regarding the Constitution:

It follows that the interpretation of the Fourteenth Amendment enunciated by this Court . . . is the *supreme law of the land,* and Article VI of the Constitution makes it of binding effect on the States "any Thing in the Constitution or Laws of any State to the Contrary notwithstanding." Every State legislator and executive and *judicial* officer is solemnly committed by oath taken pursuant to Article VI, Paragraph 3 *"to support this Constitution."* . . . (*Cooper* v. *Aaron*) [Emphasis supplied]

The phraseology employed by the Court comes, of course, from Article VI of the Constitution which lists three things only as the "supreme law of the land," the Constitution itself, laws of the United States made in pursuance thereof, and treaties. A Court decree in itself is neither Constitution, law nor treaty, but merely declaratory of one or more of them. If such a decree is to be accorded the appellation "supreme law of the land" it can only be because in a metaphysical sense it has become and is the thing it declares. In that event, it follows as night the day that the earlier declarations of the Supreme Court (confirming the meaning of the Fourteenth Amendment as pronounced by the State and lower Federal courts) became and were, to the extent involved, the amendment itself and as such subject to change only as provided for in Article V. Thus the members of the Supreme Court who decided the *Brown* case are wrong either in declaring Supreme Court opinions construing the Constitution to be the "supreme law of the land" or by undertaking to amend the Fourteenth Amendment in a way not countenanced by the Constitution. In either event, the Court, by its fiat and not by amendment of the Constitution under Article V, has effectively seized from the States a substantial portion of their remaining political power.

The Virginia Commission on Constitutional Government invites the renewed consideration of this decision by Americans everywhere, regardless of their personal convictions upon racial separation itself. Soberly, and in no mean spirit, this Commission submits that grave violence is done to the structure of constitutional government, and ominous precedents are set for further invasion of rights and powers, when the Court's action is accepted without sincere and continuing protest.

Richmond, Virginia,
May 17, 1960.

THE CONFERENCE OF CHIEF JUSTICES

REPORT OF THE COMMITTEE ON
FEDERAL-STATE RELATIONSHIPS AS
AFFECTED BY JUDICIAL DECISIONS
Adopted, August, 1958

☆ ☆ ☆ ☆ ☆ ☆ ☆ ☆ ☆ ☆ ☆ ☆ ☆

REPORT OF THE COMMITTEE ON FEDERAL-STATE RELATIONSHIPS AS AFFECTED BY JUDICIAL DECISIONS

Foreword

OUR Committee on Federal-State Relationships as Affected by Judicial Decisions was appointed pursuant to action taken at the 1957 meeting of the Conference, at which, you will recall, there was some discussion of recent decisions of the Supreme Court of the United States and a Resolution expressing concern with regard thereto was adopted by the Conference. This Committee held a meeting in Washington in December, 1957, at which plans for conducting our work were developed. This meeting was attended by Sidney Spector of the Council of State Governments and by Professor Philip B. Kurland, of the University of Chicago Law School.

The Committee believed that it would be desirable to survey this field from the point of view of general trends rather than by attempting to submit detailed analyses of many cases. It was realized however, that an expert survey of recent Supreme Court decisions within the area under consideration would be highly desirable in order that we might have the benefit in drafting this report of scholarly research and of competent analysis and appraisal, as well as of objectivity of approach.

Thanks to Professor Kurland and to four of his colleagues of the faculty of the University of Chicago Law School several monographs dealing with subjects within the Committee's field of action have been prepared and have been furnished to all members of the Committee and of the Conference. These monographs and their authors are as follows:

1. "The Supreme Court, The Due Process Clause, and the In Personam Jurisdiction of State Courts" by Professor Kurland;
2. "Limitations on State Power to Deal with Issues of Subversion and Loyalty" by Assistant Professor Cramton;
3. "Congress, the States and Commerce" by Professor Allison Dunham;
4. "The Supreme Court, Federalism, and State Systems of Criminal Justice" by Professor Francis A. Allen; and
5. "The Supreme Court, the Congress and State Jurisdiction Over Labor Relations" by Professor Bernard D. Meltzer.

These gentlemen have devoted much time, study and thought to the preparation of very scholarly, interesting and instructive monographs on the above subjects. We wish to express our deep appreciation to each of them for his very thorough research and analysis of these problems. With the pressure of the work of our respective courts, the members of this Committee could not have undertaken this research work and we could scarcely have hoped, even with ample time, to equal the thorough and excellent reports which they have written on their respective subjects.

It had originally been hoped that all necessary research material would be available to your Committee by the end of

April and that the Committee could study it and then meet for discussion, possibly late in May, and thereafter send at least a draft of the Committee's report to the members of the Conference well in advance of the 1958 meeting; but these hopes have not been realized. The magnitude of the studies and the thoroughness with which they have been made rendered it impossible to complete them until about two months after the original target date and it has been impracticable to hold another meeting of this Committee until the time of the Conference.

Even after this unavoidable delay had developed, there was a plan to have these papers presented at a Seminar to be held at the University of Chicago late in June. Unfortunately, this plan could not be carried through, either. We hope, however, that these papers may be published in the near future with such changes and additions as the several authors may wish to make in them. Some will undoubtedly be desired in order to include decisions of the Supreme Court in some cases which are referred to in these monographs, but in which decisions were rendered after the monographs had been prepared. Each of the monographs as transmitted to us is stated to be in preliminary form and subject to change and as not being for publication. Much as we are indebted to Professor Kurland and his colleagues for their invaluable research aid, your Committee must accept sole responsibility for the views herein stated. Unfortunately, it is impracticable to include all or even a substantial part of their analyses in this report.

Background and Perspective

We think it desirable at the outset of this report to set out some points which may help to put the report in proper perspective, familiar or self-evident as these points may be.

First, though decisions of the Supreme Court of the United

States have a major impact upon federal-state relationships and have had such an impact since the days of Chief Justice Marshall, they are only a part of the whole structure of these relationships. These relations are, of course, founded upon the Constitution of the United States itself. They are materially affected not only by judicial decisions but in very large measure by Acts of Congress adopted under the powers conferred by the Constitution. They are also affected, or may be affected, by the exercise of the treaty power.

Of great practical importance as affecting federal-state relationships are the rulings and actions of federal administrative bodies. These include the independent agency regulatory bodies, such as the Interstate Commerce Commission, the Federal Power Commission, the Securities and Exchange Commission, the Civil Aeronautics Board, the Federal Communications Commission and the National Labor Relations Board. Many important administrative powers are exercised by the several departments of the Executive Branch, notably the Treasury Department and the Department of the Interior. The scope and importance of the administration of the federal tax laws are, of course, familiar to many individuals and businesses because of their direct impact, and require no elaboration.

Second, when we turn to the specific field of the effect of judicial decisions on federal-state relationships we come at once to the question as to where power should lie to give the ultimate interpretation to the Constitution and to the laws made in pursuance thereof under the authority of the United States. By necessity and by almost universal common consent, these ultimate powers are regarded as being vested in the Supreme Court of the United States. Any other allocation of such power would seem to lead to chaos. (See Judge Learned Hand's most interesting Holmes Lectures on "The Bill of

Rights" delivered at the Harvard Law School this year and published by the Harvard University Press.)

Third, there is obviously great interaction between federal legislation and administrative action on the one hand, and decisions of the Supreme Court on the other, because of the power of the Court to interpret and apply Acts of Congress and to determine the validity of administrative action and the permissible scope thereof.

Fourth, whether federalism shall continue to exist, and if so in what form, is primarily a political question rather than a judicial question. On the other hand, it can hardly be denied that judicial decisions, specifically decisions of the Supreme Court, can give tremendous impetus to changes in the allocation of powers and responsibilities as between the federal and the state governments. Likewise, it can hardly be seriously disputed that on many occasions the decisions of the Supreme Court have produced exactly that effect.

Fifth, this Conference has no legal powers whatsoever. If any conclusions or recommendations at which we may arrive are to have any effect, this can only be through the power of persuasion.

Sixth, it is a part of our obligation to seek to uphold respect for law. We do not believe that this goes so far as to impose upon us an obligation of silence when we find ourselves unable to agree with pronouncements of the Supreme Court (even though we are bound by them), or when we see trends in decisions of that Court which we think will lead to unfortunate results. We hope that the expression of our views may have some value. They pertain to matters which directly affect the work of our state courts. In this report we urge the desirability of self-restraint on the part of the Supreme Court in the exercise of the vast powers committed to it. We endeavor not to be guilty ourselves of a lack of due restraint in expressing our concern and, at times, our criticisms in making the comments and observations which follow.

Problems of Federalism

The difference between matters primarily local and matters primarily national was the guiding principle upon which the framers of our national Constitution acted in outlining the division of powers between the national and state governments.

This guiding principle, central to the American federal system, was recognized when the original Constitution was being drawn and was emphasized by de Tocqueville. Under his summary of the federal Constitution he says:

"The first question which awaited the Americans was so to divide the sovereignty that each of the different states which composed the union should continue to govern itself in all that concerned its internal prosperity, while the entire nation, represented by the Union, should continue to form a compact body and to provide for all general exigencies. The problem was a complex and difficult one. It was as impossible to determine beforehand, with any degree of accuracy, the share of authority that each of the two governments was to enjoy as to foresee all the incidents in the life of a nation."

In the period when the Constitution was in the course of adoption the "Federalist" (No. 45) discussed the division of sovereignty between the Union and the States and said: "The powers delegated by the Constitution to the Federal Government are few and defined. Those which are to remain in the State governments are numerous and indefinite. The former will be exercised principally on external objects, as war, peace, negotiation, and foreign commerce. The powers reserved to the several States will extend to all the objects which, in the ordinary course of affairs, concern the internal order and prosperity of the State."

Those thoughts expressed in the "Federalist" of course are those of the general period when both the original Constitution and the Tenth Amendment were proposed and adopted. They long antedated the proposal of the Fourteenth Amendment.

The fundamental need for a system of distribution of powers between national and state governments was impressed sharply upon the framers of our Constitution not only because of their knowledge of the governmental systems of ancient Greece and Rome. They also were familiar with the government of England; they were even more aware of the colonial governments in the original states and the governments of those states after the Revolution. Included in government on this side of the Atlantic was the institution known as the New England town meeting, though it was not in use in all of the states. A town meeting could not be extended successfully to any large unit of population, which, for legislative action, must reply upon representative government.

But it is this spirit of self-government, of *local* self-government, which has been a vital force in shaping our democracy from its very inception.

The views expressed by our late brother, Chief Justice Arthur T. Vanderbilt, on the division of powers between the national and state governments—delivered in his addresses at the University of Nebraska and published under the title "The Doctrine of the Separation of Powers and Its Present Day Significance"—are persuasive. He traced the origins of the doctrine of the separation of powers to four sources: Montesquieu and other political philosophers who preceded him; English constitutional experience; American colonial experience; and the common sense and political wisdom of the Founding Fathers. He concluded his comments on the experiences of the American colonists with the British government with this sentence: "As colonists they had enough of a completely centralized government with no distribution of powers and they were intent on seeing to it that they should never suffer such grievances from a government of their own construction."

His comments on the separation of powers and the system of checks and balances and on the concern of the Founding Fathers with the proper distribution of governmental power between the nation and the several states indicates that he treated them as parts of the plan for preserving the nation on the one side and individual freedom on the other—in other words, that the traditional tripartite vertical division of powers between the legislative, the executive and the judicial branches of government was not an end in itself, but was a means towards an end; and that the horizontal distribution or allocation of powers between national and state governments was also a means towards the same end and was a part of the separation of powers which was accomplished by the federal Constitution. It is a form of the separation of powers with which Montesquieu was not concerned; but the horizontal division of powers, whether thought of as a form of separation of powers or not, was very much in the minds of the framers of the Constitution.

Two Major Developments in the Federal System

The outstanding development in federal-state relations since the adoption of the national Constitution has been the expansion of the power of the national government and the consequent contraction of the powers of the state governments. To a large extent this is wholly unavoidable and indeed is a necessity, primarily because of improved transportation and communication of all kinds and because of mass production. On the other hand, our Constitution does envision federalism.

The very name of our nation indicates that it is to be composed of states. The Supreme Court of a bygone day said in *Texas* v. *White*, 7 Wall. 700, 721 (1868): "The Constitution, in all its provisions, looks to an indestructible Union of indestructible States."

Second only to the increasing dominance of the national government has been the development of the immense power of the Supreme Court in both state and national affairs. It is not merely the final arbiter of the law; it is the maker of policy in many major social and economic fields. It is not subject to the restraints to which a legislative body is subject. There are points at which it is difficult to delineate precisely the line which should circumscribe the judicial function and separate it from that of policy-making. Thus, usually within narrow limits, a court may be called upon in the ordinary course of its duties to make what is actually a policy decision by choosing between two rules, either of which might be deemed applicable to the situation presented in a pending case.

But if and when a court in construing and applying a constitutional provision or a statute becomes a policy maker, it may leave construction behind and exercise functions which are essentially legislative in character, whether they serve in practical effect as a constitutional amendment or as an amendment of a statute. It is here that we feel the greatest concern, and it is here that we think the greatest restraint is called for. There is nothing new in urging judicial self-restraint, though there may be, and we think there is, new need to urge it.

It would be useless to attempt to review all of the decisions of the Supreme Court which have had a profound effect upon the course of our history. It has been said that the Dred Scott decision made the Civil War inevitable. Whether this is really true or not, we need not attempt to determine. Even if it is discounted as a serious overstatement, it remains a dramatic reminder of the great influence which Supreme Court decisions have had and can have. As to the great effect of decisions of that Court on the economic development of the country, see Mr. Justice Douglas' Address on *Stare Decisis*, 49 Columbia Law Review 735.

Sources of National Power

Most of the powers of the national government were set forth in the original constitution; some have been added since. In the days of Chief Justice Marshall the supremacy clause of the federal Constitution and a broad construction of the powers granted to the national government were fully developed, and as a part of this development the extent of national control over interstate commerce became very firmly established. The trends established in those days have never ceased to operate and in comparatively recent years have operated at times in a startling manner in the extent to which interstate commerce has been held to be involved, as for example in the familiar case involving an elevator operator in a loft building.

From a practical standpoint the increase in federal revenues resulting from the Sixteenth Amendment (the Income Tax Amendment) has been of great importance. National control over state action in many fields has been vastly expanded by the Fourteenth Amendment.

We shall refer to some subjects and types of cases which bear upon federal-state relationships.

The General Welfare Clause

One provision of the federal Constitution which was included in it from the beginning but which, in practical effect, lay dormant for more than a century, is the general welfare clause. In *United States* v. *Butler*, 297 U. S. 1, the original Agricultural Adjustment Act was held invalid. An argument was advanced in that case that the general welfare clause would sustain the imposition of the tax and that money derived from the tax could be expended for any purposes which would promote the general welfare. The Court viewed this argument with favor as a general proposition, but found it not supportable on the facts of that case. However, it was not long before that clause was relied upon and applied. See *Steward Machine Co.* v. *Davis,* 301 U. S. 548, and *Helvering* v. *Davis,* 301 U. S. 690. In those cases the Social Security Act was upheld and the general welfare clause was relied upon both to support the tax and to support the expenditures of the money raised by the Social Security taxes.

Grants-in-Aid

Closely related to this subject are the so-called grants-in-aid which go back to the Morrill Act of 1862 and the grants thereunder to the so-called land-grant colleges. The extent of grants-in-aid today is very great, but questions relating to the wisdom as distinguished from the legal basis for such grants seem to lie wholly in the political field and are hardly appropriate for discussion in this report. Perhaps we should also observe that since the decision of *Massachusetts* v. *Mellon,* 262 U. S. 447, there seems to be no effective way in which either a state or an individual can challenge the validity of a federal grant-in-aid.

Doctrine of Pre-emption

Many, if not most, of the problems of federalism today arise either in connection with the commerce clause and the vast extent to which its sweep has been carried by the Supreme Court, or they arise under the Fourteenth Amendment. Historically, cases involving the doctrine of pre-emption pertain mostly to the commerce clause. More recently the doctrine has been applied in other fields, notably in the case of *Commonwealth of Pennsylvania* v. *Nelson,* in which the Smith Act and other federal statutes dealing with communism and loyalty problems were held to have pre-empted the field and to invalidate or suspend the Pennsylvania anti-subversive statute which sought to impose a penalty for conspiracy to overthrow the government of the United States by force or violence. In that particular case it happens that the decision of the Supreme Court of Pennsylvania was affirmed. That fact, however, emphasizes rather than detracts from the wide sweep now given to the doctrine of pre-emption.

Labor Relations Cases

In connection with commerce clause cases, the doctrine of pre-emption, coupled with only partial express regulation by Congress, has produced a state of considerable confusion in the field of labor relations.

One of the most serious problems in this field was pointed up or created (depending upon how one looks at the matter) by the Supreme Court's decision in *Amalgamated Association* v. *Wisconsin Employment Relations Board,* 340 U. S. 383, which overturned a state statute aimed at preventing strikes and lockouts in public utilities. This decision left the states powerless to protect their own citizens against emergencies created by the suspension of essential services, even though, as the dissent pointed out, such emergencies were "economically and practically confined to a [single] state."

In two cases decided on May 28, 1958, in which the majority opinions were written by Mr. Justice Frankfurter and Mr. Justice Burton, respectively, the right of an employee to sue a union in a state court was upheld. In *International Association of Machinists* v. *Gonzales,* a union member was held entitled to maintain a suit against his union for damages for

378

wrongful expulsion. In *International Union, United Auto, etc. Workers* v. *Russell*, an employee, who was not a union member, was held entitled to maintain a suit for malicious interference with his employment through picketing during a strike against his employer. Pickets prevented Russell from entering the plant.

Regardless of what may be the ultimate solution of jurisdictional problems in this field, it appears that at the present time there is unfortunately a kind of no-man's land in which serious uncertainty exists. This uncertainty is in part undoubtedly due to the failure of Congress to make its wishes entirely clear. Also, somewhat varying views appear to have been adopted by the Supreme Court from time to time.

In connection with this matter, in the case of *Textile Union* v. *Lincoln Mills*, 353 U. S. 448, the majority opinion contains language which we find somewhat disturbing. That case concerns the interpretation of Section 301 of the Labor Management Relations Act of 1947. Paragraph (a) of that Section provides: "Suits for violation of contracts between an employer and a labor organization representing employees in an industry affecting commerce as defined in this Chapter, or between any such labor organizations, may be brought in any district court of the United States having jurisdiction of the parties, without respect to the amount in controversy or without regard to the citizenship of the parties." Paragraph (b) of the same Section provides in substance that a labor organization may sue or be sued as an entity without the procedural difficulties which formerly attended suits by or against unincorporated associations consisting of large numbers of persons. Section 301 (a) was held to be more than jurisdictional and was held to authorize federal courts to fashion a body of federal law for the enforcement of these collective bargaining agreements and to include within that body of federal law specific performance of promises to arbitrate grievances under collective bargaining agreements.

What a state court is to do if confronted with a case similar to the *Lincoln Mills* case is by no means clear. It is evident that the substantive law to be applied must be federal law, but the question remains, where is that federal law to be found? It will probably take years for the development or the "fashioning" of the body of federal law which the Supreme Court says the federal courts are authorized to make. Can a state court act at all? If it can act and does act, what remedies should it apply? Should it use those afforded by state law, or is it limited to those which would be available under federal law if the suit were in a federal court? It is perfectly possible that these questions will not have to be answered, since the Supreme Court may adopt the view that the field has been completely pre-empted by the federal law and committed solely to the jurisdiction of the federal courts, so that the state courts can have no part whatsoever in enforcing rights recognized by Section 301 of the Labor Management Relations Act. Such a result does not seem to be required by the language of Section 301 nor yet does the legislative history of that Section appear to warrant such a construction.

Professor Meltzer's monograph has brought out many of the difficulties in this whole field of substantive labor law with regard to the division of power between state and federal governments. As he points out much of this confusion is due to the fact that Congress has not made clear what functions the states may perform and what they may not perform. There are situations in which the particular activity involved is prohibited by federal law, others in which it is protected by federal law, and others in which the federal law is silent. At the present time there seems to be one field in which state action is clearly permissible. That is where actual violence is involved in a labor dispute.

State Law in Diversity Cases

Not all of the decisions of the Supreme Court in comparatively recent years have limited or tended to limit the power of the states or the effect of state laws. The celebrated case of *Erie R. R.* v. *Tompkins*, 304 U. S. 64, overruled *Swift* v. *Tyson* and established substantive state law, decisional as well as statutory, as controlling in diversity cases in the federal courts. This marked the end of the doctrine of a federal common law in such cases.

In Personam Jurisdiction Over Non-Residents

Also, in cases involving the *in personam* jurisdiction of state courts over non-residents, the Supreme Court has tended to relax rather than tighten restrictions under the due process clause upon state action in this field. *International Shoe Co.* v. *Washington*, 326 U. S. 310, is probably the most significant case in this development. In sustaining the jurisdiction of a Washington court to render a judgment *in personam* against a foreign corporation which carries on some activities within the State of Washington, Chief Justice Stone used the now familiar phrase that there "were sufficient contacts or ties with the State of the forum to make it reasonable and just, according to our traditional conception of fair play and substantial justice, to enforce the obligation which appellant has incurred there." Formalistic doctrines or dogmas have been replaced by a more flexible and realistic approach, and this trend has been carried forward in subsequent cases leading up to and including *McGee* v. *International Life Insurance Co.*, 355 U. S. 220, until halted by *Hanson* v. *Denckla*, 357 U. S. decided June 23, 1958.

Taxation

In the field of taxation the doctrine of intergovernmental immunity has been seriously curtailed partly by judicial decisions and partly by statute. This has not been entirely a one-way street.

In recent years cases involving state taxation have arisen in many fields. Sometimes they have involved questions of burdens upon interstate commerce or the export-import clause, sometimes of jurisdiction to tax as a matter of due process, and sometimes they have arisen on the fringes of governmental immunity, as where a state has sought to tax a contractor doing business with the national government. There have been some shifts in holdings. On the whole, the Supreme Court seems perhaps to have taken a more liberal view in recent years towards the validity of state taxation than it formerly took.

Other Fourteenth Amendment Cases

In many other fields, however, the Fourteenth Amendment has been invoked to cut down state action. This has been noticeably true in cases involving not only the Fourteenth Amendment but also the First Amendment guarantee of freedom of speech or the Fifth Amendment protection against self-incrimination. State anti-subversive acts have been practically eliminated by *Pennsylvania* v. *Nelson* in which the decision was rested on the ground of pre-emption of the field by the federal statutes.

The Sweezy Case—State Legislative Investigations

One manifestation of this restrictive action under the Fourteenth Amendment is to be found in *Sweezy* v. *New Hampshire*, 354 U. S. 234. In that case, the State of New Hampshire had enacted a subversive activity statute which imposed various disabilities on subversive persons and subversive organizations. In 1953 the legislature adopted a resolution under which it constituted the Attorney General a one-man legislative committee to investigate violations of that Act and to recommend additional legislation. Sweezy, described as a non-Communist Marxist, was summoned to testify at the investigation conducted by the Attorney General, pursuant to this authorization. He testified freely about many matters but refused to answer two types of questions: (1) inquiries concerning the activities of the Progressive Party in the state during the 1948 campaign, and (2) inquiries concerning a lecture Sweezy had delivered in 1954 to a class at the University of New Hampshire. He was adjudged in contempt by a state court for failure to answer these questions. The Supreme Court reversed the conviction, but there is no majority opinion. The opinion of the Chief Justice, in which he was joined by Justices Black, Douglas and Brennan, started out by reaffirming the position taken in *Watkins* v. *United States*, 354 U. S. 178, that legislative investigations can encroach on First Amendment rights. It then attacked the New Hampshire Subversive Activities Act and stated that the definition of subversive persons and subversive organizations was so vague and limitless that they extended to "conduct which is only remotely related to actual subversion and which is done free of any conscious intent to be a part of such activity." Then followed a lengthy discourse on the importance of academic freedom and political expression. This was not, however, the ground upon which these four Justices ultimately relied for their conclusion that the conviction should be reversed. The Chief Justice said in part: "The respective roles of the legislature and the investigator thus revealed are of considerable significance to the issue before us. It is eminently clear that the basic discretion of determining the direction of the legislative inquiry has been turned over to the investigative agency. The Attorney General has been given such a sweeping and uncertain mandate that it is his discretion which picks out the subjects that will be pursued, what witnesses will be summoned and what questions will be asked. In this circumstance, it can not be stated authoritatively that the legislature asked the Attorney General to gather the kind of facts comprised in the subjects upon which petitioner was interrogated."

Four members of the Court, two in a concurring opinion and two in a dissenting opinion, took vigorous issue with the view that the conviction was invalid because of the legislature's failure to provide adequate standards to guide the Attorney General's investigation. Mr. Justice Frankfurter and Mr. Justice Harlan concurred in the reversal of the conviction on the ground that there was no basis for a belief that Sweezy or the Progressive Party threatened the safety of the state and hence that the liberties of the individual should prevail. Mr. Justice Clark, with whom Mr. Justice Burton joined, arrived at the opposite conclusion and took the view that the state's interest in self-preservation justified the intrusion into Sweezy's personal affairs.

In commenting on this case Professor Cramton says: "The most puzzling aspect of the Sweezy case is the reliance by the Chief Justice on delegation of power conceptions. New Hampshire had determined that it wanted the information which Sweezy refused to give; to say that the State has not demonstrated that it wants the information seems so unreal as to be incredible. The State had delegated power to the Attorney General to determine the scope of inquiry within the general subject of subversive activities. Under these circumstances the conclusion of the Chief Justice that the vagueness of the resolution violates the due process clause must be, despite his protestations, a holding that a state legislature cannot delegate such a power."

Public Employment Cases

There are many cases involving public employment and the question of disqualification therefor by reason of Communist party membership or other questions of loyalty. *Slochower* v. *Board of Higher Education*, 350 U. S. 551, is a well known example of cases of this type. Two more recent cases, *Lerner* v. *Casey*, and *Beilan* v. *Board of Public Education*, both in 357 U. S. and decided on June 30, 1958, have upheld disqualifications for employment where such issues were involved, but they did so on the basis of lack of competence or fitness. Lerner was a subway conductor in New York and Beilan was a public school instructor. In each case the decision was by a 5 to 4 majority.

Admission to the Bar

When we come to the recent cases on admission to the bar, we are in a field of unusual sensitivity. We are well aware that any adverse comment which we may make on those decisions lays us open to attack on the grounds that we are complaining of the curtailment of our own powers and that we are merely voicing the equivalent of the ancient protest of the defeated litigant—in this instance the wail of a judge who has been reversed. That is a prospect which we accept in preference to maintaining silence on a matter which we think cannot be ignored without omitting an important element of the subject with which this report is concerned.

Konigsberg v. *State Bar of California*, 353 U. S. 252, seems to us to reach the high water mark so far established by the Supreme Court in overthrowing the action of a state and in denying to a state the power to keep order in its own house.

The majority opinion first hurdled the problem as to whether or not the federal question sought to be raised was properly presented to the state highest court for decision and was decided by that court. Mr. Justice Frankfurter dissented on the ground that the record left it doubtful whether this jurisdictional requirement for review by the Supreme Court had been met and favored a remand of the case for certification by the state highest court of "whether or not it did in fact pass on a claim properly before it under the Due Process Clause of the Fourteenth Amendment." Mr. Justice Harlan and Mr. Justice Clark shared Mr. Justice Frankfurter's jurisdictional views. They also dissented on the merits in an opinion written by Mr. Justice Harlan, of which more later.

The majority opinion next turned to the merits of Konigsberg's application for admission to the bar. Applicable state statutes required one seeking admission to show that he was a person of good moral character and that he did not advocate the overthrow of the national or state government by force or violence. The Committee of Bar Examiners, after holding several hearings on Konigsberg's application, notified him that his application was denied because he did not show that he met the above qualifications.

The Supreme Court made its own review of the facts.

On the score of good moral character, the majority found that Konigsberg had sufficiently established it, that certain editorials written by him attacking this country's participation in the Korean War, the actions of political leaders, the influence of "big business" on American life, racial discrimination and the Supreme Court's decision in *Dennis* v. *United States*, 341 U. S. 494, would not support any rational inference of bad moral character, and that his refusal to answer questions "almost all" of which were described by the Court as having "concerned his political affiliations, editorials and beliefs" (353 U. S. 269) would not support such an inference either. On the matter of advocating the overthrow of the national or state government by force or violence, the Court held (as it had in the companion case of *Schware* v. *Board of Bar Examiners of New Mexico*, 353 U. S. 232, decided contemporaneously) that past membership in the Communist party was not enough to show bad moral character. The majority apparently accepted as sufficient Konigsberg's denial of any present advocacy of the overthrow of the government of the United States or of California, which was uncontradicted on the record. He had refused to answer questions relating to his past political affiliations and beliefs, which the Bar Committee might have used to test the truthfulness of his present claims. His refusal to answer was based upon his views as to the effect of the First and Fourteenth Amendments. The Court did not make any ultimate determination of their correctness, but (at 353 U. S. 270) said that "prior decisions by this Court" indicated that his objections to answering the questions (which we shall refer to below) were not frivolous.

The majority asserted that Konigsberg "was not denied admission to the California Bar simply because he refused to answer questions." In a footnote appended to this statement it is said (353 U. S. 259): "Neither the Committee as a whole nor any of its members ever intimated that Konigsberg would be barred just because he refused to answer relevant inquiries or because he was obstructing the Committee. Some members informed him that they did not necessarily accept his position that they were not entitled to inquire into his political associations and opinions and said that his failure to answer would have some bearing on their determination whether he was qualified. But they never suggested that his failure to answer their questions was, by itself, a sufficient independent ground for denial of his application."

Mr. Justice Harlan's dissent took issue with these views—convincingly, we think. He quoted lengthy extracts from the record of Konigsberg's hearings before the subcommittee and the committee of the State Bar investigating his application. (353 U. S. 284-309.) Konigsberg flatly refused to state whether or not at the time of the hearing he was a member of the Communist Party and refused to answer questions on whether he had ever been a Communist or belonged to various organizations, including the Communist Party. The Bar Committee conceded that he could not be required to answer a question if the answer might tend to incriminate him; but Konigsberg did not stand on the Fifth Amendment and his answer which came nearest to raising that question, as far as we can see, seems to have been based upon a fear of prosecution for perjury for whatever answer he might then give as to membership in the Communist Party. We think, on the basis of the extracts from the record contained in Mr. Justice Harlan's dissenting opinion that the Committee was concerned with its duty under the statute "to certify as to this applicant's good moral character" (p. 295), and that the Committee was concerned with the applicant's "disinclination" to respond to questions proposed by the Committee (p. 301), and that the Committee, in passing on his good moral character, sought to test his veracity (p. 303).

The majority, however, having reached the conclusion above stated, that Konigsberg had not been denied admission to the bar simply because he refused to answer questions, then proceeded to demolish a straw man by saying that there was nothing in the California statutes or decisions, or in the rules of the Bar Committee which had been called to the Court's attention, suggesting that a failure to answer questions "is *ipso facto,* a basis for excluding an applicant from the Bar, irrespective of how overwhelming is his showing of good character or loyalty or how flimsy are the suspicions of the Bar Examiners." Whether Konigsberg's "overwhelming" showing of his own good character would have been shaken if he had answered the relevant questions which he refused to answer, we cannot say. We have long been under the impression that candor is required of members of the bar and, prior to *Konigsberg* we should not have thought that there was any doubt that a candidate for admission to the bar should answer questions as to matters relating to his fitness for admission, and that his failure or refusal to answer such questions would warrant an inference unfavorable to the applicant or a finding that he had failed to meet the burden of proof of his moral fitness.

Let us repeat that Konigsberg did not invoke protection against self-incrimination. He invoked a privilege which he claimed to exist against answering certain questions. These might have served to test his veracity at the Committee hearings held to determine whether or not he was possessed of the good moral character required for admission to the bar.

The majority opinion seems to ignore the issue of veracity sought to be raised by the questions which Konigsberg refused to answer. It is also somewhat confusing with regard to the burden of proof. At one point (pp. 270-271) it says that the Committee was not warranted in drawing from Konigsberg's refusal to answer questions any inference that he was of bad moral character; at another (p. 273) it says that there was no evidence in the record to justify a finding that he had failed to establish his good moral character.

Also at page 273 of 353 U. S., the majority said: "We recognize the importance of leaving States free to select their own bars, but it is equally important that the State not exercise this power in an arbitrary or discriminatory manner nor in such way as to impinge on the freedom of political expression or association. A bar composed of lawyers of good character is a worthy objective but it is unnecessary to sacrifice vital freedoms in order to obtain that goal. It is also important to society and the bar itself that lawyers be unintimidated—free to think, speak and act as members of an Independent Bar." The majority thus makes two stated concessions—each, of course, subject to limitations—one, that it is important to leave the states free to select their own bars and the other, that "a bar composed of lawyers of good character is a worthy objective."

We think that Mr. Justice Harlan's dissent on the merits, in which Mr. Justice Clark joined, shows the fallacies of the majority position. On the facts which we think were demonstrated by the excerpts from the record included in that dissent, it seems to us that the net result of the case is that a state is unable to protect itself against admitting to its bar an applicant who, by his own refusal to answer certain questions as to what the majority regarded as "political" associations and activities, avoids a test of his veracity through cross-examination on a matter which he has the burden of proving in order to establish his right to admission to the bar. The power left to the states to regulate admission to their bars under *Konigsberg* hardly seems adequate to achieve what the majority chose to describe as a "worthy objective"—"a bar composed of lawyers of good character."

We shall close our discussion of *Konigsberg* by quoting two passages from Mr. Justice Harlan's dissent, in which Mr. Justice Clark joined. In one, he states that "this case involves an area of federal-state relations—the right of States to establish and administer standards for admission to their bars—into which this Court should be especially reluctant and slow to enter." In the other, his concluding comment (p. 312), he says: "[W]hat the Court has really done, I think, is simply to impose on California its own notions of public policy and judgment. For me, today's decision represents an unacceptable intrusion into a matter of State concern."

The *Lerner* and *Beilan* cases above referred to seem to indicate some recession from the intimations, though not from the decisions, in the *Konigsberg* and *Slochower* cases. In *Beilan* the school teacher was told that his refusal to answer questions might result in his dismissal, and his refusal to answer questions pertaining to loyalty matters was held relevant to support a finding that he was incompetent. "Incompetent" seems to have been taken in the sense of unfit.

State Administration of Criminal Law

When we turn to the impact of decisions of the Supreme Court upon the state administration of criminal justice, we find that we have entered a very broad field. In many matters, such as the fair drawing of juries, the exclusion of forced confessions as evidence, and the right to counsel at least in all serious cases, we do not believe that there is any real difference in doctrine between the views held by the Supreme Court of the United States and the views held by the highest courts of the several states. There is, however, a rather considerable difference at times as to how these general principles should be applied and as to whether they have been duly regarded or not. In such matters the Supreme Court not only feels free to review the facts, but considers it to be its duty to make an independent review of the facts. It sometimes seems that the rule which governs most appellate courts in the view of findings of fact by trial courts is given lip service, but is actually given the least possible practical effect. Appellate courts generally will give great weight to the findings of fact by trial courts which had the opportunity to see and hear the witnesses, and they are reluctant to disturb such findings. The Supreme Court at times seems to read the records in criminal cases with a somewhat different point of view. Perhaps no more striking example of this can readily be found than in *Moore* v. *Michigan*, 335 U. S. 155.

In the *Moore* case the defendant had been charged in 1937 with the crime of first degree murder, to which he pleaded guilty. The murder followed a rape and was marked by extreme brutality. The defendant was a Negro youth, 17 years of age at the time of the offense, and is described as being of limited education (only the 7th grade) and as being of rather low mentality. He confessed the crime to law enforcement officers and he expressed a desire to plead guilty and "get it over with." Before such a plea was permitted to be entered he was interviewed by the trial judge in the privacy of the judge's chambers and he again admitted his guilt, said he did not want counsel and expressed the desire to "get it over with," to be sent to whatever institution he was to be confined in, and to be placed under observation. Following this, the plea of guilty was accepted and there was a hearing to determine the punishment which should be imposed. About 12 years later the defendant sought a new trial principally on the ground that he had been unfairly dealt with because he was not represented by counsel. He had expressly disclaimed any desire for counsel at the time of his trial. Pursuant to the law of Michigan, he had a hearing on this application for a new trial. In most respects his testimony was seriously at variance with the testimony of other witnesses. He was corroborated in one matter by a man who had been a deputy sheriff at the time when the prisoner was arrested and was being questioned. The trial court, however, found in substance that the defendant knew what he was doing when he rejected the appointment of counsel and pleaded guilty, that he was then calm and not intimidated, and, after hearing him testify, that he was completely unworthy of belief. It accordingly denied the application for a new trial. This denial was affirmed by the Supreme Court of Michigan, largely upon the basis of the findings of fact by the trial court. The Supreme Court of the United States reversed. The latter Court felt that counsel might have been of assistance to the prisoner, in view of his youth, lack of education and low mentality, by requiring the state to prove its case against him (saying the evidence was largely circumstantial), by raising a question as to his sanity, and by presenting factors which might have lessened the severity of the penalty imposed. It was the maximum permitted under the Michigan law—solitary confinement for life at hard labor. The case was decided by the Supreme Court of the United States in 1957. The majority opinion does not seem to have given any consideration whatsoever to the difficulties of proof which the state might encounter after the lapse of many years or the risks to society which might result from the release of a prisoner of this type, if the new prosecution should fail. They are, however, pointed out in the dissent.

Another recent case which seems to us surprising, and the full scope of which we cannot foresee, is *Lambert v. California*, 355 U. S., decided December 16, 1957. In that case a majority of the Court reversed a conviction under a Los Angeles ordinance which required a person convicted of a felony, or of a crime which would be felony under the law of California, to register upon taking up residence in Los Angeles. Lambert had been convicted of forgery and had served a long term in a California prison for that offense. She was arrested on suspicion of another crime and her failure to register was then discovered and she was prosecuted, convicted and fined. The majority of the Supreme Court found that she had no notice of the ordinance, that it was not likely to be known, that it was a measure merely for the convenience of the police, that the defendant had no opportunity to comply with it after learning of it and before being prosecuted, that she did not act willfully in failing to register, that she was not "blameworthy" in failing to do so, and that her conviction involved a denial of due process of law.

This decision was reached only after argument and reargument. Mr. Justice Frankfurter wrote a short dissenting opinion in which Mr. Justice Harlan and Mr. Justice Whittaker joined. He referred to the great number of state and federal statutes which imposed criminal penalities for non-feasance and stated that he felt confident that "the present decision will turn out to be an isolated deviation from the strong current of precedents—a derelict on the waters of the law."

We shall not comment in this report upon the broad sweep which the Supreme Court now gives to habeas corpus proceedings. Matters of this sort seem to fall within the scope of the Committee of this Conference on the Habeas Corpus Bill which has been advocated for some years by this Conference for enactment by the Congress of the United States, and has been supported by the Judicial Conference of the United States, the American Bar Association, the Association of Attorneys General and the Department of Justice.

We cannot, however, completely avoid any reference at all to habeas corpus matters because what is probably the most far reaching decision of recent years on state criminal procedure which has been rendered by the Supreme Court is itself very close to a habeas corpus case. That is the case of *Griffin* v. *Illinois*, 351 U. S. 12, which arose under the Illinois Post Conviction Procedure Act. The substance of the holding in that case may perhaps be briefly and accurately stated in this way: If a transcript of the record, or its equivalent, is essential to an effective appeal, and if a state permits an appeal by those able to pay for the cost of the record or its equivalent, then the state must furnish without expense to an indigent defendant either a transcript of the record at his trial, or an equivalent thereof, in order that the indigent defendant may have an equally effective right of appeal. Otherwise, the inference seems clear, the indigent defendant must be released upon habeas corpus or similar proceedings. Probably no one would dispute the proposition that the poor man should not be deprived of the opportunity for a meritorious appeal simply because of his poverty. The practical problems which flow from the decision in *Griffin* v. *Illinois* are, however, almost unlimited and are now only in course of development and possible solution. This was extensively discussed at the 1957 meeting of this Conference of Chief Justices in New York.

We may say at this point that in order to give full effect to the doctrine of *Griffin* v. *Illinois,* we see no basis for distinction between the cost of the record and other expenses to which the defendant will necessarily be put in the prosecution of an appeal. These include filing fees, the cost of printing the brief and of such part of the record as may be necessary, and counsel fees.

The *Griffin* case was very recently given retroactive effect by the Supreme Court in a per curiam opinion in *Eskridge* v. *Washington State Board of Prison Terms and Paroles,* 78 S. Ct. 1061. In that case the defendant, who was convicted in 1935, gave timely notice of an appeal. His application then made for a copy of the transcript of the trial proceedings to be furnished at public expense was denied by the trial judge. A statute provided for so furnishing a transcript if "in his [the trial judge's] opinion justice will thereby be promoted." The trial judge found that justice would not be promoted, in that the defendant had had a fair and impartial trial, and that, in his opinion, no grave or prejudicial errors had occurred in the trial. The defendant then sought a writ of mandate from the

Supreme Court of the state, ordering the trial judge to have the transcript furnished for the prosecution of his appeal. This was denied and his appeal was dismissed. In 1956 he instituted habeas corpus proceedings which, on June 16, 1958, resulted in a reversal of the Washington Court's decision and a remand "for further proceedings not inconsistent with this opinion." It was conceded that the "reporter's transcript" from the trial was still available. In what form it exists does not appear from the Supreme Court's opinion. As in *Griffin*, it was held that an adequate substitute for the transcript might be furnished in lieu of the transcript itself. Justices Harlan and Whittaker dissented briefly on the ground that "on this record the Griffin case decided in 1956 should not be applied to this conviction occurring in 1935." This accords with the view expressed by Mr. Justice Frankfurter in his concurring opinion in *Griffin* that it should not be retroactive. He did not participate in the *Eskridge* case.

Just where *Griffin* v. *Illinois* may lead us is rather hard to say. That it will mean a vast increase in criminal appeals and a huge case load for appellate courts seems almost to go without saying. There are two possible ways in which the meritorious appeals might be taken care of and the non-meritorious appeals eliminated. One would be to apply a screening process to appeals of all kinds, whether taken by the indigent or by persons well able to pay for the cost of appeals. It seems very doubtful that legislatures generally would be willing to curtail the absolute right of appeal in criminal cases which now exists in many jurisdictions. Another possible approach would be to require some showing of merit before permitting an appeal to be taken by an indigent defendant at the expense of the state.

Whether this latter approach which we may call "screening" would be practical or not is, to say the least, very dubious. First, let us look at a federal statute and Supreme Court decisions thereunder. What is now subsection (a) of Section 1915 of Title 28, U. S. C. A. contains a sentence reading as follows: "An appeal may not be taken in forma pauperis if the trial court certifies in writing that it is not taken in good faith." This section or a precursor thereof was involved in *Miller* v. *United States*, 317 U. S. 192, *Johnson* v. *United States*, 352 U. S. 565, and *Farley* v. *United States*, 354 U. S. 521, 523. In the *Miller* case the Supreme Court held that the discretion of the trial court in withholding such a certificate was subject to review on appeal, and that in order that such a review might be made by the Court of Appeals it was necessary that it have before it either the transcript of the record or an adequate substitute therefor, which might consist of the trial judge's notes or of an agreed statement as to the points on which review was sought. Similar holdings were made by per curiam opinions in the *Johnson* and *Farley* cases, in each of which the trial court refused to certify that the appeal was taken in good faith. In each case, though perhaps more clearly in *Johnson*, the trial court seems to have felt that the proposed appeal was frivolous, and hence not in good faith.

The *Eskridge* case, above cited, decided on June 16, 1958, rejected the screening process under the state statute there involved, and appears to require, under the Fourteenth Amendment, that a full appeal be allowed—not simply a review of the screening process, as under the federal statute above cited. The effect of the *Eskridge* case thus seems rather clearly to be that unless all appeals, at least in the same types of cases, are subject to screening, none may be.

It would seem that it may be possible to make a valid classification of appeals which shall be subject to screening and of appeals which shall not. Such a classification might be based upon the gravity of the offense or possibly upon the sentence imposed. In most, if not all, states, such a classification would doubtless require legislative action.

In the *Griffin* case, it will be recalled, the Supreme Court stated that a substitute for an actual transcript of the record would be acceptable if it were sufficient to present the points upon which the defendant based his appeal. The Supreme Court suggested the possible use of bystanders' bills of exceptions.

It seems probable to us that an actual transcript of the record will be required in most cases. For example, in cases where the basis for appeal is the alleged insufficiency of the evidence, it may be very difficult to eliminate from that part of the record which is to be transcribed portions which seem to have no immediate bearing upon this question. A statement of the facts to be agreed upon by trial counsel for both sides may be still more difficult to achieve even with the aid of the trial judge.

The danger of swamping some state appellate courts under the flood of appeals which may be loosed by *Griffin* and *Eskridge* is not a reassuring prospect. How far *Eskridge* may lead and whether it will be extended beyond its facts remain to be seen.

Conclusions

This long review, though far from exhaustive, shows some of the uncertainties as to the distribution of power which are probably inevitable in a federal system of government. It also shows, on the whole, a continuing and, we think, an accelerating trend towards increasing power of the national government and correspondingly contracted power of the state governments. Much of this is doubtless due to the fact that many matters which were once mainly of local concern are now parts of larger matters which are of national concern. Much of this stems from the doctrine of a strong, central government and of the plenitude of national power within broad limits of what may be "necessary and proper" in the exercise of the granted powers of the national government which was expounded and established by Chief Justice Marshall and his colleagues, though some of the modern extensions may and do seem to us to go to extremes. Much, however, comes from the extent of the control over the action of the states which the Supreme Court exercises under its views of the Fourteenth Amendment.

We believe that strong state and local governments are essential to the effective functioning of the American system of federal government; that they should not be sacrificed needlessly to leveling, and sometimes deadening, uniformity; and that in the interest of active, citizen participation in self-government—the foundation of our democracy—they should be sustained and strengthened.

As long as this country continues to be a developing country and as long as the conditions under which we live continue to change, there will always be problems of the allocation of power depending upon whether certain matters should be regarded as primarily of national concern or as primarily of local concern. These adjustments can hardly be effected without some friction. How much friction will develop depends in part upon the wisdom of those empowered to alter the boundaries and in part upon the speed with which such changes are effected. Of course, the question of speed really involves the exercise of judgment and the use of wisdom, so that the two things are really the same in substance.

We are now concerned specifically with the effect of judicial decisions upon the relations between the federal government and the state governments. Here we think that the over-all tendency of decisions of the Supreme Court over the last

25 years or more has been to press the extension of federal power and to press it rapidly. There have been, of course, and still are, very considerable differences within the Court on these matters, and there has been quite recently a growing recognition of the fact that our government is still a federal government and that the historic line which experience seems to justify between matters primarily of national concern and matters primarily of local concern should not be hastily or lightly obliterated. A number of justices have repeatedly demonstrated their awareness of problems of federalism and their recognition that federalism is still a living part of our system of government.

The extent to which the Supreme Court assumes the function of policy-maker is also of concern to us in the conduct of our judicial business. We realize that in the course of American history the Supreme Court has frequently—one might, indeed, say customarily—exercised policy-making powers going far beyond those involved, say, in making a selection between competing rules of law.

We believe that in the fields with which we are concerned, and as to which we feel entitled to speak, the Supreme Court too often has tended to adopt the role of policy-maker without proper judicial restraint. We feel this is particularly the case in both of the great fields we have discussed—namely, the extent and extension of the federal power, and the supervision of state action by the Supreme Court by virtue of the Fourteenth Amendment. In the light of the immense power of the Supreme Court and its practical non-reviewability in most instances no more important obligation rests upon it, in our view, than that of careful moderation in the exercise of its policy-making role.

We are not alone in our view that the Court, in many cases arising under the Fourteenth Amendment, has assumed what

400

seem to us primarily legislative powers. (See Judge Learned Hand on the Bill of Rights.) We do not believe that either the framers of the original Constitution or the possibly somewhat less gifted draftsmen of the Fourteenth Amendment ever contemplated that the Supreme Court would, or should, have the almost unlimited policy-making powers which it now exercises. It is strange, indeed, to reflect that under a constitution which provides for a system of checks and balances and of distribution of power between national and state governments one branch of one government—the Supreme Court—should attain the immense, and in many respects, dominant, power which it now wields.

We believe that the great principle of distribution of powers among the various branches of government and between levels of government has vitality today and is the crucial base of our democracy. We further believe that in construing and applying the Constitution and laws made in pursuance thereof, this principle of the division of power based upon whether a matter is primarily of national or of local concern should not be lost sight of or ignored, especially in fields which bear upon the meaning of a constitutional or statutory provision, or the validity of state action presented for review. For, with due allowance for the changed conditions under which it may or must operate, the principle is as worthy of our consideration today as it was of the consideration of the great men who met in 1787 to establish our nation as a nation.

It has long been an American boast that we have a government of laws and not of men. We believe that any study of recent decisions of the Supreme Court will raise at least considerable doubt as to the validity of that boast. We find first that in constitutional cases unanimous decisions are comparative rarities and that multiple opinions, concurring or dissenting, are common occurrences. We find next that divisions in result on a 5 to 4 basis are quite frequent. We find further that on some occasions a majority of the Court cannot be mustered in support of any one opinion and that the result of a given case may come from the divergent views of individual Justices who happen to unite on one outcome or the other of the case before the Court.

We further find that the Court does not accord finality to its own determinations of constitutional questions, or for that matter of others. We concede that a slavish adherence to *stare decisis* could at times have unfortunate consequences; but it seems strange that under a constitutional doctrine which requires all others to recognize the Supreme Court's rulings on constitutional questions as binding adjudications of the meaning and application of the Constitution, the Court itself has so frequently overturned its own decisions thereon, after the lapse of periods varying from one year to seventy-five, or even ninety-five years. (See the tables appended to Mr. Justice Douglas' address on *Stare Decisis*, 49 Columbia Law Review 735, 756-758.) The Constitution expressly sets up its own procedures for amendment, slow or cumbersome though they may be.

These frequent differences and occasional overrulings of prior decisions in constitutional cases cause us grave concern as to whether individual views of the members of the court as from time to time constituted, or of a majority thereof, as to what is wise or desirable do not unconsciously override a more dispassionate consideration of what is or is not constitutionally warranted. We believe that the latter is the correct approach, and we have no doubt that every member of the Supreme Court intends to adhere to that approach, and believes that he does so. It is our earnest hope which we respectfully express, that that great Court exercise to the full its power of judicial self-restraint by adhering firmly to its tremendous, strictly